9 PRESIDENTS WHO SCREWED UP AMERICA

"Every once in a while American historians will be polled regarding the men they consider the greatest presidents. Without fail, they choose those people most dedicated to the expansion of government. In this outstanding book, Brion McClanahan blasts these historians to smithereens and reveals the true history of the dangerous men who are known as our great presidents. It's about time someone did!"

—Thomas E. Woods Jr., author of *Nullification: How to Resist Federal Tyranny in the 21ˢᵗ Century* and *The Politically Incorrect Guide® to American History*

"James Madison's fealty to the Constitution led him to veto a bill he had asked Congress to pass and to issue a 'war message' not asking Congress to declare war, and Barack Obama rewrote his own signature law, made 'recess' appointments when the Senate was not recessed, and launched an aggressive war without so much as asking Congress what it thought. Brion McClanahan's latest blockbuster book shows how we got from there to here by recounting the most important offending presidencies along the way. Many sacred cows are slain. This book is both a fascinating read by a master historian and a necessary guide for any voter."

—Kevin R. C. Gutzman, author of *James Madison and the Making of America* and *The Politically Incorrect Guide® to the Constitution*

"Many people think of our American history as a series of 'Great Presidents.' We like to rank them: Great, Near Great, Mediocre, Bad. Lincoln, Wilson, FDR, and Kennedy (or Reagan if you prefer) are on most lists as Great Presidents, inspiring heroes who overcome the past and lead America ever higher. Brion McClanahan applies a different measure of what makes a Great President—to what extent does he adhere to the constitutional role of the Chief Executive of the Union that was intended by the

Founding Fathers? Applying this standard yields some mighty surprises. There are hundreds of books on the American presidency. This is the most original one you will ever read."

> —Clyde N. Wilson, distinguished professor of history emeritus, University of South Carolina

"This is an insightful study which presents well McClanahan's characterizations of thirteen presidents, four praised, nine castigated as dangerous to freedom. Readers may differ with him on a few of his conclusions, but everyone committed to freedom within an orderly and just society should read it."

> —John Pafford, professor of history at Northwood University and author of *Cleveland: The Forgotten Conservative* and *John Jay: The Forgotten Founder*

"Congratulations to Brion McClanahan. As a true American historian, he tells the truth about the rogues' gallery of U.S. presidents, who have stolen our freedoms, and killed millions in the process. And what great prose!"

> —Llewellyn H. Rockwell Jr., founding chairman of the Ludwig von Mises Institute

9 PRESIDENTS WHO SCREWED UP AMERICA

ANDREW JACKSON   ABRAHAM LINCOLN   THEODORE ROOSEVELT

HARRY S. TRUMAN   FRANKLIN D. ROOSEVELT   WOODROW WILSON

LYNDON B. JOHNSON   RICHARD M. NIXON   BARACK OBAMA

9 PRESIDENTS

WHO SCREWED UP

AMERICA

and four who tried to save her

BRION McCLANAHAN

REGNERY
HISTORY

Regnery History™ is a trademark of Salem Communications Holding Corporation; Regnery® is a registered trademark of Salem Communications Holding Corporation

Library of Congress Cataloging-in-Publication Data

Names: McClanahan, Brion T., author.
Title: 9 presidents who screwed up America : and four who tried to save her / Brion McClanahan.
Other titles: Nine presidents who screwed up America
Description: Washington, DC : Regnery Publishing, 2016. | Includes bibliographical references and index.
Identifiers: LCCN 2015048188 | ISBN 9781621573753
Subjects: LCSH: Presidents--Rating of--United States. | United States--Politics and government. | Presidents--United States--History.
Classification: LCC E176.1 .M145 2016 | DDC 973.09/9--dc23
LC record available at http://lccn.loc.gov/2015048188

Published in the United States by
Regnery History
An imprint of Regnery Publishing
A Division of Salem Media Group
300 New Jersey Ave NW
Washington, DC 20001
www.RegneryHistory.com

Manufactured in the United States of America

10 9 8 7 6 5 4 3 2

Books are available in quantity for promotional or premium use. For information on discounts and terms, please visit our website: www.Regnery.com.

Distributed to the trade by
Perseus Distribution
250 West 57th Street
New York, NY 10107

To Samantha, Shannon, Savannah, Virginia, and Charlotte

CONTENTS

INTRODUCTION

P residents have been judged on their job performance since George
Washington took the first oath of office on April 30, 1789. Not even he
was immune from criticism, some of it harsh. The essayist Tom Paine
wrote a stinging rebuke of the Washington administration—and of Washington's character—just before the first president left office in 1797. Every
administration has had its critics. We can often learn more from opponents of an administration than from those who supported the president.
Not that the critics are always correct. Hardly. But criticism shouldn't be
dismissed as simply a partisan political maneuver. Partisan critics can be
prescient. We fear those in power who think and act least like us and
therefore scrutinize their every decision. This would be the Founders'

position as well. Jealously guarding constitutional limitations on the executive is a healthy reaction from the American polity.

With each successive administration, Americans have compared and measured the man in office against his predecessors. Even presidents themselves have attempted to attach their administration to supposed greats of the past. These comparisons provide perspective in the maelstrom of American politics. In the modern era, last week's news might as well have been two hundred years ago, but by showing continuity between Abraham Lincoln and Barack Obama, for example, politicians hope to persuade the American public to buy their pitch and support their policies. If Franklin Roosevelt did it, then it should be good enough for George W. Bush or Bill Clinton.

THE RIGHT PRESIDENTIAL YARDSTICK

But how do Americans measure presidential success? By popularity? Effective communication? Success in achieving foreign or domestic policy goals? Energy and activity in the office? Leadership? The overall health of the country during and immediately after a president's administration? An ideological disposition similar to that of the person ranking the president? This is a difficult question and one that Americans have pondered for decades.

The historian Arthur Schlesinger Sr. conducted the first academic poll that attempted to rank the presidents for a 1948 issue of *Time* magazine. The fifty-five academics surveyed found six presidents to be "great": Abraham Lincoln, George Washington, Franklin Roosevelt, Woodrow Wilson, Thomas Jefferson, and Andrew Jackson. Schlesinger followed up in a 1962 poll of seventy-five historians for the *New York Times Magazine*. This poll dropped Jackson from the "great" category, but otherwise the list remained static.

The historians Schlesinger surveyed were generally left-of-center academics who favored the policies and qualities of the men on the list.

Lincoln, Wilson, and FDR were reformers; Jackson presided over the "Age of Democracy"; Jefferson, as the first "people's president," is always portrayed (incorrectly) as a modern liberal, and Washington was the glue that held the federal Republic together. On this list, only Jefferson's administration could be classified as less than energetic, at least in regard to the public perception of the office: Jefferson deliberately downgraded the presidency during his first term in office. Washington's careful implementation of executive powers had established precedents for executive conduct, but few followed his advice, and even he disregarded the Constitution during his second term.

With the exception of Grover Cleveland, the "great" and "above average" presidents in each poll were cut from the same cloth. Teddy Roosevelt, John Adams, and James K. Polk, along with Cleveland, were in the "above average" category in the 1948 poll, and Harry Truman and Jackson joined that category in the 1962 poll. Roosevelt was a progressive who believed in an energetic executive; Adams, though a member of the founding generation, had a much more active executive office than any other member of that generation; in one term, Polk acquired California and most of the desert southwest through a war with Mexico and secured the Oregon territory from Great Britain; Truman was a World War II president, stared down communists in Asia, and gave Americans a "Fair Deal." Cleveland is the only outlier. He used the office of president the way the founding generation intended by vetoing unconstitutional legislation and avoiding foreign entanglements. This, however, would be the best Cleveland would fare in any poll until 2005.

Polls in subsequent years by different academics and publications remained fairly consistent, perhaps because of the fact that the historians surveyed generally used the same criteria for determining the "greatness" of the president, namely leadership qualities, vision, and success in achieving their desired foreign or domestic policy goals. Every "great" president in the Schlesinger polls remained in the top group in the polls. Opinions varied for the rest of the presidents, but there was also a consistent trend in the bottom group. John Tyler, James Buchanan, Franklin Pierce, Warren G. Harding, Andrew Johnson, Zachary Taylor, and Calvin Coolidge were generally held in low esteem in every academic poll conducted from 1948 to 2005. The "below average" to "poor" presidents tend to be those who had forgettable administrations—they did not have grand foreign or domestic policy accomplishments—or those who supposedly blundered through a crisis such as the early stages of the Great Depression or the start of the Civil War.

The problem with these academic polls is not the questions but the perception of the executive office, a perception that has been skewed by the success of the United States in the twentieth century and the growth of the power of the executive branch vis-à-vis the other branches and levels of government. The historians who participated in these polls lacked an originalist perspective on the Constitution. So they ranked the presidents based on the outcome of their policies, not on how they upheld the oath they took when sworn into office, "to preserve, protect and defend the Constitution of the United States."

A ranking of the presidents on that basis would be a bit more difficult. The historian would have to understand how the proponents of the Constitution in 1787 and 1788 argued executive powers would be implemented once the Constitution was ratified. Most don't. Certainly, historians read the famous *Federalist* essays, but the real debates took place in the ratifying conventions themselves and among less conspicuous but equally important members of the founding generation, men such as John Dickinson, Roger Sherman, James Wilson, James Iredell, William Richardson Davie, John Rutledge, Oliver Ellsworth, and Edmund Randolph. These men argued that the president was not to be a king, nor would he have the power George III had in England. But the understanding of the executive branch among most Americans—including historians—has been distorted. We ask what we think the president *should* do in office, not what he is *constitutionally permitted* to do in office. The latter should be the measure of the man.

TURNING THE RANKINGS UPSIDE DOWN

Under those criteria, the traditional presidential rankings should be inverted, with just a few exceptions. Generally, those at the bottom of the lists tended to hew to greater constitutional restraint than those at the top. If we judge presidents not on their policies or ideas, but simply on their actions measured against the definition of the office of president in the Constitution, as it was sold to reluctant delegates at the state ratifying conventions and in the press, then the "great" executives look more like John Tyler or Calvin Coolidge than Franklin Roosevelt or Abraham Lincoln. We may admire the policy outcomes of the anointed great presidents—indeed some of these policies have had a dramatic and beneficial effect on American society—but that does not mean these men were adhering to their oath. In most cases, they weren't. Some of the men who would fare better under an originalist evaluation held views repugnant to modern Americans, but that does not make their stand for limitations on central power any less important. Potential executive abuse was one of the most feared results of the ratification of the Constitution. The founding generation considered an out-of-control executive to be the greatest bane to liberty.

The Constitution was ratified on a certain understanding of the office of president—of its powers, and above all of its limitations. The men who hold that office have no right to exceed those limits. When they do so, they are breaking their inaugural oath and straining to the breaking point the very compact that our government is founded on. Achieving other goals, however laudable, can never excuse actions that violate the fundamental understanding to which "the consent of the governed" was accorded when our constitutional government was established.

And the violation of that principle has very practical consequences. As we shall see throughout this book, unconstitutional government is irresponsible government. When the executive arrogates to itself powers that the Constitution does not grant, when unelected bureaucrats usurp the powers that the states and the people delegated only to their elected representatives, then the general government is no longer responsible to the states or the people. As the history laid out below demonstrates, what follows inevitably on the abandonment of constitutional principle is irresponsible policy, dangerous to the health and even the survival of the Republic—from ruinous deficits to out-of-control foreign adventurism. In the Constitution, the founding generation left us a vehicle for preserving self-government. We ignore it at our peril.

This book was born during the marketing campaign for my *Founding Fathers' Guide to the Constitution*. My assertion that nearly every president in the last one hundred years should be impeached created quite a stir. I had to explain, and one or two sentences were not enough to do the argument justice. This work is not a comprehensive "ranking" of all the presidents. It is designed to shed light on those who "screwed up America" and those who "tried to save her" using a simple formula: Did the man in office adhere to his oath to defend the Constitution as ratified by the founding generation? And, if not, where did he go off the rails?

The identities of the nine men who "screwed things up" may shock the modern reader. After all, many of them have been called "great" presidents, including Jackson, Lincoln, Wilson, and Franklin Roosevelt, while Teddy Roosevelt and Truman are always regarded as "near great." I listed Jackson as a true American hero in my book *The Politically Incorrect Guide® to* <u>Real</u> *American Heroes*, but that does not mean he should get a free pass for violating his oath. Jackson established precedents that allowed future presidents to deviate even further from the Constitution. He was a good general but a terrible president.

The other men in the list of those who "screwed things up"—Lyndon Johnson, Richard Nixon, and Barack Obama—have been generally ranked based on the politics of the person reviewing their records in office. Conservatives may rate Nixon highly but condemn the administrations of Johnson and Obama, while those on the Left would champion Obama and perhaps Johnson while classifying Nixon as a crook and a war criminal. But none of these men followed their oath, and in fact all of them established dangerous patterns that have created the modern "imperial presidency," a thinly veiled elected monarchy with more power than George III exercised at the time of the American War for Independence.

The four men who "tried to save" America are of a different stripe. Each of the four took office in a transitional period. Jefferson called his election in 1800 a "revolution." Tyler assumed office after the sudden death of President William Henry Harrison, proceeded to reverse the policies of the party which had elected him vice president in 1840, and as a result was booted from the party. Cleveland was the first Democrat elected since 1856, and he set out to undo nearly two decades of unconstitutional Republican legislation. Coolidge, like Tyler, took office through succession, and though his administration continued some of the policies of his predecessor, Coolidge was his own man and a far more effective originalist president than anyone else in the twentieth century.

Yet of this group only Jefferson is generally held in high esteem by the historical profession and the public at large. In contrast, I give him credit only for his first term. The second was a disaster, at least according to the Constitution as ratified. Tyler, Cleveland, and Coolidge are typically either forgotten or shunned by presidential "experts," considered to be abject failures, or characterized as spineless "do-nothings" who accelerated political or economic ruin. These charges are not only false but are indicative of a larger problem. Many historians—and too many Americans in general—seem to believe that presidential authority is virtually unlimited, that it is both necessary and competent to "solve" the crisis of the hour, and that the unconstitutional usurpation of power is admirable executive "energy."

In reality, all four men who "tried to save" America displayed a resolve in executive *restraint*, a much more difficult but necessary achievement in a federal Republic designed to have limited enumerated powers. The founding generation considered self-control a key measure of character. Anyone with enough political clout can abuse power. Restraint requires more tenacity and backbone than rampant, damaging, and often narcissistic autocratic rule. Executive restraint is a republican virtue, passed down from the great example of the Roman Cincinnatus, the general who saved Rome from collapse but then gave up power willingly to return to his fields and resume his life as a farmer. It is essential for the health and stability of our federal Republic. Following the Constitution and the oath of office is often not the popular path. The four presidents who "tried to save" America took this perilous trail. That should be admired, not condemned.

It also should be noted that none of the men who "tried to save her" were pushovers in office. They typically deferred to Congress when the Constitution required they do so, and they let Congress lead the legislative process—that was the proper course constitutionally. But Congress often characterized them as *too strong* and too willing to wield executive power. That should say something about the charge that they were executive lightweights. These four men exercised power not for political gain but to "defend the Constitution" from radical departures from its original intent. They defended their oath.

If Americans believe in a federal Republic with limited powers, defined by a written constitution, with checks and balances—not only between the three branches of the general government but also between the general and state governments—then the four men who "tried to save" constitutional government in our Republic should be regarded as the greatest presidents in American history. They must be our standard. Our future executives should be more like Tyler than either Roosevelt in the use of executive powers and more like Cleveland or Coolidge than Obama in regard to character. The presidency is a potentially dangerous office that, regardless of which party controls it, should always be viewed with suspicion. A return to this type of vigilance would protect both individual liberty and the liberty of the community from executive abuse. As we enter another presidential election season, that should be our goal. A proper understanding of the president's limited powers under our Constitution should guide the way all Americans vote.

THE FOUNDERS' EXECUTIVE

The Founders left clues in the historical record, some of them more conspicuous than others, which defined their vision for the executive branch. They articulated that vision in the Constitution for the United States and specifically in the enumerated powers of the new presidency. A written constitution established constraints because history had proven that the executive—whether a king, a dictator, a tsar, a tyrant, a pharaoh, or an emperor—was the greatest threat to liberty. Thus, in order to "secure the Blessings of Liberty to ourselves and our Posterity," the Founders believed a codification of executive powers was needed. In fact, not all of them were convinced it would be enough.

In the years leading to the American War for Independence, the founding generation implored George III to intercede on their behalf and stop unconstitutional parliamentary acts. They thought that only the king had dominion over the colonies, that they had no representation in the Parliament, and that any attempt to legislate for them—with the exceptions of trade and defense—was repugnant to the unwritten British constitution. The American colonists regarded King George III as the final check on the legislative branch. His veto could stop Parliament's tyrannical acts. Several times the colonists appealed directly to the king. He failed to act, and therefore the Declaration of Independence was a direct indictment of the king. George III became the lightning rod for colonial discontent, the despot and tyrant who had refused to intercede and use his constitutional powers to arrest the hand of Parliament.

There were precedents in British history. The barons who forced King John to sign the Magna Carta in 1215 emphasized that the king was not above the law. The English Civil War (1642–1651) was in part a struggle for power between the king and Parliament. King Charles I lost his head during the war. But then Oliver Cromwell, the Lord Protector, assumed greater power than King Charles ever had in England. The English people belatedly recognized this fact, deposed Cromwell's son in 1660, and exhumed and mauled the Lord Protector's body. He had been dead and buried for only two years. Heavy-handed executive rule was not welcome in England. Finally, the bloodless Glorious Revolution of 1688 placed restrictions on the king. William III had to formally recognize restrictions on his power as a condition of assuming the throne. The English Bill of Rights of 1689 was an attempt to place limitations on executive power and preserve the ancient rights of Englishmen—rights the colonists would insist they retained even after their emigration to the New World. Thomas Jefferson copied some of the language and form for the Declaration of Independence from the English Bill of Rights.

All this history played a part in the drafting of the several state constitutions during the American War for Independence and in the structure of the Articles of Confederation, the first governing document for the United States of America. The 1780 Constitution of Massachusetts, for example, granted little power to the executive branch. The governor of Massachusetts faced annual elections and had to concede to the supremacy of the Massachusetts General Court. Other state constitutions charted a similar course, and most of them checked executive power through an advisory council. The constitutions of the several states charged the executive branch with enforcing the laws, directing the state militias, and appointing civil officers, but the state governors were constrained by the declared powers and could not exceed their constituted authority. That was the point of a written constitution.

The Articles of Confederation, proposed in 1776 and ratified by all the states in 1781, did not have an executive branch (or a judicial branch), and executive tasks were carried out by the presiding officer of Congress. Each state had a republican form of government including an executive, but the members of the founding generation had been fighting a long and bloody war with Great Britain partially over executive usurpation of power. Thus the colonists deemed it inexpedient to place the new Union of states under the thumb of another powerful central government with substantial executive authority.

Several events led some members of the founding generation to reconsider their opposition to executive authority. Under the Articles of Confederation, the United States lacked a unified foreign policy; states could negotiate different treaties with foreign powers. The lack of an executive branch was also blamed for the inability for the general government to quiet unrest in the states, particularly during Shays' Rebellion in 1786. An independent executive branch came to be seen as a potential panacea for a government deemed too weak to operate effectively in both foreign and domestic policy.

AVOIDING AN ELECTIVE MONARCHY

The need for an executive branch became one of the rallying cries for a new constitution at the Philadelphia Convention in 1787, but the prospect of a federal executive also aroused considerable opposition. In the Constitutional Convention of 1787, James Madison called for a "national executive" to be elected by the "national legislature" in his famous Virginia Plan. But Charles Pinckney of South Carolina feared that the Convention might create the worst kind of executive, an elected king. And when James Wilson of Pennsylvania proposed that the executive consist of a single person, the Convention sat in stunned silence, assuredly frightened that such a move smacked of the tyranny they had just seceded from in 1776. The American Sage Benjamin Franklin broke the silence by asking the Convention for its opinion on the subject.[1]

John Rutledge of South Carolina suggested that a single executive was probably best, but he was against investing the power of the sword in the new branch of government. Even Wilson, who pursued a single executive with more vigor than any man in the Convention save Alexander Hamilton, thought that the *only* powers the executive should have were "executing the laws and appointing officers." Roger Sherman of Connecticut agreed. According to Madison's notes on the Convention, Sherman "considered the executive magistracy as nothing more than an institution for carrying the will of the legislature into effect."[2] Simply put, to these proponents of the new constitution, the president would execute the laws of Congress, nothing more.

But this promise of an executive with limited powers did not effectively persuade several of the delegates to the Convention to support the new Constitution. Its opponents consistently pointed out the potential for executive abuse. During the Convention, Edmund Randolph of Virginia claimed the executive branch was "the foetus of monarchy." When the Constitution was sent to the states for ratification, George Mason of Virginia warned that unless there was some sort of check on the executive branch's power, "the Government will...degenerate...into a Monarchy—a Government so contrary to the Genius of the people that they will reject even the Appearance of it...." He also thought that without a council of advisors chosen to represent the various sections of the Union, the new president "will generally be directed by Minions & Favorites—or He will become a Tool of the Senate—or a Council of State will grow out of the principal Officers of the great Departments; the worst & most dangerous of all Ingredients for such a Council, in a free Country...."[3] Such a warning seems prescient today, particularly after the last half of the twentieth century, when presidents continually relied on friends for advice and appointed close associates to the most powerful positions in the cabinet.

But what can the president do *constitutionally*? Article II of the Constitution is brief and the language seemingly vague. If we are to evaluate the president from an originalist position, then we must understand what powers the proponents of the Constitution said the executive would possess and what powers they claimed were denied to him by the document. This is the understanding of the presidency that was proposed to the people of the states when the Constitution was ratified.

LIMITED POWERS

Wilson considered the powers of the British monarch to be too extensive, for they extended to "prerogatives...of a legislative nature [and] that of war and peace, &c. . . ." The new president, he claimed, would not have such authority. Madison suggested that the president should have "power to carry into effect the national laws, to appoint to offices in cases not otherwise provided for, and to execute such other powers 'not legislative nor judiciary in their nature' as may from time to time be delegated by the national legislature."[4] The phrase "not legislative nor judiciary in their nature" is crucial. The president was not to have legislative power, meaning he is not *constitutionally* the "chief legislator"—as too many Americans today believe.

Nor does the president have unlimited power in regard to foreign policy. According to the Constitution as ratified, the president is the "commander in chief" of the armed services when they are called into service and the head of state with treaty making authority and appointment powers, but even these powers have limitations. The founding generation feared that that "commander in chief" power, extending to personal command of the army, would open the door to a military dictatorship. In fact, the majority of the founding generation considered placing the power of the sword in the hands of one man to be potentially the most dangerous provision of the new constitution.

But proponents of the Constitution argued that Americans should not be anxious in this regard; they reassured doubters by pointing to the constitutional limitations on the president's powers in foreign affairs. James Iredell of North Carolina argued fervently, "The President has not the power of declaring war by his own authority, nor that of raising fleets and armies." He also emphasized that only Congress could call up the militia and provide for the military. The military would be controlled by the civil power. So according to the Constitution as ratified, the president cannot make war unilaterally, nor can he raise the army and navy without congressional consent. In *The Federalist* No. 74 Hamilton suggested that the "propriety" of making the president commander in chief was "so evident in itself; and it is at the same time so consonant to the precedents of the State constitutions in general, that little need be said to explain or enforce it." But George Mason still had concerns; he reasoned that though Congress would have had to call up the militia and the army, the president would have no restrictions on his power once in command of the armed forces.[5] This fear has been justified in the modern era.

As for the powers of treaty making and appointment, the founding generation was confident the Senate, and by default the states, could check any abuse by the executive branch. Rutledge thought that allowing the president sole authority over appointments would smack of "Monarchy." The decision to give the Senate "advice and consent" was a compromise between those who favored executive authority and those who thought the Senate should have complete control in this area. The same was true of the president's treaty making powers, subject to approval by the Senate. Only a handful of the leading members of the founding generation thought the president should have unilateral control in foreign policy, and they didn't prevail. Francis Corbin of Virginia remarked in the Virginia Ratifying Convention that "It would be dangerous to give this power [treaty making] to the President alone, as the concession of such power to one individual is repugnant to republican principles." The Constitution includes this senatorial check on executive abuse because, in the words of James Iredell, "the great caution of giving the states an equality of suffrage in making treaties [that is, requiring Senate approval], was for the express purpose of taking care of that sovereignty, and attending to their interests, as political bodies, in foreign negotiations."[6]

Perhaps the most flagrant distortion of the Constitution as ratified is the modern executive use (or abuse) of the veto power. When James Wilson proposed that the president should have an absolute negative over congressional legislation, the rest of the delegates collectively gasped. Benjamin Franklin, who said very little during the entire Convention, made two speeches against Wilson's proposal. In the first he said, "if a negative should be given as proposed, that more power and money would be demanded, till at last eno' would be gotten to influence & bribe the Legislature into a compleat subjection to the will of the Executive." In the second he was even more direct. "The executive will be always increasing here, as elsewhere, till it ends in a monarchy." That was the greatest fear among the founding generation: the creation of an American king with powers beyond those of George III. George Mason hoped "that nothing like a monarchy would ever be attempted in this Country" because "an elective one" would be "a more dangerous monarchy" than in the British system.[7]

The first drafts of the Constitution established a three-fourths requirement for overriding a presidential veto. It remained this way until five days before the Constitution was approved in Philadelphia. On September 12, 1787, Hugh Williamson of North Carolina moved to strike the three-fourths requirement and replace it with two-thirds, stating that "the former puts too much in the power of the President." Roger Sherman agreed. "In making laws regard should be had to the sense of the people, who are to be bound by them, and it was more probable that a single man should mistake or betray this sense than the Legislature." Other delegates feared the veto would prevent "proper laws" or block "the repeal of [bad] laws." James Madison insisted that the veto should only be used to "defend Executive Rights [and] to prevent popular or factious injustice." Translation: the president should use the veto in order to protect the executive branch from legislative encroachment and to prevent unconstitutional legislation. To a man, the founding generation thought all else should pass without his interference.[8]

The best summary explanation of the executive branch as ratified in the Constitution comes from the pen of Alexander Hamilton in *The Federalist* No. 69. The president, he wrote, would have concurrent power with the Senate over appointments and treaties. He would not be able to unilaterally declare war or raise and regulate the armed forces. He would lack an absolute negative over legislation, and he would not be able to "prescribe...rules concerning the commerce or currency of the nation."[9] In short, the president would have very little authority beyond executing the laws of Congress and serving as head of state, and even those powers would be limited by the Senate. The president's oath of office is based on *this* conception of the Constitution. That is the executive according to the Constitution as ratified by the founding generation. Americans should measure the man in office by this standard. This book will do just that.

PART I

THE NINE WHO SCREWED UP AMERICA

CHAPTER 1

ANDREW JACKSON

AND THE ANTECEDENTS OF THE IMPERIAL PRESIDENCY

From the Founding to Andrew Jackson, Seventh President, 1829–1837

xecutive overreach did not begin overnight. While many Americans, liberals and conservatives alike, have recoiled at the actions of the Barack Obama administration, the seeds of his unconstitutional actions were planted long ago. Any study of executive abuse must begin at its source, and the roots of our out-of-control twenty-first-century presidency run deep. To understand how we got here, it is necessary to go back to the first deviations from the principles of the Constitution, which so wisely limit the powers of the president—checking the executive's natural tendency to accrue ever more power to itself and balancing the power of Congress and the courts against executive power and the power of the states against that of the general government.

THE FIRST IMPERIAL PRESIDENCY

It has been nearly two hundred years since the first presidency that can rightly be called imperial. That's how long ago an early nineteenth-century president "screwed up America" by arrogating to his office enormous powers that are not authorized by the Constitution. Andrew Jackson's presidency is the model for our lawless twenty-first-century executive. And, tragically, Jackson was able to get away with unconstitutional uses of the president's power in part because of abuses even before his time. Great men of the founding generation (including even that "indispensable man," the father of our country) deviated from their republican principles in a few crucial instances that opened the door to unconstitutional government just a crack—and then Jackson drove a horse and buggy through the opening.

George Washington's first administration was a model for the constitutional exercise of the presidential powers. But in his second term he followed some very bad advice, particularly from Alexander Hamilton, who, as we shall see, had played a key role persuading the state conventions to ratify the Constitution on the understanding that the federal executive would be a limited one—and then turned around and advised the first president to flout those limits. The choices Washington made may have been justified as policy. But the consequences that followed from them, from Andrew Jackson's blatant abuses of power to Barack Obama's flagrant attempts to govern without Congress, amply demonstrate the danger of any violation of the constitutional limitations on presidential power. No president, no matter how good his intentions, and no matter how pressing the crisis, is justified in exercising powers that the Constitution simply does not give him.

THE FATHER OF HIS COUNTRY

No one was better suited for the newly crafted office of president of the United States than the great statesman from Virginia. George Washington had willingly relinquished power following the American War for

Independence—an unprecedented move in the eighteenth century—and described assuming office as the first president of the United States as going to his execution. Washington was regarded as the glue that held the federal Republic together in both war and peace, the man who transcended section and whose unselfish loyalty to the cause helped the states achieve independence in 1783. He was not only the most famous man in America; he was the most famous American in the world.

The executive office was designed with him in mind. Benjamin Franklin said during the Philadelphia Convention in 1787 that "the first man put at the helm will be a good one. No body knows what sort may come afterwards."[1] Washington's first cabinet contained some of the best minds in the states: Thomas Jefferson, Alexander Hamilton, Henry Knox, and Edmund Randolph. Yet Washington spent much of his first term feeling his way around the newly established office. Some of the executive powers were vague.

What did the "advice and consent" of the Senate actually mean? At first Washington thought that he had to meet the Senate in person to discuss treaties, but that visit ended in disaster and Washington never again set foot on the Senate floor.

How was the veto power to be used? Washington thought that it should only be used to nullify unconstitutional legislation. He also believed that, once signed, every bill had to be accepted and enforced *in toto*.

The president serves a four-year term, but should he serve until he dies, or can the president retire? Washington chose the latter path and established the two-term precedent that every subsequent president followed until Franklin Roosevelt in 1940.

A REPUBLICAN AT HEART

Washington was restrained by the constant tug of republicanism. He believed in a strong central government, but he also understood that the American public would not support an American king—nor did he want to be that man. He sought to balance executive energy with liberty. Washington also knew that both the framers of the Constitution and the ratifiers in the state conventions feared potential abuse from the executive branch above all else. As a result, during his first term, Washington cautiously implemented executive authority.

That changed in 1793. The French Revolution had a lot to do with Washington's policy shifts. By 1793, the revolution had turned violent. In January of that year, Louis XVI was beheaded, and the French government was quickly embroiled in war with all of Europe. This presented a problem for American diplomacy. United States treaty obligations to the French government due to French support for the American War for Independence complicated matters. French wars became an American problem. Thomas Paine, the author of *Common Sense* and *The American Crisis*, wound up in revolutionary France and eventually became a bitter critic of the Washington administration, in part because he blamed it for leaving him to rot in a French prison.

Secretary of State Jefferson was an early supporter of the revolution and even helped the "hero of two worlds," the Marquis de Lafayette, craft a French declaration of rights. Jefferson thought the United States should uphold its treaty obligations and support the new government in France. Hamilton disagreed and urged Washington to pursue an independent course. Washington sided with Hamilton, but because the Constitution placed all war-making powers in the legislative branch and treaties had to have the "advice and consent" of the Senate, the Congress had to be consulted. The president was head of state and could receive ambassadors, but he could not act unilaterally.

PRESIDENTIAL PROCLAMATION

Washington sidestepped the problem—and the Constitution—by issuing what has been called the "Proclamation of Neutrality" in May 1793. He did not use the word neutrality in the document, but that was the intent.

The United States, Washington decreed, would adopt a "friendly and impartial" policy in regard to all belligerent powers in Europe. Any American caught serving a foreign government would be hung out to dry by the Washington administration. The message was clear. Washington was not going to become involved in a European war. This was the prudent and correct course to take. An alliance with France would have been disastrous for the fledgling American federal Republic. Washington, however, had no constitutional authority to unilaterally issue a "proclamation" determining the foreign policy of the United States. This was the type of power only kings possessed—and many Americans feared.

Only five years removed from their famous partnership in *The Federalist* essays, Hamilton and James Madison authored a series of essays on the controversy for the press, this time on opposite sides. Hamilton, writing under the *nom de plume* "Pacificus" defended Washington's unilateral decree. It was true, he conceded, that the legislature alone could declare war or move the United States "from a state of Peace to a state of War," but "it belongs to the 'Executive Power,' to do whatever else the law of Nations cooperating with the Treaties of the Country enjoin in the intercourse of the U[nited] States with foreign Powers." Hamilton reasoned that from the fact that the executive power alone could execute the laws and treaties of the United States, it could be deduced that the executive had the power *not* to execute the provisions of a treaty, and thus to maintain a neutral position vis-à-vis a foreign power. That was the intent of Washington's proclamation.[2]

THE CASE FOR THE CONSTITUTION

Neither Jefferson nor Madison bought it. After reading Hamilton's essays, Jefferson urged Madison to respond, stating, "For god's sake, my dear Sir, take up your pen, select the most striking heresies, and cut him to pieces in the face of the public. There is nobody else who can & will enter the lists with him."[3]

Madison obliged his friend and political ally. He rejoined under the pseudonym "Helvidius," verbally pummeling Washington's proclamation, arguing it contained a hint of monarchy and could not be constitutionally defended:

> ... an independent exercise of an *executive act* by the legislature *alone*, or of a *legislative* act by the executive *alone*, one or other of which must happen in every case where the same act is exerciseable by each...is contrary to one of the first and best maxims of a well-organized government, and ought never to be founded in a forced construction, much less in opposition to a fair one. Instances, it is true, may be discovered among ourselves, where this maxim has not been faithfully pursued; but being generally acknowledged to be errors, they confirm, rather than impeach the truth and value of the maxim.

In fact, Washington's proclamation could only be viewed as an extension of British "royal prerogatives." Madison argued that because the Constitution vested legislative powers in the Congress alone, the proclamation, which was essentially legislative in nature, violated the compact on which the United States government was founded and violated the separation of powers. He wrote, "Those who are to *conduct a war* [meaning the executive branch] cannot in the nature of things, be proper or safe judges, whether *a war ought* to be *commenced, continued,* or *concluded*. They are barred from the latter functions by a great principle in free government, analogous to that which separates the sword from the purse, or the power of executing from the power of enacting laws...."

Madison was correct. He pointed out that Washington had unilaterally infringed upon congressional powers because the power of making peace or war was outlined only in Article I, Section 8, of the Constitution, delineating the powers of Congress. Thus the president could request congressional authorization but could not declare either neutrality or war on his own. And Congress could never give that power to the executive branch through legislation. That transfer of power could only be accomplished by a constitutional amendment. Because the Proclamation of Neutrality had the force of a treaty, and because the Senate had played no role in its creation, it was, and still is, unconstitutional. Later, Madison had Congress draft and pass a neutrality act. Washington signed it in 1794, and it still remains in effect. But as of 2016, no amendment granting proclamation power to the executive exists. Custom and precedent do not equate to a constitutional right.

HAMILTON VS. HAMILTON

The debate over the issue of neutrality is instructive. Only five years into the new government under the Constitution, the only man most in the founding generation considered up to the role of the presidency of the Republic had already assumed undelegated powers that rivaled those of a European monarch. To make matters worse, many Americans defended the move. And yet even Hamilton had written in *The Federalist* No. 69 that the president could not unilaterally make foreign policy decisions. He had to have the "advice and consent" of the Senate. Had the delegates in the state ratifying conventions known that within less than a decade the executive would make such unconstitutional moves, the Constitution would never have been ratified.

The constant friction between Hamilton and Jefferson forced Jefferson to resign as secretary of state in 1793. This was an important development for the powers of the executive branch. Once Jefferson was out of the cabinet, Hamilton had free rein to influence Washington's policy decisions. No event better illustrated Hamilton's influence—and its threat to the limitations on executive power established in the Constitution—than the federal response in 1794 to the so-called "Whiskey Rebellion."

As secretary of the treasury, Hamilton had urged Congress to adopt a series of excise taxes to help fund the general government, including a tax on distilled liquor. This was a targeted tax on farmers who needed to distill liquor in order to turn a profit on unsold cash crops, mainly corn and rye. None of these farmers supported Hamilton's policies, and many had gravitated to the new Democratic-Republican clubs that had sprung up during Washington's first term in office. Hamilton considered these groups dangerous to the stability of the federal Republic, particularly when they began calling for farmers to resist paying the whiskey tax.

For nearly three years, the whiskey tax was a matter of intense public debate. Farmers in Western Pennsylvania organized committees that openly flaunted non-compliance with the tax, formed ad hoc courts, erected liberty poles, and armed themselves against federal tax collectors, who were harassed and their property destroyed. Kentucky refused to collect the tax, and there was widespread opposition along most of the American frontier, particularly in the Carolinas. This was an open challenge to federal authority, and both Hamilton and Washington fumed over the defiance.

Hamilton drafted a presidential proclamation in September 1792 not only denying the fundamental right of citizens to meet and petition the government for redress but demanding compliance with the law under the threat of military coercion. Attorney General Edmund Randolph, worried that Hamilton's move would make the situation worse, did his best to tone down the language of the proclamation. He was right. Washington had also urged caution and signed Randolph's modified proclamation, but he ultimately followed Hamilton's lead in the matter. This turned out to be a mistake.

The proclamation was circulated in newspapers throughout the Union, but tensions did not subside. Farmers in Western Pennsylvania continued to disregard federal tax law, and in 1794 the federal government issued subpoenas demanding that tax dodgers appear in federal court. The subpoenas reached their intended destination just after the whiskey tax was modified, thus rendering the orders impotent, but no one in Western Pennsylvania knew that the law had been changed. Opposition was immediate and violent.

FLOUTING A CONSTITUTIONAL REQUIREMENT

Washington feared that such open resistance to federal authority could lead to a wider rebellion against the general government. His cabinet, with the exception of Attorney General Randolph, supported military action against the tax "rebels." The Militia Act of 1792 required the Supreme Court to certify that the local authorities were incapable of quelling violence before the president could muster the militia into service. Supreme Court Justice James Wilson of Pennsylvania, a nationalist who had wanted to abolish the states in the Philadelphia convention in 1787, complied with a request to issue such a ruling. Washington delivered a proclamation in August 1794 calling up the militia to crush the "insurgents" and restore order in the state. He then led a twelve-thousand-man army into Pennsylvania to put down the rebellion. It worked. All of the leaders fled or were hidden by friends and relatives. Twenty-four men were arrested, two were tried for treason—one being a man with poor mental capacity—and both were pardoned by Washington. Jefferson wrote after the event, "An insurrection was announced and proclaimed and armed against, but could never be found."[4]

But did Washington violate the Constitution by raising an army and marching into Pennsylvania? Yes, according to the Constitution as ratified in 1788. Congress passed the Militia Act in 1792 in order to give the president the authority to call up the militia to repel invasions and oppose "combinations too powerful to be suppressed by the ordinary course of judicial proceedings." Yet the Constitution purposely vested this power in Congress alone, and the Congress could not grant an expressly delegated power to another branch of government. The Militia Act itself, then, was unconstitutional. But even if it had been constitutional, Washington's decision to lead the army into Pennsylvania violated the Constitution in other ways.

The governor of Pennsylvania, Thomas Mifflin, insisted that state authorities had the "rebellion" under control and that federal intervention was unnecessary. Article IV, Section 4, authorizes the general government to "guarantee to every State in this Union a Republican Form of Government" and protect the states against invasion. The general government can also protect "against domestic violence" but only on the "Application of the Legislature, or of the Executive (when the Legislature cannot be convened)." In other words, unless a state legislature or governor requests federal military intervention, the general government cannot legally send in the army.

Governor Mifflin knew this. He was present at the Philadelphia Convention of 1787 and was a proponent of the Constitution in the Pennsylvania State Ratifying Convention. He had also served as Washington's aide-de-camp during the American War for Independence. Neither he nor the Pennsylvania legislature requested federal troops. And it's difficult to argue that a "[combination] too powerful to be suppressed" existed in Pennsylvania. No other states had sent troops to aid the "rebellion." State leaders believed they had the issue under control and did not need federal intervention. State consent was and is a constitutional requirement for federal involvement in a state matter. Washington did not have it.

The Congress had illegally punted its authority to the executive branch, and the president had unconstitutionally usurped power from the state of Pennsylvania. These two wrongs by a good man acting on bad advice combined to set a dangerous precedent for future presidents. But it wasn't until the tenure of Andrew Jackson—not such a sterling character—that the real outlines of the imperial presidency can be seen.

OLD HICKORY

Jackson is an American hero, and while some of the more unseemly elements of his administration have been condemned—his actions in regard to American Indian tribes, for example—Jackson's reputation has been recently revived by popular histories. In fact "Old Hickory" was a great general, a true American hero, but a reckless president. Jefferson divined as much when he knew Representative Jackson in the 1780s: "I feel much alarmed at the prospect of seeing General Jackson President. He is one of the most unfit men I know of for such a place. He has had very little respect for laws and constitutions, and is, in fact, an able military chief. His passions are terrible. When I was President of the Senate, he was Senator; and he could never speak on account of the rashness of his feelings. I have seen him attempt it repeatedly, and as often choke with rage. His passions are, no doubt, cooler now; he has been much tried since I knew him, but he is a dangerous man."

Jackson assumed office in 1829 after one of the most brutal campaigns in American history. He had been called a "jackass," a Western man with no conception of American government; and his wife Rachel had been labeled a bigamist in the opposition press. She died of a heart attack just days before Jackson's inauguration.

Jackson reveled in personal politics, and the man behind the slander of his wife, Henry Clay, became Jackson's archenemy. He wasn't the only one. Jackson hated Vice President John C. Calhoun, because then Secretary of War Calhoun had supported reprimanding then General Jackson for unauthorized military actions in Florida in 1818. Jackson also despised Missouri Senator Thomas Hart Benton; the president carried a bullet in his shoulder from a duel between the two men. David Crockett, Nicholas Biddle, John Marshall, and a host of other men also fell out of favor with Jackson. His "personal enemies" list trumped both Richard Nixon's and the Clintons' in regard to the stature of the people on it.

Jackson preferred the title of "General" to "Mr. President," and he believed the formal cabinet should be nothing more than a rubber stamp for his will. Jackson thought of himself as a commanding officer, not a public servant, and his actions would show it.

THE SECOND BANK OF THE UNITED STATES

Jackson's 1832 veto of a bill re-chartering the Second Bank of the United States is often hailed as one of the great victories for the original

Constitution. His veto message, which was nothing short of rhetorical brilliance, included the same type of language Jeffersonians had used for years in their opposition to the Bank. Jeffersonians, most importantly John Taylor of Caroline, had articulated the anti-Bank position for years. Taylor considered the fusion of government and finance capital to be the greatest threat to liberty. Jackson agreed. He called the Bank "subversive of the rights of the States, and dangerous to the liberties of the people...."[5] Why? Because it placed too much power and influence in an institution that had no accountability to the American people. So Jackson had a duty to do everything possible to render the Bank powerless. (Marxist-leaning historians often read Jackson's attacks on "privilege" as a nod to the American proletariat, a way to unite the working people of America in a cause against special interests. But principled opponents of the Bank of the United States should never be confused with Marxists.)

Proponents of the Bank argued that its constitutionality had been settled by the famous—or infamous—*McCulloch v. Maryland* decision of 1819 and by precedent. Jackson retorted:

> It is maintained by the advocates of the bank that its constitutionality in all its features ought to be considered as settled by precedent and by the decision of the Supreme Court. To this conclusion I can not assent. Mere precedent is a dangerous source of authority, and should not be regarded as deciding questions of constitutional power except where the acquiescence of the people and the States can be considered as well settled. So far from this being the case on this subject, an argument against the bank might be based on precedent. One Congress, in 1791, decided in favor of a bank; another, in 1811, decided against it. One Congress, in 1815, decided against a bank; another, in 1816, decided in its favor. Prior to the present Congress, therefore, the precedents drawn from that source were equal. If we resort to the States, the expressions of legislative, judicial, and executive

opinions against the bank have been probably to those in its favor as 4 to 1. There is nothing in precedent, therefore, which, if its authority were admitted, ought to weigh in favor of the act before me.[6]

Jackson maintained that it was his duty as president to interpret the Constitution in a manner he saw fit. If he considered a bill to be unconstitutional, he was not duty bound to enforce it. This is the correct originalist position.

A PERSONAL VENDETTA

But while it certainly seemed that Jackson was Jefferson's heir apparent in relation to constitutional construction, his position on the bank was not really based on an ideological disposition against the clearly unconstitutional government corporation. Jackson hated the Bank because Henry Clay supported the Bank. Jackson, in fact, had been an ardent *proponent* of the Bank while standing for election for United States senator from Tennessee. His inconsistency on the matter is one reason why David Crockett became an anti-Jacksonian.

Though Jackson vetoed the re-charter bill and Congress failed to override his veto, the Bank's original charter allowed it to continue to operate until 1836. Jackson was determined to "kill it." This was a personal crusade to rid the United States of not only the Bank but its stubborn president, Nicholas Biddle. To Jackson, the Bank was already dead, but Biddle continued to fight even as the Bank was on life support and coughing up blood. Biddle's intractability became more pronounced when Jackson decided in 1833 to act unilaterally—and both unconstitutionally and illegally—by removing all federal deposits from the Bank without congressional approval. Biddle dug in his heels, with the result being one of the more bitter political "wars" of the nineteenth century.

Jackson began polling his cabinet in March 1833 about the potential removal of bank deposits. His secretary of the treasury, Louis McLane, was against the move until a substitute for the Bank could be established. Attorney General Roger Taney, however, favored removing the deposits as quickly as possible. This was an opportunity to destroy the Bank before Congress could get involved and before Biddle had the chance to buy support with Bank loans. Taney appealed to Jackson's manly resolve by equating the situation to a war and by flattering the president, arguing Jackson alone had the courage to confront the powerful American institution. Jackson was like a moth to a candle.

There was one problem. McLane had already agreed to become secretary of state and his incoming successor, William John Duane, was opposed to removing the Bank deposits. No matter. Jackson simply fired him for refusing to comply with an order from the president and appointed Taney as his successor while Congress was out of session. This gave Taney time to begin the process of withdrawing federal deposits from the Bank before Congress had a chance to act. Taney's recess appointment was going to face congressional obstacles, but the president did have the constitutional authority to appoint him during a recess. But Taney failed to follow the letter of the law in making the withdrawals, and once back in session, Congress quickly pounced.

A JUSTIFICATION THAT WASN'T

The 1816 bill chartering the Bank of the United States allowed for the secretary of the treasury to withdrawal federal deposits from the Bank as long as he provided written justification to Congress. Taney did write to Congress, but his argument teetered on autocracy. It was less a justification than a claim that he didn't owe Congress one. Taney claimed that as secretary of the treasury he alone could determine whether "the general interests and convenience of the people" were being met by the Bank. Therefore, even if the Bank was solvent, even if it could meet its contractual obligations, Taney contended that he could act without Congress to remove the deposits.

Once the Senate was back in session, Senator Henry Clay of Kentucky quickly offered a resolution condemning the move. Taney, he argued, had arrogated unconstitutional power to himself. He had bypassed Congress, the creator of both the Bank and the Treasury Department, and considered himself to be above the law. This was a fight over executive power and Clay, for once, was on the right side of the issue, at least according to the original Constitution as ratified in 1788.

True, Congress had unconstitutionally given the executive branch legislative authority through the Treasury Department in the 1816 Bank Bill, but that authority was qualified by congressional oversight and approval, making it an issue of "advice and consent." Then Taney claimed he did not need congressional approval to remove the deposits. This was, he argued, his exclusive authority as secretary of the treasury. But Article II of the Constitution clearly did not grant such power to the executive branch or its agents. Jackson and Taney were using a "loose construction" method to destroy a Bank that had been created by "loose construction" arguments in the first place.

Clay, for all of his faults in regard to policy, understood that according to the original Constitution, the legislature was intended to be the most powerful branch of government. It had to be able to check the executive branch. If not, the executive would be able to continually expand its power at the expense of American liberty. The "Bank War" was simply a battle in a larger struggle between the executive and legislative branches for constitutional supremacy. Though Clay eventually orchestrated a Senate censure of Jackson (which was later expunged from the record), Congress ultimately lost the battle with "Old Hickory"—and the war with the executive branch. So Jackson's victory in the "Bank War" should not be confused with a triumph for a Jeffersonian vision of America. The issue was hardly settled, Jackson's part in the crisis was more of a personal quarrel than an ideological crusade, and his treasury secretary's actions with regard to the Bank were at least as clearly unconstitutional as Congress's establishment of the Bank in the first place.

THE NULLIFICATION CRISIS

Jackson's unilateral moves during the "Bank War" were appalling, but his political war with South Carolina during the "Nullification Crisis" earned him the nickname "King Andrew." When he assumed office in 1829, Jackson inherited a conflict over the protective tariff. The Congress had passed the "Tariff of Abominations" in 1828, and the South Carolina legislature had responded by issuing a series of resolutions declaring the tariff "unconstitutional, oppressive, and unjust." Vice President Calhoun secretly authored a pamphlet entitled *The South Carolina Exposition and Protest*, which made the case for "State interposition" or "nullification" of federal legislation. This was not a new idea. Jefferson and Madison had articulated the same approach in opposing the Sedition Act of 1798 through the famous Virginia and Kentucky Resolutions. Thirty years later Calhoun, channeling Jefferson and Madison, argued that when the general government passed a law that was clearly unconstitutional, the states had a duty to protect their citizens and veto the violation through their respective legislatures. Calhoun called this the "conservative" position.

He was right. During the state ratifying debates in 1787 and 1788, proponents of the Constitution sought to allay the fear that the document would destroy the states through unconstitutional usurpations of power by insisting that an unconstitutional law was no law and therefore void. Even Alexander Hamilton agreed. During the New York Ratifying Convention of 1788, Hamilton insisted that "the laws of Congress are restricted to a certain sphere, and when they depart from this sphere, they are no longer supreme and binding."[7] Roger Sherman of Connecticut, one of the greatest statesmen of the founding generation, argued that if the general government passed an unconstitutional law the states would be "powerful enough to check it."[8] So the pressing question in 1828 was whether the Tariff of 1828 was unconstitutional.

South Carolina believed it was, and they had a point. Article I, Section 8, granted the general government the ability to levy taxes through a tariff "to pay the Debts and provide for the common Defence and general

Welfare of the United States; but all Duties, Imposts and Excises shall be uniform throughout the United States...." The "general Welfare," at least according to the original Constitution, meant that all legislation had to be of equal benefit and burden to the Union. Thus no one section should profit or be excessively burdened at the expense of another state or group of states. A protective tariff had that effect. The South was almost universally opposed to the 1828 tariff because it raised the price of their imported manufactured goods, while the Middle Atlantic states and a large part of New England favored the bill because it protected their fledgling industries from foreign competition. This was a tax that while "uniform" in rates would not be "uniform" in application.

Jackson was generally sympathetic to the Southern position before taking office, but he bristled at "nullification." At an 1830 Jefferson Day dinner, Jackson reportedly toasted the Union, insisting that "it must be preserved." Calhoun responded that the Union, "next to our liberty" was "most dear." But Calhoun was not a disunionist. He always insisted that his position was consistent with the *preservation* of the Union, not its demise. He privately wrote in 1831 that, "I do not wish to destroy the Union! I only wish to make it honest!"[9] The real underlying issue for Jackson was not the tariff but his personal hatred for Calhoun and his fundamental belief in executive and federal supremacy.

In 1832, Jackson signed a modified tariff bill that reduced some of the rates but retained the tariff's protectionist character. To Jackson, this seemed like a logical compromise. The North would retain protection for their infant industries but at lower rates, which would appease those in the South who were clamoring for a more neutral revenue-raising tariff. South Carolina countered by insisting that as a protective measure the tariff was still unconstitutional. As a result, a convention of the people of South Carolina voted to nullify the tariff and refuse to collect the duties.

Because of the growing tension between President Jackson and Vice President Calhoun over the issue of nullification, the latter determined to retire in 1832. Perhaps Calhoun made the situation more difficult when he gave his famous "Fort Hill Address" in July 1831. From the front porch of his plantation, Calhoun insisted:

> The great and leading principle is, that the General Government emanated from the people of the several States, forming distinct political communities, and acting in their separate and sovereign capacity, and not from all of the people forming one aggregate political community; that the Constitution of the United States is, in fact, a compact, to which each State is a party, in the character already described; and that the several States, or parties, have a right to judge of its infractions; and in case of a deliberate, palpable, and dangerous exercise of power not delegated, they have the right, in the last resort, to use the language of the Virginia Resolutions, "to interpose for arresting the progress of the evil, and for maintaining, within their respective limits, the authorities, rights, and liberties appertaining to them." This right of interposition, thus solemnly asserted by the State of Virginia, be it called what it may—State-right, veto, nullification, or by any other name—I conceive to be the fundamental principle of our system, resting on facts historically as certain as our revolution itself, and deductions as simple and demonstrative as that of any political, or moral truth whatever; and I firmly believe that on its recognition depend the stability and safety of our political institutions.[10]

Jackson didn't agree. Nullification was an open threat to his authority, and he wanted to stretch Calhoun's neck. While Calhoun may have feared for his life, when South Carolina sent him to the United States Senate, he went to Washington, D.C., with a manly resolve to defend his state and his principles. The ensuing debate would help illuminate not only the constitutional limits of executive power but the relationship between the states and the general government.

Congress received South Carolina's "Ordinance of Nullification" in November 1832. Jackson responded with a proclamation that outlined his position on both nullification and the potential secession of South Carolina. "The Constitution of the United States," he wrote, "forms a government, not a league, and whether it be formed by compact between the States, or in any other manner, its character is the same. It is a government in which all the people are represented, which operates directly on the people individually, not upon the States.... To say that any State may at pleasure secede from the Union, is to say that the United States are not a nation...." Moreover, if South Carolina continued down this path, particularly in regard to armed resistance to federal law, Jackson declared, "Their object is disunion, but be not deceived by names; disunion, by armed force, is TREASON."[11] Washington had used the same line of reasoning in 1794 during the "Whiskey Rebellion," and Abraham Lincoln would echo Jackson in 1861 with a similar defense of federal supremacy.

A THREAT OF FORCE

Jackson then dispatched an armed flotilla to South Carolina and threatened force if the state did not comply with federal law. The situation was tense. South Carolina, which had begun arming its militia for a potential conflict between the general and state governments, insisted that it was only doing so because Jackson had been overtly hostile to the state's position. Jackson wasn't bluffing. He went to Congress and asked for legislation authorizing him to use force to collect the tariff, if necessary. In doing so, Jackson was departing from his original stance that he would only enforce the laws already on the books. What became known as the Force Bill gave Jackson wide-ranging powers to shut down ports in South Carolina and send in the army to protect customs officials or other government employees charged with collecting the tariff. Moreover, if local law enforcement proved inadequate to hold the "nullifiers" accountable, United States marshals would be granted arresting powers. This would have amounted to a full-scale federal takeover of South Carolina, ostensibly with congressional support but orchestrated by the executive branch.

On the surface, Jackson's actions seemed constitutional. The president takes an oath to "defend the Constitution" and has a constitutional duty to enforce or execute the laws of the United States. Calhoun countered that the "Supremacy Clause" of the Constitution did not give the United States government, including the executive branch, a blank check to do whatever it wanted. "It is...undeniable that laws *not* made in pursuance [of the Constitution] are not only not of paramount authority, but are of no authority whatever, being of themselves null and void...."[12] The tariff, Calhoun argued, was unconstitutional. But the real issue at hand centered on who would be the final judge in such matters: "I would ask him [Daniel Webster] on what principle, if the departments of General government are to possess the right of judging, finally and conclusively, of their respective powers, on what principle can the same right be withheld from the State Governments, which, as well as the General Government, properly considered, are but departments of the same general system, and form together, properly speaking, but one government[?]"[13]

If the states could not serve as the "restraining influence" on the general government, Calhoun feared that the net result would be a system in which the executive would be the "*sole* interpreter of the powers of the government. It is the *armed* interpreter, with powers to execute its own construction, and without the aid of which the construction of the other departments will be impotent."[14] Calhoun proved to be prophetic. Jackson's Force Bill was an unconstitutional expansion of executive authority not only at the expense of the states, but at the expense of the entire federal system and the Constitution itself.

Congress passed a modified Force Bill in 1833, along with a compromise tariff that reduced rates. South Carolina responded by rescinding their Ordinance of Nullification of the tariff but then nullified the Force Bill. Critics claimed this was a victory for the Jackson administration. Perhaps so, in the long term—because as Calhoun correctly estimated, the executive branch would eventually consume the powers of the other branches of government along with those of the states. Hence Jackson can be viewed as one of the presidents who "screwed things up" for the original Constitution.

In the short term, however, nullification won. The tariff was reduced and the Union was preserved. Nullification had proved to be a viable option for resistance to unconstitutional federal authority. It worked in 1798 and again in 1833, and it has since been dusted off in the twenty-first century as a potential remedy for unconstitutional federal usurpations of power. The issue, then, has never been completely settled. Time will tell if Jackson or Calhoun will win the day.

CHAPTER 2

ABRAHAM LINCOLN

Sixteenth President, 1861–1865

After Abraham Lincoln was assassinated in April 1865, he became the symbol of America, the personification of the American ideal. Lincoln sits atop Mount Rushmore with the two most beloved founders of the Republic, and including him in a list of the presidents who "screwed up America" may come as a shock to the modern reader.

Today, Lincoln is considered sacrosanct by most Americans regardless of political persuasion. His was a rags-to-riches story of a self-educated man of humble roots who rose to prominence and who presided over the most traumatic and defining moment in American history. The War Between the States has properly been labeled the Second American Revolution by both participants and modern historians. Dramatic changes took place in American social institutions, in the economy, and most importantly to the Constitution. Lincoln's critics—there were many—consistently walloped the sixteenth president for his careless disregard for executive restraint and the wholesale transformation of the American political system from a federal Republic to a consolidated nation. The war represented a watershed in American constitutional history. Every president who "screwed things up" could use Lincoln's example to justify his actions. Lincoln, more than any president who came before him, created the blueprint for the modern presidency.

DECLARING "ANARCHY"

Lincoln assumed office in 1861 amid the worst constitutional crisis in American history. Seven states had already seceded from the Union and the other Southern states were watching Lincoln's actions closely. In his first inaugural address he promised to faithfully "execute the laws." He then refused to acknowledge the right of secession, claiming that the Union was "perpetual" and that in order for any dissolution *all* states must agree to part company. To Lincoln, the "Constitution and the laws of the Union" remained "unbroken." This was an important legal stand. As Lincoln did not recognize the Confederate states as a legitimate government, he could declare a state of rebellion and insist that it was the South, not the Union, which was in violation of the law and therefore that force could be used to put down the insurrection against legal authority. Lincoln classified the situation as a state of "anarchy."

By pronouncing the Union "perpetual" and indissoluble, Lincoln channeled every nationalist from the founding period forward, but most importantly Associate Supreme Court Justice Joseph Story, whose *Commentaries on the Constitution of the United States* formed the philosophical underpinnings for the nationalist interpretation of the Constitution. In what is often called the "one people" thesis, Story asserted that the Constitution had been formed and ratified by the American people at large, not as a compact between individual states. In one sentence, Story reduced the states to the status of mere counties, provinces, or shires: "The constitution of a confederated republic, that is, of a national republic, formed of several states, is, or at least may be, not less an irrevocable form of government, than the constitution of a state formed and ratified by the aggregate of the several counties of the state."[1] In addition, he claimed that the Union had already existed *before* independence was achieved in 1783 and therefore predated both the Articles of Confederation and the Constitution. Lincoln made the same claim during the war.

There are two problems with this position. First, Story ingeniously and incongruously claimed that a "confederated republic" is the same as a "national republic." Not true. A confederated republic consists of sovereign political bodies joined for a particular set of purposes, as in the case of the United States for commerce and defense. A national republic is a singular unitary state, like France, with complete and indivisible sovereignty.

Second, in reducing the states to the status of mere departments of the federal government and by claiming that the Union predated the states, Story ignored the entire legal history of the United States. The British recognized the independence of each state individually in the 1783 Treaty of Paris, as did Jefferson in the Declaration of Independence when he used the same term for them as for the "State of Great Britain." Article II of the Articles of Confederation expressly declared that each state retained its "sovereignty and independence." Article VII of the Constitution for the United States affirms that it was an agreement (compact) "between the States so ratifying the same"—not between an amorphous mass of people. John Adams called the members of the Continental Congress and the Congress under the Articles of Confederation "ambassadors" from their respective states. Based on the historical record, the Union was a federal Republic comprised of independent sovereign states. No other claim can be accurately or honestly made.

"PERPETUAL UNION"

Both Lincoln and Story insisted that the Union was permanent because of the term "perpetual." And yet that term is not in the Constitution, but rather in the Articles of Confederation—whose title, in full, was The Articles of Confederation and Perpetual Union. In a general way, all legal contracts are thought to be "perpetual" unless an express cessation date or terms of termination are inserted in the document, but that does not mean they cannot be voided by any party to the agreement at will. Both the Articles of Confederation and the Constitution were no different. In fact the Constitution itself voided the Articles of Confederation—Article VII of the Constitution was in clear violation of the earlier compact. Unanimous consent of all the states was required to amend or alter the Articles; only nine states were needed to ratify the Constitution. Therefore, with the adoption of the Constitution, the states essentially seceded from the Articles of Confederation and formed another government. Lincoln and Story built their legal argument against secession on quicksand.

The Confederate States of America in 1861 was legally an independent government. The Southern states seceded by popular conventions of the people of each state, the same method they had used to ratify the Constitution. The causes underpinning the secession of the Southern states can be debated, but not the principle or legality of secession. If a state acceded to the compact it could then logically secede from the compact. The states reserved all powers not delegated to the central authority or prohibited by Article I, Section 10. The right of secession is not a prohibited power in Article I, Section 10. Forming alliances with other states is prohibited but only as long as the state(s) remain in the Union. None of the Southern states that seceded from the Union were legally bound by the Constitution from 1861 to 1865.

Lincoln was playing a dangerous balancing act with the Constitution and his oath of office. His call for seventy-five thousand troops to put down the "rebellion" in April 1861 was constitutionally dubious in more than one way. The Confederate states were legally out of the Union, so according to the Constitution the president needed a declaration of war from Congress to invade the South, blockade her ports, and begin military operations against the foreign government. Of course, the people of the South considered the Confederate States of America their legitimate government and the government dispatched foreign agents to Europe to establish diplomatic intercourse. No European governments officially recognized the Confederate government, but they did treat Confederate emissaries as legal representatives of the Confederate states. Both in and out of government, Northern Americans recognized that secession had in fact taken place. For example, United States Senator Jesse Bright of Indiana was expelled from the Senate for writing a private letter addressed to "His Excellency Jefferson Davis, President of the Confederate States of America" before hostilities began in 1861. His crime was a *de facto* recognition of the title Davis and millions of Southerners claimed to be his legal position. Lincoln's refusal to accept *de jure* secession was by no means universal in the North.

UNILATERAL EXECUTIVE ACTION

According to the Constitution, the United States government should have recognized the Confederate states. But even assuming for the sake of argument that secession was, as Lincoln classified it, an illegal act of "anarchy" or "rebellion," his unilateral actions were still unconstitutional. The Constitution authorizes the *Congress*—not the president—to call "forth the Militia to execute the Laws of the Union, suppress Insurrections," suspend the writ of *habeas corpus* "when in Cases of Rebellion or Invasion the public Safety may require it," and "guarantee to every State in this Union a Republican Form of Government...and on Application of the Legislature, or of the Executive (when the Legislature cannot be convened) against domestic Violence."

Lincoln violated the Constitution and his oath by unilaterally calling up the "militia" to subdue "combinations too powerful to be suppressed by the ordinary course of judicial proceedings or by the powers vested in the marshals by law." His legal justification came from the Militia Act of 1792, the law Washington had used to quell the "Whiskey Rebellion." Lincoln did not have a request for federal troops from any legislature or governor of Southern states, any more than Washington had from Pennsylvania. Worse, Lincoln did not even have an order from a Supreme Court justice like the one Washington had. The move was illegal, both in regard to established law and the Constitution. Lincoln could have used the regular army and navy to repulse the attack on Fort Sumter constitutionally, but contrary to his proclamation, he had no legal authority to suspend *habeas corpus* or raise a militia to march south. In fact, according to Article III, Section 3, of the Constitution, Lincoln's actions bordered on treason as his move was calculated to levy "war against them," the "them" being the states.

FLAGRANT ABUSES OF POWER

And these violations of the Constitution were only the beginning. Lincoln presided over the most oppressive and lawless general government in American history to that point, one that has only been surpassed by the imperial presidencies of the twentieth century. His unilateral suspension of *habeas corpus* was ruled unconstitutional by Supreme Court Chief Justice Roger Taney in the 1861 *Ex parte Merryman* case. Lincoln ignored the ruling, and throughout the war the Lincoln administration arrested over ten thousand *Northern* Americans for their opposition to the war, mostly newspaper editors and politically well-connected citizens, including a United States congressman, Clement Vallandigham of Ohio.

Troops were sent to polling places in elections across the North—in some cases allowed to vote illegally in states where they did not reside and in others used to intimidate Democratic voters. In Delaware, election officials stuffed ballot boxes with Republican votes and forced Democrats to take an oath of allegiance before voting. Additionally, the army arrested and disarmed private citizens for "suspected" pro-Southern activity and for wearing "secession badges," a clear violation of the First and Second Amendments to the Constitution. One of the men affected was future United States Senator, Secretary of State, and Ambassador to Great Britain Thomas F. Bayard Sr. Lincoln may not have had direct knowledge of the arrests, but he was in the loop concerning troops at the polls. United States Representative George P. Fisher directly appealed to Lincoln in 1862 to send troops into Delaware during the election in order to prevent a Democratic victory. They showed up not long after.[2]

In September 1862, Lincoln issued the Emancipation Proclamation, generally hailed as a seminal moment in American history, the day that "Lincoln freed the slaves." Morally emancipation was just, but even Northern legal scholars at the time questioned whether it was legal for the president, by decree, to invalidate state laws in regard to property rights.

A PRINCIPLED SUPPORTER OF THE UNION

Massachusetts-born Supreme Court Justice Benjamin Robbins Curtis, for example, considered the Emancipation Proclamation a grave violation of the Constitution. He supported the war, believed secession to be illegal, and advocated abolition. Curtis had resigned his seat on the bench after his dissent in the Dred Scott case in 1857. But he balked at unilateral executive action in this regard. Lincoln had said, "I raise no objection against it [executive emancipation] on legal or constitutional grounds; for, *as commander-in-chief of the army and navy, in time of war, I suppose I have a right to take any measure which may best subdue the enemy* [emphasis added]."[3] (This is the same argument George W. Bush made in regard to the War on Terror.) But Curtis argued that the Emancipation Proclamation flouted the Constitution and reduced the government to a petty tyranny:

> It has never been doubted that the power to abolish slavery within the States was not delegated to the United States by the

Constitution, but was reserved to the States. If the President, as commander-in-chief of the army and navy in time of war, may, by an executive decree, exercise this power to abolish slavery in the States, which power was reserved to the States, because he is of opinion that he may thus "best subdue the enemy," what other power, reserved to the States or to the people, may not be exercised by the President, for the same reason that he is of opinion he may thus best subdue the enemy? And, if so, what distinction can be made between powers not delegated to the United States at all, and powers which, though thus delegated, are conferred by the Constitution upon some department of the Government other than the Executive?[4]

Curtis wondered how any American citizen would be able to resist the unveiled attack on constitutional government by the administration, particularly if citizens could be thrown in jail for openly voicing their opposition to the war. He lamented that many Americans were oblivious to the legal issues raised by Lincoln's wartime actions—one leading Northern newspaper wrote that "nobody cares whether it is legal or not."[5] Lincoln issued the Proclamation, the military supported it, and the Northern people sustained it, but as Curtis defiantly pointed out, that did not make it legal.

ALL-PURPOSE EXCUSE

The justification of "best [subduing] the enemy" was used to defend other unconstitutional actions as well. The postal service, presumably at the direction of Lincoln's Postmaster General, searched and confiscated mail from suspected Lincoln opponents. United States Senator James A. Bayard of Delaware had his mail searched and a bag of printed speeches go missing. The speech in question was titled "Executive Usurpation," and it was a damning account of the Lincoln administration's actions in the early months of the war. Newspapers were shut down and martial law was declared in Chicago and eventually throughout the United States. Lincoln had a hand in all of this.

Lincoln also abrogated his responsibility to uphold and defend the Constitution by signing a number of bills into law (bills that, for constitutional reasons, would have never made it out of the Congress had secession not taken place in 1861). The National Bank Acts, for example, established another central banking system for the United States, an institution that Jefferson and other members of the founding generation had deemed unconstitutional and that both Andrew Jackson and John Tyler vetoed in part on constitutional grounds. Lincoln signed into law the first income tax in American history, the Revenue Act of 1861. Because the income tax was not levied uniformly, this law violated Article I, Section 9, which states that all direct taxes have to be made in "proportion to the Census or Enumeration herein before directed to be taken." (The Supreme Court invalidated an 1894 income tax for just this reason in *Pollock v. Farmers Loan Trust Co.*) Only the Sixteenth Amendment made the income tax constitutional. Lincoln had a constitutional duty to veto the bill as unconstitutional, but the general government needed revenue to "subdue the enemy." The emergency took precedence over the Constitution—as became commonplace during the war.

WE WERE WARNED

Lincoln didn't stop with a new central bank or an income tax. He signed protective tariff legislation into law early in his first term. The tariff had long been one of the most contentious issues between the North and South, with Southern opposition dating to the debates over the ratification of the Constitution in 1787 and 1788. In the Philadelphia Convention in 1787, George Mason had argued, "By requiring only a majority to make all commercial and navigation laws (tariffs), the five Southern states will be ruined; for such rigid and premature regulations may be made, as will enable the merchants of the northern and eastern states not only to demand an exorbitant freight, but to monopolize the purchase of the commodities at their own price, for many years...."[6] As a result, Virginia proposed an amendment to the Constitution requiring a two-thirds majority to pass "navigation laws." Though the amendment didn't become part of the Constitution, during the "Nullification Crisis" South Carolina persuasively argued that protective tariffs were unconstitutional. But these arguments cut no ice with President Lincoln, who had been one of the more ardent protectionists in the United States before the War.

Lincoln violated the Constitution because as commander in chief he believed he had to "subdue the enemy," no matter the collateral damage. And his violations created a blueprint for more executive abuse in the future. Had the founding generation anticipated an executive like Lincoln—or any of the men "who screwed things up" in the following chapters—the Constitution would never have been ratified. Opponents of ratification warned against this very outcome, but their cries fell on deaf ears. The American people have paid the price.

CHAPTER 3

THEODORE ROOSEVELT

Twenty-Sixth President, 1901–1909

Teddy Roosevelt called the presidency the "bully pulpit." He believed that the Constitution, rather than limiting executive power to those codified in the document, established unlimited implied powers. Silence equated permission. Roosevelt was the first president to have a comprehensive legislative agenda (the Square Deal), and he thought that the president should be chief legislator, an informal member of the legislative branch. Roosevelt helped write legislation, promoted legislation to the American people at large, became involved in every minor issue—even "simplified spelling"—and pressured Congress to act on his recommendations. His foreign policy involved unilateral executive action. In short, Roosevelt expanded presidential power far beyond what the founding generation intended, and he did so openly.

Roosevelt is an easy man to admire, particularly for conservative Americans. He was a war hero, a man of principle, and a firm proponent of American "exceptionalism." But that does not make his decisions in office, some of which are lauded for their salutary effect on American policy, constitutional or legal. If originalists insist on lambasting leftist progressives who abuse the Constitution, then they must be consistent and also take to task men whom they would otherwise admire when they do the same. As the first "progressive" president and the progenitor of several of the prerogatives presidents now use to justify their actions, TR represents a turning point in American history. He must be held accountable.

There is a commonly repeated anecdote that Republican Party bosses feared adding Roosevelt to the ticket as the vice presidential candidate in 1900, since that would put him one bullet away from the executive office. After all, two presidents in the preceding thirty-five years had been killed in office, so there was a real possibility Roosevelt could assume the presidency. And that's exactly what happened on September 14, 1901, not even one year into President William McKinley's second term.

But why did Party bosses fear Roosevelt? He had been a lifelong Republican, a man dedicated to Party core principles, but Roosevelt was a renegade who could not be corralled by corrupt political kneecappers or smoke-filled backroom politics. He was not a Party man, but an independent man. This made him both admirable and dangerous.

THE BULLY PULPIT

Roosevelt exuded energy and confidence. He drank a gallon of coffee a day and sucked the air out of any room he entered. Roosevelt had been involved in politics since the 1880s. His six years on the Federal Civil Service Commission had given him a reputation as a reformer—he detested the spoils system—and his headline-grabbing actions during the Spanish-American War had endeared him to the American people, but his overall political philosophy was generally unknown, at least to the American public at large. That changed quickly. Roosevelt's first public address, a weighty twenty thousand words, outlined his political philosophy in regard to both executive power and constitutional policy.

Roosevelt thought the president should lead both the people and the government and considered the Constitution a hindrance to needed reform. That was the progressive mantra. Roosevelt now had the power— supposedly "implied" in the Constitution—to act on his progressive principles, and no element of American society was off limits to "reform." Roosevelt labeled his philosophy "Applied Idealism" in his autobiography. Ideas have consequences. He made that clear.

"When the Constitution was adopted, at the end of the eighteenth century, no human wisdom could foretell the sweeping changes, alike in industrial and political conditions, which were to take place by the beginning of the twentieth century."[1] As a good progressive, Roosevelt argued that modern emergencies and economic conditions called for wide-ranging government action. He called on Congress to pass legislation for the regulation of corporations while tempering his demand with the request that Congress find "constitutional authority" to pass such measures. If they did not, Roosevelt requested a constitutional amendment. But if Congress did not act, Roosevelt would act alone.

Roosevelt understood that the executive office had a clear advantage over Congress in messaging. He had learned that from William McKinley. One man with a platform can articulate an agenda better than over four hundred discordant voices. Like McKinley, Roosevelt held daily press briefings in an effort to drive his agenda and spin it to the American people. Such unilateral action was not lost on his opponents, and it set the stage for future presidents of both parties who wanted to make an end run around Congress. Though Congress was dominated by fellow Republicans, they did not always agree with Roosevelt's progressive idealism and his belief that—as Roosevelt's friend Herbert Croly advocated—the Constitution was an outdated piece of parchment subject to elastic interpretation and the will of the executive. Democrat Champ Clark of Missouri spoke for many Americans when he said in 1904 that "the President is not the country. The time has not yet arrived—I pray Almighty God that it never will arrive—when the American people will accept the arrogant dictum of Louis XIV, if repeated by an American president, 'I am the State!'"[2]

SQUARE DEAL DEMAGOGUE

Roosevelt spent much of his first message to Congress railing against large corporations on behalf of the working class, namely farmers, mechanics, and small businessmen. This was typical "Main Street vs. Wall Street" progressive demagoguery, but now that it was the president taking up the rhetoric, it had teeth. By 1904, Roosevelt was insisting that the common man needed a "square deal" from the government and outlining the first presidential legislative agenda in American history. Other presidents had called for Congress to act; Roosevelt laid out his own legislative program and pursued it with vigor. He was the first "chief legislator" in American history, a job that is not defined in the original Constitution as ratified by the states.

Roosevelt's first step was to call on the federal bureaucracy to rigidly enforce the Sherman Anti-Trust Act of 1890. This law was constitutionally dubious, and the president has a responsibility to enforce only *constitutional* legislation. Both the Sherman Anti-Trust Act and its predecessor the Interstate Commerce Act of 1887 broadened the scope of the "Commerce Clause" found in Article I, Section 8, of the Constitution. The founding generation understood the language, "To regulate Commerce with foreign Nations, and among the several States, and with the Indian Tribes" to mean that Congress should maintain a free trade zone among the states. Alexander Hamilton wrote in *The Federalist* No. 11, "An unrestrained intercourse between the States themselves will advance the trade of each...not only for the supply of reciprocal wants at home, but for exportation to foreign markets." Edmund Pendleton of Virginia was much more direct. "Trade & manufacturers," he said, "should both be Free...."[3]

The Supreme Court ruled in 1895 that the Sherman Anti-Trust Act was constitutional, but only in a limited sense. The general government still could not regulate manufacturing or any "intrastate" commerce; that type of economic activity was solely under the purview of the state governments. This decision followed Court precedent. In the 1824 *Gibbons v. Ogden* decision, Chief Justice John Marshall, a member of the founding generation and one of the most ardent nationalists in the United States, opined that the "Commerce Clause" of the Constitution did not apply to "intrastate" commerce. He agreed with what Hamilton and Pendleton said in 1788. But Roosevelt did not, and in short order he unleashed the Justice Department on American business.

Roosevelt promised to use the power of the general government to rein in big business. By the end of his almost two terms in office, his Justice Department had sued forty-five American corporations for violation of the Sherman Anti-Trust Act. The most significant case involved the Northern Securities Company, a corporation that could have, in theory, acquired a monopoly on railroad transportation in the Northwest.

This was a high-profile case. Roosevelt labeled the railroad industry a "public servant" in his first address to Congress, and he wanted to make the potential trust an example and scare future business leaders out of activities that could be perceived as potentially cornering a large percentage of the market.[4] That was the main thrust of the Sherman Act. The law made it illegal for anyone to conspire to form a monopoly. How that would be measured was never decided. This was nineteenth-century progressive thought control. The object of all business is to eliminate the competition and gain market share. The general government had made that illegal in 1890; now Roosevelt would ensure that the law was enforced.

The case against the Northern Securities Company appeared to be a clear-cut use of constitutional federal power. After all, railroads engaged in "interstate commerce" by shipping products over state lines, and thus could be regulated by the federal government. That precedent had been established by the aforementioned *Gibbons v. Ogden* decision, though the founding generation generally, if not to a man, had argued that all interstate commerce should be *free* from *prohibitive* regulation, meaning that all commercial "intercourse" should be unencumbered by economic penalties such as state-imposed tariffs and taxes levied against other *states*. That was the point of the "Commerce Clause" of the Constitution. The "intercourse" it was meant to apply to was actual trade and exchange between states, not the mere transportation of goods from one state to another.

The Supreme Court took up the issue in 1903 in the case of *Northern Securities Co. v. United States*. Roosevelt was unsure whether the Court would follow his lead and break up the company. He had only two appointees on the bench, and historically the Court had been hesitant to uphold punitive legislation against American business. But Roosevelt believed he had a mandate, and the Court, though designed to be non-partisan and politically independent, often rides the wave of popular opinion. At the very least, Roosevelt had skillfully used his "bully pulpit" to shame those who believed in an unrestrained free market.

Though the justices would never admit it, the Court bowed to the political pressure of the day and upheld the decision to break up the Northern Securities Company. But it was a split decision with four dissenters, and though Roosevelt's Justice Department won, it was a bittersweet victory for the president.

The lead dissent in the case came from Justice Edward D. White. He systematically shredded the expansive power of the Sherman Anti-Trust Act by correctly pointing out that interstate commerce, under an originalist definition, could not simply be transportation. It had to be commercial *intercourse*. And it had to be between *states*, not individuals. So Congress could not, constitutionally, regulate the sale and purchase of stock in companies, a purely individual action outside the purview of federal authority. To White, the Sherman Anti-Trust Act was a clear violation of the Tenth Amendment to the Constitution, an unprecedented and unconstitutional power grab by the general government that would render property rights void.

Shockingly, one of Roosevelt's appointees, Justice Oliver Wendell Holmes, agreed with White. Holmes had been chosen for the bench for the sole purpose of upholding progressive legislation. He would follow through in most instances, but in this case, Holmes sided with "big business"—or perhaps he simply had constitutional clarity for once. Holmes concluded his dissent by asserting that the majority interpretation of the Sherman Act would allow an "attempt to reconstruct society" and that would lead to a "war of all against all."[5] If that was the case, Congress had no constitutional power to enact it. Roosevelt was furious and quipped that a banana had more backbone than Holmes. But this says more about Roosevelt than Holmes. Roosevelt was willing to use the Court as a tool in his progressive arsenal, as a political weapon of last resort, and as a way of circumventing the Constitution and the states. Roosevelt was not the first president to do so, but his behavior demonstrated that for him ideology trumped the legal boundaries of the original Constitution, a document he had sworn to defend.

By the time Roosevelt left office in 1909, his sweeping labor reforms had transformed the relationship between the general government and business, but more importantly between private property and the long arm of the Justice Department. Roosevelt acted where he had no constitutional authority, intervening in matters that had once been the sole purview of the states.

The 1902 Coal Strike exemplifies Roosevelt's "Square Deal" demagoguery. The anthracite coal industry shut down in May 1902 when almost 80 percent of the mining force in Pennsylvania walked off the job. (Many of the rest went back to Europe. It is estimated that almost 90 percent of the miners were European immigrants.) Coal mine owners refused to negotiate, and Roosevelt and the progressives began stumping on the theme that the strike threatened to cut off the heat for American cities...in the summer. Of course, coal supplies needed to be stocked for the winter, but there were already huge reserves and as a result low prices for the product.

Regardless, Roosevelt began wringing his hands over the issue only three weeks into the strike. He wanted to use the power of the federal government to end the strike but was advised by Attorney General Philander Knox that such a move would be unconstitutional. So instead, Roosevelt called a meeting in Washington with the heads of labor and business. If Roosevelt could not use the force of government to break the strike, he would act as a mediator. The general government had intervened in labor disputes before, for example during the Great Railway Strike of 1877, but only to open transportation or keep goods moving. It had never come down on the side of labor. Roosevelt was ready to change that, for, in his mind, he was attempting to prevent "a social war." He may have had a point. The miners did riot and attack "scabs" and private police forces hired to protect mine property. Strikes in this period were often bloody.

Roosevelt charged the Bureau of Labor chief Carroll Wright with undertaking a fact-finding mission. Wright's report was favorable to the coal miners but not entirely anti-business. He made several recommendations to improve labor conditions—shorter work day, better protection for the over one hundred forty thousand non-union men, almost all of whom were immigrants, and a committee composed of both labor and management and charged with mediation. Roosevelt sent Wright's findings to Attorney General Knox. Again Knox insisted that under the Constitution Roosevelt could do nothing to stop the strike. Roosevelt wanted to act, and as the strike dragged on into the fall, he threated to nationalize the coal fields and send in the army. That move would have been unprecedented and in no way constitutional, but Roosevelt thought "national" action was necessary to defend the interests of the American people at large.

Roosevelt's October meeting did little to stop the strike, and it wasn't until business tycoon J. P. Morgan stepped in that business and labor sat down at the negotiation table to hammer out their differences. But progressives hailed Roosevelt's involvement as a turning point in the history of business and labor. Labor leader Samuel Gompers called it the most important moment in the history of labor relations. It was indeed a turning point, but only because Roosevelt had to stretch his constitutional powers to act and the general government assumed a role between business and labor that was never contemplated when the Constitution was drafted and ratified. Roosevelt would insist that the founding generation could not have foreseen the problems of an industrial society and that they would have supported his aggressive executive action. Probably not. Labor disputes were not uncommon in the founding period, but they were left to the private sector, or at most for state and local governments to handle; in the Founders' day, neither the Congress nor the president would have had any interest in intervention. Roosevelt's open disregard for the Constitution as ratified and his penchant for demagoguery had led to a radical transformation of the executive branch. And he was just getting started.

FALSE FOOD POLICE

In 1906, the muckraking journalist Upton Sinclair published *The Jungle*, a novel he hoped would serve as an expose of the working conditions of meat packing workers in American factories. It was an attack on big business designed to help the working class. His friend and socialist "comrade," author Jack London, wrote,

> It is written of sweat and blood, and groans and tears. It depicts not what man ought to be, but what man is compelled to be in this, our world, in the Twentieth Century. It depicts not what our country ought to be or what it seems to be in the fancies of Fourth of July spell-binders, the hoax of liberty and equality, of opportunity; but it depicts what our country really is, the home of oppression and injustice, a nightmare of misery, an inferno of suffering, a human hell, a jungle of wild beasts.... And take notice and remember, comrades, this book is straight proletarian.... It is written for the proletarian.[6]

London and others called Sinclair's novel the *Uncle Tom's Cabin* of their time. They were correct. Abraham Lincoln had suggested that Harriet Beecher Stowe helped start the Civil War. At the very least, her fictionalized depiction of American slavery—though rife with inaccuracies—led to a broader movement for federal action. Stowe had never visited the South, and her research generally came from secondhand accounts. But Americans believed her story and began agitating for reform. The same can be said for *The Jungle*.

Like Stowe, Sinclair had limited experience with his subject. He had never visited a meat packing plant, had never seen the working conditions in one, and based his conclusions on hearsay rather than concrete fact. That didn't matter. What Sinclair intended to be a book aimed at challenging working conditions instead led to a call for food reform in America. People could not believe what was in their meat. And in fact Sinclair had made most of it up. But Roosevelt enthusiastically supported federal intervention in the food and drug industry and began pushing for more restrictions on meat packing and other consumables in the name of regulating "interstate commerce." With one success under his belt under a broad definition of federal regulatory power, Roosevelt refused to call it quits.

He acted unilaterally, sending his newly appointed Bureau of Labor chief Charles Neill (Neill had succeeded Wright and served on the mediation board charged with ending the Coal Labor Strike) to investigate. This method had born fruit before, and Roosevelt, to his credit, was suspicious of Sinclair and his socialist agenda. Neill selected a New Yorker named James Bronson Reynolds to accompany him to meat packing plants in the Midwest. Neither had even set foot inside a meat packing plant and knew little to nothing about such plants' operations, but they produced the Neill-Reynolds Report critical of the working conditions and sanitation in the factories. Roosevelt believed it and signed the Meat Inspection Act into law in 1906. This unconstitutional federal usurpation of both citizens' property and contract rights and the states' powers turned out to be a boon for the large corporations, as most federal regulatory programs tend to be.

Most Americans don't realize that meat inspectors already existed in 1906 and that the "reform" process Roosevelt put the full force of the general government behind was promoted by the *meat inspection industry* itself! With the Meat Inspection Act now in effect, smaller companies faced expensive regulatory barriers to continuing in business and the taxpayer was on the hook for the $3 million required to implement the new rules—a gift to the big meat packing corporations. Many of the smaller meat packing companies shut down while the rich got richer. The same held true for other food production companies after Roosevelt signed the Pure Food and Drug Act of 1906. Inspections were no more rigid, but they were more costly, and now Americans had a little stamp on their food, which supposedly proved its purity. Roosevelt had expanded both federal and executive power in the name of commerce and the common man—based on the fabricated lies of a socialist. Commerce did not increase, but federal power did, and the office of the president had inched a little further away from the Founders' understanding of the executive branch.

SAVE THE FOREST!

Theodore Roosevelt is perhaps the most well-known conservationist in American history. He, more than any other public figure, placed the "preservation" of natural resources at the forefront of public policy. In his opening address to Congress, Roosevelt called forests the basis of "national wealth" and pledged to preserve these "national reservoirs" for both human beings and animals alike. He initially defended using government power to seize land as a way to protect the resources for "business neces-sity." But that wasn't the real reason behind the land grabs. Roosevelt and his primary conservationist advisor, Gifford Pinchot, believed in the conservationist ethic—in short, that government protects and preserves land while private industry and individuals destroy it. Therefore, the only way to ensure that future generations could enjoy forests, mountains, waterways, or any other worthwhile land was for the government to gobble it up and set it aside. How and when it would be used or enjoyed was to be determined by Washington bureaucrats.

Roosevelt aggressively used "proclamations" to set aside almost 150 million acres of "forest land," issuing in excess of one hundred such proclamations in his nearly eight years as president. By the end of his presidency, Roosevelt had moved over 200 million acres of land into government hands. These decisions were theoretically constitutional because in 1891 Congress had passed legislation authorizing the president, from time to time, to set aside public land through proclamation. Congress added to this power in 1906 with the Antiquities Act, a bill that allowed the executive to designate natural monuments, provided that the land be "confined to the smallest area compatible with proper care and management of the objects to be protected." There was one problem with this line of reasoning. There is no executive proclamation power in the Constitution, and Congress cannot create an executive power through legislation. This supposed power had been used by preceding administrations, but much more sparingly, with the most consistent use being for declaring a day of Thanksgiving.

Roosevelt's public land confiscation scheme was not only a bad policy that would be perpetuated and expanded by successive administrations, it was an unconstitutional abuse of power in which Congress was complicit in the crime. But their complicity is no excuse. The president takes an oath to defend the Constitution. Implicit in that oath is the responsibility to ignore, oppose, or veto unconstitutional acts of Congress. But ideological agendas never mesh with constitutional restraint or the Constitution as ratified.

THE WHITE HOUSE AND THE SPELLING BOARD

Before Roosevelt's administration, the president did not get involved in many issues outside of the executive purview. That was by design. As Hamilton insisted in *The Federalist* No. 69, the president was not to be a king and had limited delegated authority. But Roosevelt was different. He was a crusader, and he understood the impact the office could have on popular opinion. Sometimes his executive energy backfired.

In October 1901, Roosevelt invited Booker T. Washington to the executive mansion for dinner. Washington was probably the most respected African American in the United States at the time. His work in advancing education for black Americans at Tuskegee Institute and his 1895 speech at the Atlanta Cotton States and International Exposition had made him an influential spokesman for the African American community. No black American had ever been invited to dine with the president. Frederick Douglass had had Abraham Lincoln's ear, and in one interesting episode Douglass arrived unannounced with a group of black leaders during Andrew Johnson's administration, but this was different. Roosevelt was extending a courtesy that had been reserved for white Americans. He was making a statement, and he issued a press release about the event.

The reaction was less than enthusiastic—even hostile among some Americans. Roosevelt's staff downplayed the event, but the "people's president" was becoming more involved in social issues than any of his predecessors, save perhaps Lincoln. This was an important shift in public policy, and while the president's intentions were laudable, his determination to reform racial attitudes moved the executive further from the original intent of the office. No longer was the president simply the head of the executive branch; he was the chief social engineer of America, a man who drove public opinion on a variety of issues, including some of the most hotly contested matters of the day.

Paradoxically, at the same time, Roosevelt wanted to make the office of the president more "democratic." The day following Washington's visit, Roosevelt instructed his secretary to inform the government that all future correspondence from the president's house would be labeled from "The White House." Up to that point, the president's residence had been known as "The Executive Mansion." That sounded aristocratic and pretentious. Roosevelt did not leave a record as to why he initiated the change, but it can be deduced that he was trying to downgrade the office of the president, even if only semantically, by describing his residence as a simple white house for the people's president. The "White House" nickname had been used for almost a century, but it made sense to officially change the name now. Though his actions were more monarchical and his attitude more aristocratic than those of most men who had previously held the office, to the public at large Roosevelt was bringing power back to "the plain people." He allowed weekly access to his office to ordinary Americans so long as they bathed and brought a calling card. If Roosevelt could swing public opinion, he could drive his agenda. Image was more important than substance. As he said, following his reelection in 1904, "I would literally, not figuratively, rather cut off my right hand than forfeit by any improper act of mine the trust and regard of these people."[7]

Roosevelt attempted to use his political capital and newly established "bully pulpit" to support reform activities that had never been considered a component of executive power. In 1906, Andrew Carnegie established the Simplified Spelling Board. Its purpose was to reform and "simplify" the English language. Several prominent Americans sat on the board, including Mark Twain, Melvil Dewey (creator of the Dewey Decimal System), and publisher Henry Holt. The Board found three hundred words that needed to be changed. They wanted, for example, to drop the "ed" from "addressed" and add a "t" to make it "addresst" and to change the spelling of "honour" to "honor." The "simplified" spelling code aimed to make words phonetic, or "fonetic." (Modern American texters would rejoice!)

Unknown to the Board, Roosevelt enthusiastically supported "simplified spelling" and without congressional approval instructed the Government Printing Office to adhere to its recommendations. The American public and the Congress, however, did not find the new rules appealing. Just four months later, Congress passed a resolution that rejected implementation of Roosevelt's order for congressional documents, and the spelling changes made no impact in American education, at least not at the time. Roosevelt was forced to rescind his order. Yet, as in other areas of reform, Roosevelt was driving the agenda.

Many of the spelling changes have been adopted over time. More significant was Roosevelt's pursuit of reform through unconstitutional means. He could have recommended to Congress that the changes be implemented by legislation. Instead, Roosevelt decided to act unilaterally. That would be a hallmark of his administration. If Congress could be circumvented, Roosevelt would circumvent it in the name of reform. Such practices have become commonplace in modern American government, but in 1906 Roosevelt was not only violating the Constitution as ratified, but breaking protocol and establishing dangerous precedents. The "people's president" assumed power to advance his progressive program.

THE BIG STICK

Roosevelt is best known today for his foreign policy. His message of national strength, vigorous defense of the Western Hemisphere, and pursuance of American interests abroad resonates with modern Americans, particularly conservatives. We live in the aftermath of Roosevelt's vision, and as citizens of the only "superpower" in the world, Americans see Roosevelt as the progenitor of the American age, the intellectual godfather of American exceptionalism and the Pax Americana. What we call "Peace through Strength" was summed up in Teddy Roosevelt's motto: "Speak softly, and carry a big stick." The "big stick" was the United States Navy.

Roosevelt engaged in what may now be called foreign adventurism, typically without congressional authorization. Certainly, the president has a constitutional responsibility to act as head of state and chief diplomat, but executive powers are limited and concurrent with the Senate in foreign relations. The president does not have unilateral power. Those constitutional restrictions, however, did not stop Roosevelt or hinder his progressive idealism in foreign affairs any more than in domestic policy.

Roosevelt's most flagrant abuse of power occurred in 1903. For years, European powers, including the United States, had attempted to build a canal across Central America. In 1850, the United States and Great Britain signed the Clayton-Bulwer Treaty, an agreement that obligated both governments to neutrality in regard to a future canal. This was reinforced by the Hay-Pauncefote Treaty of 1902, written and ratified during the Roosevelt administration. In 1850 the United States needed the Clayton-Bulwer Treaty as a hedge against British power in the region, but by the early twentieth century, the geo-political situation had changed. The United States had a larger role in the Caribbean after the Spanish-American War of 1898, and in the first two years of his administration Roosevelt was already formulating what was later called the Roosevelt Corollary to the Monroe Doctrine. In the name of security, the United States would police the Western Hemisphere, and the executive branch would be central to the task. An isthmian canal controlled by the United States would solidify American hegemony in the Caribbean and make the United States a global power. Roosevelt had a grand vision, but there were obstacles, including that pesky Constitution he had sworn to defend.

Roosevelt supported a plan to cut the British out of Central America and build a canal controlled solely by the United States. The key was Colombia. In 1902 the United States Congress authorized Roosevelt to pursue a Panamanian option in regard to a future canal. But Colombia controlled Panama, and though in 1903 the United States Senate ratified the Hay-Herran Treaty, granting the United States perpetual control of a future canal zone through Colombian territory, the Colombian government refused to ratify it.

The French were complicating matters for Colombia. Like other Latin American countries in the nineteenth century, Colombia had its share of political unrest. A large faction of the Panamanian people had been pushing for independence since the 1880s. When the Hay-Herran Treaty failed ratification, Frenchman Philippe-Jean Bunau-Varilla informed the Roosevelt administration that Panama was ripe for revolution and eventual separation from Colombia. The Panamanians just needed assistance. Bunau-Varilla had a vested interest in a revolt. He was a soldier and engineer who had not lived in Colombia in years, but he had a $40 million interest in promoting a canal through Panama. His company was selling the land to the United States. Roosevelt seized the opportunity to act and sent several gunboats to the region to block the movement of Colombian troops that might be able to suppress an armed insurrection. The plan worked. The following day, November 3, 1903, Panama declared its independence; and three days later the United States and Panama signed the Hay-Bunau-Varilla Treaty which gave the U.S. the right to build a canal and indefinite control of the canal zone.

Roosevelt's participation in the Panamanian revolution exemplifies his faith in power and order and most importantly in America's role in the Caribbean. In 1904, Roosevelt issued the Roosevelt Corollary to the Monroe Doctrine. Europe was put on notice. If the United States—meaning Roosevelt—deemed Latin American unrest a threat to its peace and security, the United States would intervene. This happened in the Dominican Republic, in Cuba, and in Panama. In each case Roosevelt argued that the native population was incapable of addressing its own problems. Like his domestic policy initiatives, his foreign adventures showed that Roosevelt believed in a centralized, top-down approach. He couched his intentions in the language of democracy, but Roosevelt hardly believed in popular sovereignty. Roosevelt thought *he* knew what was best for the general population. This is monarchy and aristocracy, not democracy, but it fit perfectly with TR's conception of American government.

Roosevelt's direct involvement in the Panamanian revolution in 1903 expanded executive power greatly—and unconstitutionally. Years later, Roosevelt addressed the Panama incident, and by implication his entire foreign policy, in a speech at the University of California at Berkeley:

> But the Panama Canal would not have been started if I had not taken hold of it, because if I had followed the traditional or

conservative method I should have submitted an admirable state paper occupying a couple of hundred pages detailing all of the facts to Congress and asking Congress' consideration of it.

In that case there would have been a number of excellent speeches made on the subject in Congress; the debate would be proceeding at this moment with great spirit and the beginning of work on the canal would be fifty years in the future.

Fortunately the crisis came at a period when I could act unhampered. Accordingly I took the Isthmus, started the Canal and then left Congress not to debate the canal, but to debate me.[8]

EMPOWERING THE EXECUTIVE

Roosevelt was not the first president to use the powers of the office in a way the founding generation feared, but he represented a watershed in American politics. Roosevelt *was* the agenda in both domestic and foreign policy. Earlier administrations had driven public policy, but Roosevelt actively seized the initiative in an unprecedented way, all the while insisting that his directives were inspired by and responsive to the "plain people." His populist message obscured the arrogation of power to the executive branch. Roosevelt mirrored the ancient Greek leader Pericles, the good tyrant who ran Athens into a long period of decline through expansive government programs and long foreign wars. Roosevelt was loved by the people, but his policies inaugurated a century-long plunge into foreign wars in the name of "democracy" and "security" while his "Square Deal" provided the blueprint for future progressive presidents in domestic policy. The president had become both commander in chief in an everlasting quest to expand American power and legislator in chief of a perpetually bloated bureaucracy.

Roosevelt did all of this unconstitutionally in an unprecedented usurpation of power. He did not see it that way, but he understood that his critics did, and he used the pen to defend his actions in his *Autobiography*:

The most important factor in getting the right spirit in my Administration, next to the insistence upon courage, honesty, and a genuine democracy of desire to serve the plain people, was my insistence upon the theory that the executive power was limited only by specific restrictions and prohibitions appearing in the Constitution or imposed by the Congress under its Constitutional powers. My view was that every executive officer, and above all every executive officer in high position, was a steward of the people bound actively and affirmatively to do all he could for the people, and not to content himself with the negative merit of keeping his talents undamaged in a napkin. *I declined to adopt the view that what was imperatively necessary for the Nation could not be done by the President unless he could find some specific authorization to do it.* My belief was that it was not only his right but his duty to do anything that the needs of the Nation demanded unless such action was forbidden by the Constitution or by the laws. Under this interpretation of executive power I did and caused to be done many things not previously done by the President and the heads of the departments. *I did not usurp power, but I did greatly broaden the use of executive power. In other words, I acted for the public welfare, I acted for the common well-being of all our people, whenever and in whatever manner was necessary, unless prevented by direct constitutional or legislative prohibition.*[9] [emphasis added]

This view fits perfectly with progressive ideology. The Constitution is an elastic document with open-ended implied powers, and if it is silent on a given power, the president, Congress, or the Supreme Court can assume that power is granted. This interpretation is diametrically opposed to the way proponents of the Constitution insisted the document would be interpreted when it was ratified in 1788. But with Theodore Roosevelt,

America was only starting down the slippery slope to unlimited executive power.

CHAPTER 4

WOODROW WILSON

Twenty-Eighth President, 1913–1921

Wilson was a twentieth-century pioneer in unconstitutional executive authority. His book on the Constitution lamented that the founding generation did not have the foresight to call for a closer link between the executive and legislative branches. But he found a silver lining. Wilson reasoned that time and practice had made coordination of the two branches possible, and since the Constitution was in his mind an "organic" document, President Wilson could usurp power from the other branches and levels of government because that is what the people wanted.

Wilson argued that the president should be more like a prime minister, and that's how he governed. Of course, no constitutional amendments had been made to codify this change, but Wilson didn't care. He drove the legislative agenda, often keeping Congress in session until they bent to his wishes. He supported several unconstitutional laws—actively lobbying for many of them—most conspicuously during World War I. These included legislation for the federal control of the economy and the nationalization of the railroads and an infamous Sedition Act. In fact, Franklin Roosevelt copied much of his World War II wartime legislation from Wilson. If Roosevelt was "King Franklin," then Wilson was no less "Dictator Wilson," a term he actually took a shine to.

No president to this point in American history had a better academic pedigree. Wilson held a Ph.D in government from Johns Hopkins University; he had titled his dissertation, "Congressional Government: A Study in American Politics." He later authored a book titled *Constitutional Government in the United States.* He was an academic—his primary biographer counted this against his leadership style—and he relied on other academics for advice, though they were typically "yes men." Wilson once said that "he did not prepare . . . to become President."[1] He had never held a position in government until elected governor of New Jersey in 1910, just two years before his candidacy for president in 1912. He was a real outsider. But Wilson was talking about ideological preparation. Wilson, like Theodore Roosevelt, was a progressive, and ideology drove his administration. But he did not solidify his views on the presidency until only a few weeks before he took office, and much of Wilson's thinking on the executive office was formed under the influence of "Colonel" Edward M. House, Wilson's most trusted political advisor.

After the 1912 election, Wilson spent several weeks in Bermuda reading a little known utopian novel entitled *Philip Dru: Administrator.* The plot of the novel, penned anonymously by House, foreshadowed much of Wilson's legislative agenda, aptly titled the "New Freedom," and ultimately Wilson's foreign policy as well. The main character, a West Point graduate named Philip Dru, becomes dictator of the United States and implements a radical domestic program intended to "save" America from collapse. At the same time, Dru wages a war in Europe against the enemies of democracy. The result is a complete restructuring of the American economy, arrogation of power by the executive branch, a restructuring of Europe, and the centralization of government in Washington, D.C. By the end of Wilson's two terms in office, all of this had come to fruition.

This is not to suggest that Wilson did not have his own ideas. He was considered to be a conservative Democrat before becoming governor of New Jersey, and in 1896 he had supported the National Democratic Party, a conservative splinter group opposed to the nomination of William Jennings Bryan. But there were clues that could be read long before he became president suggesting that Wilson rejected the American political system. He was particularly critical of the separation of powers, the limited role of the executive branch in the legislative arena, and the overall concept of federalism. To Wilson, only the central government, not the states, could be trusted to move the American political process; it should all be done from the top down.

Back in 1885 Wilson had expressed a less expansive idea of the president's role. He wrote then that he considered, "the business of the President, occasionally great, is usually not much above routine. Most of the time it is *mere* administration...." subject to congressional standing committees.[2] He considered state governors as best suited for the job of president and thought that men should be selected not on their intellectual merits but by how well they could "run" the office. Congress, he said, did the heavy lifting and the president simply executed the laws, a job that took skill, but not great energy or creativity.

By 1908, his opinion had changed dramatically. In his *Constitutional Government in the United States*, Wilson complained that the "theory" behind the Constitution limited the potential of the executive branch. The founding generation had designed the executive to be "only the legal executive, the presiding and guiding authority in the application of law and the execution of policy. [The president's] veto upon legislation was only his 'check' on Congress,—was a power of restraint, not of guidance. He was empowered to prevent bad laws, but he was not to be given an opportunity to make good ones." To Wilson, the founding vision was outmoded and inconsistent with the realities of twentieth-century America. The times required action, and thus the Constitution and its limits on the presidency could be ignored. Wilson wrote, "Greatly as the practice and influence of Presidents has varied, there can be no mistaking the fact that we have grown more and more inclined from generation to generation to look to the President as the unifying force in our complex system, the leader both of his party and of the nation. To do so is not inconsistent with the actual provisions of the Constitution; it is only inconsistent with a very mechanical theory of its meaning and intention. The Constitution contains no theories. It is as practical a document as Magna Carta."[3]

This rejection of the "mechanical" application of the Constitution's actual words defining the executive office in favor of a "practical" application of whatever general principles Wilson claimed to have distilled from it—along with House's blueprint, in *Philip Dru*, for a presidency so energetic that it was really a dictatorship—formed the basis of the Wilson administration. President Wilson openly rejected an originalist interpretation of the Constitution. Thus, though he took an oath to defend the Constitution, he was really loyal only to his own theories about it. This alone makes him one of the worst presidents in American history. Not everything Wilson did as president was unconstitutional, but there is not much that can be vindicated by the understanding of the executive branch that prevailed during the ratification of the Constitution.

THE "NEW FREEDOM" AGENDA

Wilson's defining achievement as president was his legislative agenda, the "New Freedom." He had written in 1908 that the president was "the political leader of the nation." Wilson took it upon himself to be a new type of executive, a prime minister more than a president, to guide the legislative process so that "no other single force can withstand him, no combination of forces will easily overpower him."[4] The New Freedom represented his plan for a new America, with the government, the Constitution, and

the relationship between the central authority and the people all remade—
to give the president new, sweeping powers. Teddy Roosevelt had started
this process in 1901. Wilson put an exclamation point on the effort. And
the presidents who followed him built on Wilson's theoretical designs and
program directives.

With the publication of a pamphlet entitled *The New Freedom* in 1913,
Wilson appealed directly to "the people." He reiterated his position that
the Constitution had become outdated and ill equipped to handle the
problems of the modern age. "All that progressives ask or desire," he wrote,
"is permission—in an era when 'development,' 'evolution,' is the scientific
word—to interpret the Constitution according to the Darwinian principle; all they ask is recognition of the fact that a nation is a living thing and
not a machine."[5]

Wilson took the first step toward increasing the role of the executive
branch by calling Congress into special session the day after his inauguration and then by appearing in person to deliver a special message to both
houses on April 8, 1913. No president since John Adams had personally
appeared before the legislative branch. This made a statement. By calling
Congress into session and speaking to them, Wilson did nothing unconstitutional, but these actions were taken in pursuit of his very unconstitutional project to make himself the chief legislator. If Congress did not want
to act on legislation Wilson wanted passed, he would whip and grind them
until they followed through. He would do so through the Democratic
Party, now in power for the first time since Grover Cleveland had left office
in 1897.

Wilson's New Freedom called for tariff and banking reform and
stronger anti-trust laws. On the tariffs, he was following the traditional
line of the Democrat Party, which had always supported low, revenue-only
tariffs. Here Wilson was in line with the Constitution. Protective tariffs
had been controversial for years. The South had long insisted that protective measures violated Article I, Section 8, Clause 1, which requires all
taxes to be uniform. Protective measures that singled out certain goods

or industries were not uniform. By reducing the tariff in response to Wilson's pressure, the Congress acted more in line with the Constitution than it had in decades.

But the means that Wilson used to get the tariff reform passed were unprecedented. He was directly involved in the drafting of the legislation. He called the head of the Ways and Means Committee, Oscar Underwood of Alabama, to the White House to devise a strategy for the bill's provisions and even its language. Previous presidents, dating to the founding generation, had made their ideas clear when Congress considered legislation, but no one had been as directly involved as Wilson. The Underwood Tariff, as it became known, was in reality the Wilson Tariff. While there is no specific provision in the Constitution prohibiting the role Wilson assumed in the process, he was certainly breaking precedent and relying on a broad use of implied powers to hammer out the tariff proposal. Of course, when the Constitution was ratified, proponents consistently denied that the president would have this kind of power. But Wilson believed in a "living" Constitution—so the Founders' assurances were irrelevant.

Progressives in the Congress wanted a redistributive tax, with higher burdens on the wealthiest Americans. And the revenue from an income tax, which was made possible by the ratification of the Sixteenth Amendment earlier in 1913, would offset the revenue lost to a lower tariff. So the first graduated income tax in American history was written into the Underwood tariff and the tax bill. When it bogged down in the Senate, Democrats called in Wilson and his Secretary of State, William Jennings Bryan, for reinforcement. The original proposal set very low rates, and progressives balked, with one congressman calling for a 75 percent rate on the highest incomes. Wilson wrote several letters to prominent Democrats urging them to seek a more moderate resolution. Their intervention worked, and the Congress settled on a compromise bill that lowered the tariff and provided a "reasonable" graduated income tax.

Wilson had succeeded in infusing his personal beliefs into the legislative process—something that did not go unnoticed. The press remarked that Wilson had become the man of the hour, a man of action who had transformed the role of the president. That was certainly the intent—the Constitution be damned. Wilson also pioneered the ingenious strategy of cloaking unconstitutional programs in language that made them *seem* constitutional—and justified the innovations as necessary in a moral crusade to save America. During the debate over the Underwood bill, Wilson had gone directly to the American people for support, claiming that the government had responsibility to arrest the corrupt special interest groups that swarmed around Washington, D.C. "It is of serious interest to the country that the people at large should have no lobby and be voiceless in these matters, while great bodies of astute men seek to create an artificial opinion and to overcome the interests of the public for their private profit."[6] Wilson was not the first to use such democratic language, nor was he the first president to act as a demagogue, but he had interceded in the legislative process in a way no previous president had.

Wilson had promised anti-trust reform as part of his New Freedom agenda, complaining during the 1912 campaign that Roosevelt's anti-trust activities were ineffective in disrupting the monopolistic practices of big business. Large corporations needed more than regulation. They needed to be destroyed. Wilson believed that the Sherman Anti-Trust Act and Interstate Commerce Act, while steps in the right direction, did not have enough teeth. Roosevelt actually agreed, and during the same campaign presented a sweeping plan to establish a powerful interstate trade commission charged with reviewing all "illegal" trade practices. But Wilson thought the same effect could be achieved with a few minor changes to existing anti-trust legislation. As president, he began working closely with Henry D. Clayton of Alabama to craft a bill that satisfied both his campaign pledge and those who wanted more extensive reform, but that contained exemptions for labor unions and agricultural organizations, two large constituencies of the Democrat Party.

Wilson signed the Clayton Anti-Trust Act into law in 1914. Like other "anti-trust" legislation, the law contained vague language that made it

difficult to enforce, but more importantly difficult for businesses to interpret. That may have been the point. The Clayton Act would ultimately find
its muscle in the federal court system. Progressive judges would mold the
law to fit their ideology and in the process create the massive American
regulatory state. But even before the Clayton Act was passed, Wilson had
already decided that his piecemeal approach to business regulation did not
go far enough and quickly adopted Roosevelt's plan for a regulatory oversight committee charged with reviewing *all* "interstate commerce" in the
United States.

Though signed three weeks before the Clayton Anti-Trust Act, the
Federal Trade Commission Act did not find its legs until after Wilson
signed the Clayton Act and the Federal Trade Commission (FTC) was
established. The FTC throttled American business. It was the brainchild
of Oklahoma Republican Dick Thompson Morgan, an agrarian-minded
ally of the progressive movement. Morgan saw the federal government as
a vehicle to effect change, particularly to curtail the power of large corporations. Morgan was fighting a war on wealth and privilege, with the
federal government playing offense for the "common man"—at least that
is how the government sold the legislation to America.

The Justice Department had already broken apart the Standard Oil
Company and the American Tobacco Company in 1911, but Morgan
thought more needed to be done. Wilson agreed. The FTC became one of
the most powerful regulatory agencies in Washington, D.C., with the ability to act as all three branches of the general government. Like other regulatory agencies, the FTC could craft rules, enforce the rules, and decide
who broke the rules with virtually no oversight by the American people.
This is not how the founding generation promised the congressional power
to "regulate" business would be wielded. Wilson's direct involvement in
the legislative process, his personal appeals to members of Congress, and
his enthusiastic support for both pieces of legislation and the FTC violated
presidential precedent and his oath of office. Wilson was not defending
the Constitution. He was shredding it.

The final plank in Wilson's New Freedom agenda was banking reform. One of the great progressive mantras, then and now, is that "big banks" and "big business" rob Americans of their hard-earned cash. There is some truth to this claim, but mostly because "big banks" and "big business" get in bed with "big government." There is no clearer link between financial capital and the general government than the Federal Reserve System, created during Wilson's first year in office.

Designed by an exclusive group of bankers led by Republican Senator Nelson Aldrich of Rhode Island at Jekyll Island, Georgia, in 1910, the Federal Reserve System is the latest in the list of American central banking systems. It is also the most powerful in our history. Aldrich, as chairman of the Monetary Commission, had presented recommendations for adopting the Federal Reserve System to Congress in 1912, but the plan was shelved with Wilson's victory in the presidential election that year and the ascension of Democrats to power in Congress during the same election cycle. Not only was Aldrich a Republican; he was also criticized on account of his ties to wealthy financiers. He was close to John P. Morgan, and John D. Rockefeller Jr. was his son-in-law. Both men had been present at the Jekyll Island conference.

The following year, Congressman Arsène P. Pujo of Louisiana, a one-time member of the Monetary Commission who had bolted to investigate the activities of the "money trust," published a report from his ad hoc Pujo Committee placing the blame for the concentration of wealth in New York City at the feet of John P. Morgan. A "money trust," Pujo said, existed and was working against the interests of the common American. Pujo concluded that Morgan controlled both the monetary supply and American credit. Morgan denied these claims, but Pujo had dented the credibility of the big Wall Street bankers and businessmen, and as a result a renewed effort was made to curtail their control of the American economy. Unfortunately, the plan Congress adopted only served to *increase* and *strengthen* the ties between the finance community and the general government—at the expense of the American people. That was the Jekyll Island idea all along.

Wilson had little knowledge of banking and money. He was a political theorist, not an economic historian. But he was a progressive, and in 1912 he had promised to challenge the hegemony of the banking industry in the United States. To Wilson, the "money trust" was simply another illegal and powerful monopoly that needed to be destroyed, and he thought banks should be under public, not private, control. Things did not work out that way.

Wilson's fingerprints were all over the Federal Reserve Act of 1913. He worked closely with leading members of Congress to draft a piece of legislation that met the promises of the New Freedom program. Carter Glass of Virginia slightly modified the original Aldrich proposal by outlining a decentralized "Federal Reserve System" that would have complete control over credit and the monetary supply. In theory, the member banks in the Federal Reserve System would remain under private control but with government checks. The American banking system was divided into twelve regions, and a five-member board was created to oversee the entire system. All "national" banks had to join the system and, though not required to do so, virtually all local and regional banks did as well.

The idea was to break the hold New York had on the banking system and evenly distribute wealth throughout the United States, providing a safeguard in financial emergencies when access to cash and credit became a problem particularly in rural America. Banks could monetize their debt—in other words, inflate the monetary supply—but there were some requirements on how much gold they had to keep in reserve to back the loans. (These would be relaxed over the years until very little was required.) Banks could also rediscount commercial loans and interest rates.

Cash and credit flowed freely under the Federal Reserve System. And though the early aim was supposedly to restrict the power New York had over American banking, the politically appointed board was almost always led by a former head of the New York division of the Federal Reserve System, and the banking lobby eventually wormed its way into the entire process. A system purportedly designed to cut the power of New York gave more power over credit and money to New York bankers than J. P. Morgan had ever hoped to have.

At the time the Federal Reserve legislation was being debated, progressives complained the bill did not nationalize and control the banking system enough and the banking industry whined about concessions to agricultural groups, but in the end, with Wilson's direct involvement in the legislative process, using strong-arm tactics on fellow Democrats, the Federal Reserve Act passed by crushing majorities in both the House and Senate. The historian Arthur S. Link called it "the crowning achievement of the first Wilson administration."[7] This shortsighted statement seems to assume that the legislation was somehow constitutional. It wasn't.

Since the Philadelphia Convention in 1787, there had been considerable debate concerning the general government's role in the banking industry. Members of the Pennsylvania delegation to the 1787 Convention urged the delegates to consider giving the general government the power to charter a central bank. That idea was rejected outright, and no one during the ratification period of 1787 and 1788 argued that a central banking system would be remotely constitutional. Proponents of the Constitution had assured the ratifying conventions in the states that only enumerated and clearly delegated powers would be wielded by the new general government that the Constitution would create. A bank was not one of those delegated powers.

Alexander Hamilton's proposal for a First Bank of the United States met resistance from Thomas Jefferson and James Madison because the power to charter a bank or any other corporation was not a delegated power of the general government. When Hamilton suggested that Jefferson read between the lines, Jefferson responded that he could find only blank space. The Bank ultimately passed with George Washington's signature, but the constitutional question was unresolved. The First Bank of the United States failed re-charter in 1811 precisely because opponents of the Bank held the high ground on the constitutional question (and a majority in Congress), but following the War of 1812, President Madison signed a Second Bank of the United States into law. He justified his flip-flop on the issue with a poor argument: the Bank, he said, was now constitutional because custom and precedent had made it so. Chief Justice John Marshall ruled in the 1819 *McCulloch v. Maryland* case that the Bank was constitutional because the Necessary and Proper Clause of Article I, Section 8, allowed for the chartering of a Bank—on the theory that a bank was a "necessary and proper" means for the exercise of the powers actually delegated to the general government. Thus the Bank, he concluded, was within the letter and spirit of the Constitution. This was the same argument Hamilton had made in 1791. Not everyone bought it, and when in 1832 Henry Clay made re-chartering the Bank a campaign issue, Andrew Jackson went to war with the Bank. As we have seen, Jackson eventually prevailed by vetoing a bill that would have given the Bank another twenty-year lease on life. The Bank ceased to exist in 1836.

During the James K. Polk administration, Congress established an Independent Treasury (long the vision of several leading Democrats), which served the American public well until the War Between the States. Hamiltonians in the Whig and later the Republican Party still insisted a central banking system was necessary, but Southern Democrats constantly blocked any proposal to alter the financial system. Once these Southerners were out of the Congress in 1861, Republicans passed the National Banking Acts in 1863 and 1864, centralizing the American banking system. The constitutional question had not changed, but without opposition the Hamiltonians made a central banking system a permanent feature of the American economy.

In that regard, Southerners like Pujo and Glass were simply trying to reform and break up a banking and financial system that the South had long opposed. But their solution ultimately pinched working Americans by eventually creating a condition of perpetual inflation and cheap credit. These Southerners, Wilson included, had made the mistake of trying to check unconstitutional central banking through unconstitutional regulation. One unconstitutional move cannot correct another. Wilson should have followed his oath to defend the Constitution and vetoed any banking legislation short of an outright repeal of the central banking system. That would have been the proper constitutional move, but instead Wilson operated like a prime minister, helped move legislation based on an ideological agenda through Congress, and signed this unconstitutional legislation to please the constituents he cared about most—that is, progressives and the Democrat Party.

Wilson had a temporary bout of clarity early in his administration in regard to labor laws. Progressives had long agitated for federal regulation of child labor and working conditions, and they assumed that Wilson, as a staunch progressive, would support legislation to that aim. They were wrong, at least initially. Wilson wrote in 1914 that he thought all child labor legislation proposed to that point "seemed to me unconstitutional" and refused to engage Congress or influence congressional leaders to support such legislation.[8] But this did not mean the issue was dead. By the outbreak of World War I, Wilson had decided that extensive executive control of the economy, both of production and consumption, was needed to win the war in Europe and that constitutional restraint hampered a potential victory abroad. In the process, the Constitution was ground to pulp.

WORLD WAR I

No issue defined the Wilson administration like World War I. Wilson wrapped both his foreign and domestic policy into a comprehensive program designed to centralize power in Washington, D.C., and to aggrandize the role of the president in both areas. What Wilson could not accomplish with the New Freedom or was hesitant to implement because of supposed constitutional constraints became possible with American involvement in the Great War in 1917. Perhaps that was by design.

Historian John Morton Blum portrays Wilson as an unprepared novice in the months leading to war in Europe, particularly in relation to mobilization of the American economy and the military resources needed to win a comprehensive modern war. If he was, Wilson quickly caught up—using tactics that would make any modern dictator take notice. Much of the mobilization was done without congressional approval, though when necessary Wilson would ask for their rubber stamp.

Wilson brought the United States into World War I through under-handed tactics, insisting publicly that "He Kept Us Out of War" while privately moving the United States ever closer to the conflict. This devious behavior drove his Secretary of State, William Jennings Bryan, to resign. Wilson followed proper constitutional procedures by asking Congress to declare war on Germany in April 1917, but his War Message was filled with grand pronouncements of a broad strategy to "make the world safe for democracy." The democracy Wilson wished to establish in Europe he trampled on at home. Civil liberties, even the most basic safeguards such as freedom of speech and of the press, were disregarded during the War for the sake of "the public good." And while American doughboys were being slaughtered on the battlefield fighting for "freedom," Americans on the home front were being soaked for taxes, their travel restricted, their information redacted, and their food and industrial products manipulated. Democracy in America gave way to totalitarianism.

The process of mobilization began with the Selective Service Act of 1917 in May of that year. Wilson eagerly signed the bill into law. He should have vetoed it. While it was not the first conscription law in American history—Abraham Lincoln and the Republican Party hold the "honor" for that—the constitutionality of such legislation had never been settled. Article I, Section 8, of the Constitution contains no language authorizing a military draft—which stretches even an expansive understanding of the phrase "to raise and support armies"—and the Thirteenth Amendment explicitly prohibits involuntary servitude. The draft can be described as nothing less. The Selective Service Act sent 3 million American young men into service during the War and allowed the general government to dictate which branch they entered and what duties they were required to perform.

It served its purpose. General John J. "Blackjack" Pershing believed that 3.5 million men would be required to win the War in Europe. Five hundred thousand Americans volunteered. The rest were drafted. The Selective Service Act has never been repealed, and to this day American men are required to register for the draft. As a result, Wilson placed an indelible stamp on American society.

Large scale mobilization requires financial resources, and so Congress, with Wilson's approval, ramped up income tax collections, spiked rates to some of the highest levels in American history, and began a borrowing program that allowed government expenditures to increase tenfold during the two years the United States was at war. Much of this was facilitated by the new Federal Reserve. The Fed increased the monetary supply by over 1,000 percent and cut reserve requirements for member banks in half. The net result was inflation and higher debt for both the American government and the American consumer. Tax rates were at minimum doubled and broadened to catch more wage earners in the net while corporations saw their taxes tripled. All of this activity was accomplished through legislation, but without Wilson's signature on the laws—and on the Federal Reserve Act and the Underwood Tariff—the Congress would not have had the tools to gouge average Americans or finance such a large-scale war effort, one many Americans were still unsure needed American blood or money.

And the real work for the war effort was done by means not authorized in the Constitution. Wilson began appointing "boards" charged with broad powers over industry, commerce, agriculture, and transportation. Some were created by Congress, for example the Food Administration, but these boards had no congressional oversight and they reported directly to Wilson. The chairman of each board was essentially a dictator over a segment of the American economy.

The War Labor Board had no conceivable role in war mobilization other than as a payback to labor unions for supporting Wilson in 1916. Samuel Gompers, the leader of the American Federation of Labor, was on the Board, as were four other union leaders out of twelve members, and the net result of board activities was a doubling of union membership during the War. Overall American wages only increased enough to keep up with inflation, but union workers saw their wages double during the War. Without Wilson and the War, the unionization of workers would have remained stagnant in the early twentieth century.

The two most powerful and important government boards were the War Industries Board and the Food Administration. Wilson tapped financier Bernard Baruch to head the War Industries Board, with the charge to do everything possible to streamline the American economy and supply needed war materials. Baruch complied. He controlled industrial production, fixed prices, expedited and restricted the supply of raw materials when necessary, and could shut down renegade industrialists with the swipe of a pen. Nothing in the Constitution authorized this type of government control of the economy, but no one effectively sounded the alarm or resisted. The progressive historian John Morton Blum has lauded Baruch's work for its efficiency in removing "bottlenecks," eliminating waste, and for moving factories into "essential work."[9] To Blum, constitutional arguments against the War Industries Board or any board created during the War were inconsequential. The ends justified the means. Wilson thought just the same.

Wilson called on future president Herbert Hoover to run the Food Administration. Though he publicly denied it, Hoover had actively campaigned for the job. Contrary to popular belief, Hoover was no fan of small government either before or after becoming president in 1929. Hoover believed "Food Will Win the War"—a slogan the Wilson administration would wallpaper around America and Europe. Like its industrial counterpart, the Food Administration had broad powers, ranging from price fixing and improved production—accomplished by setting the minimum price of an agricultural good higher than the market value—to the regulation of distribution. The Administration also encouraged Americans not to eat certain foods by setting rations on specific articles. Newspapers advocated meatless Tuesdays and meatless breakfasts or wheatless Mondays. The idea was to save food for the army. Wilson greased the wheels by issuing several executive orders to make Hoover's work "legal."

But these boards were only three of several. Two others were established to purchase American grain and sugar and distribute them to the allies in Europe. Americans were encouraged to use no more than one scoop of sugar for their coffee so the boys on the Western Front could enjoy two. Wilson used the power of the Railroad War Board to control transportation, and the railroads were nationalized by the government in 1917 and remained under the direction of Washington bureaucrats until 1920. This did not lower transportation costs. On the contrary, the government *raised* rates 25 percent during the War while treating the rail industry as one large monopoly. All of this was prohibited by law, but that didn't matter in a national "emergency." Everything government regulation had prohibited in the years leading to World War I was speedily accomplished by...government. The federal government also seized control of international shipping with the War Trade Board and the Emergency Fleet Corporation. Wilson signed off on both. "Regulation" of trade carried a whole new meaning under the Wilson administration.

When opponents began to raise concerns that the government had exceeded its constitutional authority, Wilson pressured Senator Lee Slater Overman of North Carolina to draft a bill "legalizing" all of the work of the previous year. The Overman Act of 1918 made Wilson a virtual dictator of the United States (like the fictional hero Philip Dru) with power to coordinate and animate all of the wartime boards and agencies at will. It did not pass without opposition. Senator Frank Brandegee of Connecticut proposed a contemptuous amendment to the bill that would have granted Wilson unlimited power, the language of which read, "If any power, constitutional or not, has been inadvertently omitted from this bill, it is hereby granted in full."[10] The bill passed without the Brandegee amendment.

Wilson also made regulating information and speech a top priority. Less than two weeks after his request for a declaration of war, Wilson nationalized the "wireless" industry (radios) in order to control information. He established a Committee of Public Information charged with advancing the correct interpretation of the War for schools, the press, and the public at large and promoting his war aims at home and abroad. A December 1917 executive order established a division to create and distribute motion pictures to troops in Europe for their entertainment and education. Wilson's propaganda knew no bounds.

The director of the committee, George Creel, was a former newspaperman and understood the effect the news could have on the population. He organized over thirty divisions charged with swaying public opinion. "Four-minute men" appeared across the country to rally support for government programs and borrowing initiatives, and to "support the troops." But Creel also worked to censor any dissent, and he had congressional backing and Wilson's signature to assist him in that mission.

Congress, at Wilson's prodding, fired two deadly salvos at free speech and a free press during World War I. First, just two months after the United States declared war on Germany, the Espionage Act of 1917 was intended to target activities that might harm the American war effort, principally protests against the draft and any "support" for U.S. enemies or criticism of American allies. The language of the law was loose and the application aggressive. Federal authorities cast a wide net for "traitors," many of whom simply disagreed with American policy during the War. Socialist Eugene Debs was rounded up and sent to prison for his wartime opposition to the draft. He later ran for president while incarcerated. Other socialists faced jail time and fines for their anti-war speeches. Southerner Tom Watson, a populist Jeffersonian from Georgia, faced potential prosecution under the law because his newspaper often opposed Wilson's war aims and policies. Several movie directors were arrested or fined, one because his film on the American War for Independence cast the British in a negative light.

While critics of the law complained that the Espionage Act destroyed civil liberties—it did—the Wilson administration and Congress doubled down with the Sedition Act of 1918. Passed a short time before the end of the War, the Sedition Act clarified vague language in the Espionage Act and made any speech, in print or not, illegal if it was critical of the American war effort or the aims of the government. This is the law Wilson had wanted from the beginning. Several war opponents were sent to jail or fined for their "seditious" opposition to the War under the Sedition Act, and even after the war some American leaders pressed for a peacetime application of the law. Wilson had no problem with either move. One historian wrote, "The President turned his back on civil liberties not because he loved them less but because he loved his vision of eventual peace much more.... there was coming a great day. So intensely did Wilson believe this, so determined was he to convince the people of the world, the American people included, that he had room within him for few other worries, tolerance for no conflicting evidence or thoughts."[11]

Wilson had always been an ideologue and his actions during the War proved it. The Constitution and his oath to uphold and defend it were a hindrance to his war aims and the radical transformation of the United States and the executive branch. The War provided a vehicle that Wilson gladly rode to his intended destination—the subversion of the Constitution. This makes Wilson one of the worst presidents, if not the worst president, in American history. If Theodore Roosevelt was the watershed in American presidential history, Wilson provided the blueprint for every future architect of executive usurpation to follow. And most future presidents followed enthusiastically.

CHAPTER 5

FRANKLIN D. ROOSEVELT

Thirty-Second President, 1933–1945

Roosevelt wasn't nicknamed "King Franklin" by his detractors because he believed in executive restraint. The only man to be elected president four times, Roosevelt dramatically altered both the power and the perception of the executive branch. The foundations for the newly expanded executive office had been established by several predecessors, but Roosevelt made it all work. His New Deal was not really different in concept from Woodrow Wilson's New Freedom or Teddy Roosevelt's Square Deal, but Roosevelt rammed his agenda through Congress with a personal zeal unmatched by anyone who had held the office before him. All of the New Deal programs were constitutionally dubious, and so was the means— acting as legislator in chief—by which Roosevelt managed to achieve them. Closing banks through executive decree, check. Confiscating private gold, check. Attempting to pack the Supreme Court with political sycophants, check. Roosevelt made little effort to hide his unconstitutional power grab. And he had public support and congressional blessing until 1937. The Roosevelt administration marked a watershed in American history. It is no coincidence that every successive president—with just one possible exception—has failed to adhere to the Constitution as ratified. Roosevelt greased the wheels and set the standard.

Roosevelt is often considered to be one of the top three presidents in American history. He "rescued" America from the Depression, "rescued" the world from the Nazis and the Japanese, and "rescued" the American people from "fear." Such a man, according to historians, deserves a place in the pantheon of American heroes, regardless of the methods used to accomplish these tasks. His trampling of the Constitution can be ignored because the ends justified the means. But Roosevelt took an oath when he assumed office in 1933. That is how Americans should measure the man. Under constitutional criteria, Roosevelt would be dropped significantly in any presidential ranking—to the bottom three, rather than the top.

"THE ONLY THING WE HAVE TO FEAR . . ."

During the 1932 campaign, Roosevelt classified Herbert Hoover as a reckless tax-and-spend aristocrat intent on bankrupting the United States—which in retrospect seems like a case of the pot calling the kettle black. Hoover's ideas, in fact, anticipated Roosevelt's New Deal. Hoover had advocated several programs designed to increase agricultural prices, supported subsidies for banks and railroads, and signed legislation to pay for them with higher income and excise taxes. After Roosevelt won the election, Hoover reached out to the president-elect, hoping they could come up with a plan to solve the banking crisis together. Roosevelt stuffed Hoover's note in his pocket and coyly refused to act. He wanted to be the white knight riding into Washington, D.C., to save the day. Hoover could go down in flames.

Unfortunately, what transpired after Roosevelt's inauguration was nothing short of the most unprecedented expansion of the executive branch in the history of the United States. Roosevelt did an about-face and adopted Hoover's blueprint for government involvement in the economy—then juiced it on steroids. And Roosevelt's first inaugural address made it clear that this had been his plan from the beginning.

Roosevelt's first speech to the American public as president is often regarded as one of the most important orations in American history. It was beautifully written and artistically delivered, and while it lacked specifics, it foreshadowed what a Roosevelt administration would do to the Constitution. Roosevelt contended that the "dark realities of the moment" called "for action, and action now." He introduced a catchphrase used by every American politician in the last half of the twentieth century. Roosevelt pledged to "put people to work" by using the government as the employer of last resort. This proposal, in concert with a slew of ideas designed to control prices, keep people in their houses, reduce the cost of government, nationalize communications and transportation, and control banking, credit, and speculation, became the focal point of Roosevelt's first "hundred days" in office, a term the media latched onto in Roosevelt's first term and used as a yardstick for presidencies ever since. Roosevelt declared war on the "emergency" and mobilized the American people into a "loyal army willing to sacrifice for the good of a common discipline, because without such discipline no progress is made, no leadership becomes effective." Naturally, Roosevelt was ready to "assume unhesitatingly the leadership of this great army of our people dedicated to a disciplined attack upon our common problems." How comforting—and monarchical.

Roosevelt understood that what he proposed could not be done constitutionally, or at least that his program was not consistent with the Constitution as ratified in 1787 and 1788. Thus he distorted history and argued that, "this end is feasible under the form of government which we have inherited from our ancestors. Our Constitution is so simple and practical that it is possible always to meet extraordinary needs by changes in emphasis and arrangement without loss of essential form." Translation: *The Constitution is a malleable, living document that can be amended without amendments. Trust me. The founding generation designed it this way.* Roosevelt had found the technique that the progressive movement could use to put their unconstitutional agenda into effect. If you can't prove it's compatible with the Constitution, lie about our founding document, and keep lying until the lie becomes the truth.

Roosevelt did concede that he needed the Congress to be a complicit partner in his unbridled takeover of the federal government. But then he warned that if they refused to act and pass legislation to quell the "crisis," he was determined to take a "temporary departure from the normal balance of public procedure" and ask for "broad executive power to wage a war against the emergency, as great as the power that would be given to me if we were in fact invaded by a foreign foe."[1] This last sentence described a plan of attack from which Roosevelt would not deviate during his over twelve years in office.

THE FIRST HUNDRED DAYS

Since Roosevelt's first term in office, every succeeding president has been measured by his "first hundred days" at the helm of the executive branch. If Roosevelt had done nothing else in office, this precedent for executive "energy" alone would make him a pivotal figure in American political history, but the substance of his agenda during those first "hundred days" also radically expanded the implied powers of the presidency. If our modern journalists had any clue about the original Constitution, no future president would again be asked, "Mr. President, what are you going to do in your first hundred days?"

Roosevelt called Congress into a special session after his inauguration and with a stroke of the pen shut down all banks in the United States for a "Bank Holiday." Most banks had already closed, but Roosevelt forcibly shuttered the rest. The first act was constitutional; the second, illegal. But Roosevelt had already openly declared that he would act alone in his war on the economic crisis. Executive decrees became part of the plan. Roosevelt acted first and asked permission later. When it came to the "Bank Holiday," he acted like Wilson and Teddy Roosevelt before him, writing the legislation granting him the power and jamming it down Congress's throat. They agreed—in fact, rumor has it they first passed a rolled-up newspaper in lieu of an actual bill until the Roosevelt White House could write one. It was a particularly extreme case of Congress having to pass the bill before they could see what was in the bill.

The next few weeks saw a procession of bills cascade down to Congress from Pennsylvania Avenue. Roosevelt set the agenda in his first speech to Congress on March 9. He called for a reduction in the deficit and a 25 percent cut in federal spending. This, he said, was a necessary move to trim inflation and refresh the private sector. Good. But then, shockingly, Roosevelt turned around and recommended an *increase* in federal spending. He suggested a budget with the highest deficit in American history to that point, over three billion dollars. At the time the projected deficit for 1934 was only *one* billion dollars. Roosevelt was speaking out of both sides of his mouth. His plan was to woo the American public, Congress included, and lull them into accepting his schizophrenic utopian dream called the New Deal.

What did three billion in red ink buy? Unconstitutional legislation, all crafted by Roosevelt and a host of academics, advisors, and intellectuals. The Ivy League had taken over the executive branch, and most of their theories had never been tested in practice. Every piece of New Deal legislation had Roosevelt's fingerprints on it. The president and his trusted academics were pragmatists who believed that "reform" constituted "progress." This was nothing new. Both his cousin Theodore Roosevelt and Woodrow Wilson had believed in this mantra, but Franklin Roosevelt pursued it with unprecedented vigor. If Wilson was the first "prime minister" president, Roosevelt was the first dictator in chief. And Congress hid its tail between its legs for years, generally unwilling or unable to challenge "King Franklin."

Roosevelt's first order of business was the first of what would become a host of "alphabet soup" agencies, the Agricultural Adjustment Act (AAA). Crafted by the newly appointed Secretary of Agriculture Henry Wallace, the AAA imposed rigid restrictions on American agriculture, from price-fixing to the unpopular practices of livestock and crop destruction. To Wallace, the problems in American agriculture sprung from the stupidity of the American farmer. Low cotton prices were the result of too many Southerners planting cotton. The solution: plow the crops under and pay farmers with taxpayer dollars *not* to plant cotton. The price of ham and bacon dropped during the Great Depression. The solution: slaughter thousands of hogs and pay farmers *not* to have hog farms.

The crop and livestock destruction policy applied to all types of farms, from small family-owned subsistence ventures to large commercial enterprises. The eventual net result was the virtual disappearance of the family farm. Wallace had long been an advocate of commercial farming. There were subsidies designed to help small farmers, but many just closed shop and took up another occupation. Those who thrived were the large farming operations. When small farms disappeared, the larger farmers picked up the slack and the market. The Supreme Court, in a rare case of clarity, eventually declared the AAA unconstitutional, but Roosevelt's agricultural central planning had already had long-term consequences for the American economy. The small farmer, once the backbone of America, was ground down by the wheels of New Deal adventurism and American "progress." Joseph Stalin's centralized "Five Year Plans" had an American counterpart in the AAA.

Roosevelt's pen stayed hot. His next order of business in "ending the Depression" was the Civilian Conservation Corps (CCC), to which he had alluded in his first inaugural address. The plan was to put young men to work on "needed" environmental projects for a buck a day, most of which had to be sent back to their families. They were sheltered, clothed, fed, and marched out like soldiers to do the necessary work of the American peo-ple—such "essential" jobs as building hiking trails at the Grand Canyon and a golf course in Texas; landscaping in Mississippi; creating camping and picnicking areas in Delaware, swimming pools in Maine, and rest-rooms in California; and clearing bat dung in Montana occupied their days. How did Americans survive before? Roosevelt had basically made private citizens soldiers in a "war" against weeds, erosion, bad hiking trails, and substandard picnic areas, all under executive direction. He was now conservationist in chief of an "army" of landscapers. No such power existed (it still doesn't) in the Constitution, but Roosevelt had become the driving force in the American economy, or so he assumed.

The real *coup de grâce* against the Constitution was the National Industrial Recovery Act (NIRA), crafted by Secretary of the Interior Har-old Ickes. Created as the industrial companion to the AAA, the NIRA attempted to regulate the non-agricultural side of the American economy, from price controls and production to wages, working conditions, and the length of the work day. The plan was lauded by the American public and landed one of its architects, Hugh Johnson, on *Time* magazine as the "Man of the Year." This was a massive takeover of the American economy, in line with progressive ideas about labor and the nature of business and capital. The NIRA also created the Public Works Administration (PWA) in an effort to funnel federal tax dollars into public works projects across the United States. During the Depression only three counties failed to receive PWA money, and it was responsible for building schools, post offices, roads, and bridges.

As labor boss in chief, Roosevelt forced businesses to accept NIRA regulations under threat of penalty. But rather than promoting "fair competition," as the authors of the bill had hoped it would do, the NIRA *created* monopolies with government protection. Even Roosevelt later admitted this to be true. NIRA-compliant companies were freed from competition. In essence, Roosevelt was acting as the CEO of one large industrial and commercial corporation with control over the entire

American economy. The Congress had enthusiastically, if illegally, punted their legislative duties up to the White House and thus established new executive powers out of thin air.

If Roosevelt had been true to his oath, the NIRA, along with every other piece of legislation passed during the first hundred days, would have quickly met the veto pen. Instead, Roosevelt signed every one of them, using dozens of pens to do so in order for each sponsor to receive a pen as a token of the achievement. No debates were held on the constitutionality of any of these measures, at least not at first. Congress had given Roosevelt dictatorial powers and Roosevelt acted. He met little to no opposition from the Congress or the American people at large for several years. He was the toast of the town, the man of the hour. Roosevelt had planned it that way. When the smoke cleared after his first hundred days in office, the Congress—with Roosevelt's signature affixed to each bill—had created dozens of new federal programs designed to end poverty, unemployment, and ultimately the Depression. They certainly ended the original executive branch, but their effect on the overall health of the American economy was marginal at best.

In 1935 Roosevelt, motivated by a Supreme Court decision that had knocked out the pillars of the first New Deal, the AAA and the NIRA, pressed Congress to enact another round of New Deal programs. Roosevelt again acted as legislator in chief and had his administration write the even more aggressive batch of unconstitutional legislation. Roosevelt leaned on communist Harry Hopkins for advice on "job creation" for people who had "fallen through the cracks," including artists, writers, and actors. Hopkins had already written legislation in New York designed to find jobs for the unemployed and those on government assistance. Now that he had federal resources, Hopkins beefed up the plan. What became known as the Works Progress Administration (WPA) started out as the Federal Emergency Relief Administration (FERA) and then became the Civil Works Administration (CWA). American taxpayers ultimately spent billions on cleaning up parks; sweeping sidewalks; restoring swimming pools; constructing playgrounds, golf courses, and sports stadiums; free plays; public murals; collecting American folklore; and job training programs for American youth. Of course, in their publicity about the program both Roosevelt and Hopkins focused on WPA efforts to build roads, schools, sewers, and bridges and emphasized that the WPA was the "employer of last resort"—only those already in distress could find a job with the organization. The WPA and still-active PWA, however, were charged with the same tasks, the end result being two bloated government bureaucracies bidding for the same jobs. The constitutionality of the Works Progress Administration was questionable at best, but Roosevelt was at war with "fear" and he acted without regard to constitutional restraint.

Roosevelt also had his secretary of labor, Frances Perkins, draw up a new type of social program for the disabled and elderly. Called "Social Security," it became the largest entitlement program in American history and a mandatory Ponzi scheme. No constitutional authority existed either for the Congress to pass the legislation or for Roosevelt to sign it. No matter. Roosevelt had built up considerable political capital and he was not going to let anything as small as separation of powers or delegated authority stop his steamrolling of traditional American government. Social Security was sold as a tax that would put "savings" in an impenetrable lock box for later use. What it really did was tax the employed to pay for retired Americans; the "lock box" was later raided by Congress and added to the general fund.

GOVERNMENT BY EXECUTIVE ORDER

On top of this mountain of unconstitutional legislation, Roosevelt also pushed his New Deal agenda through executive orders, a dubiously constitutional tool that had rarely been used before the middle of the nineteenth century, but had become the method of choice to circumvent the Congress, when needed. Roosevelt insisted that he was simply executing the will of the people as expressed in legislation that had been passed by Congress, but even a cursory analysis of his over three thousand executive orders reveals something different. Roosevelt was setting policy. While his cousin Teddy had used the power of the executive branch to confiscate millions of acres of land, FDR used executive orders to grab private gold in the United States and ultimately to complete the fusion of finance and government in America. FDR's use of the power of the pen was much more sinister.

Many people blamed the banking crisis on the "stringent" monetary policy of the United States, in which the paper currency was tied to precious metals. When the Depression began to take hold of the American economy, Americans rushed to the banks to withdraw their money with many demanding payment in specie. They wanted their gold. Unfortunately, the banks did not have the gold to give them and refused. And this was legal. Banks could lend more money than they had on hand because of a system called fractional reserve banking. Typically, banks only had 10 percent of the total money deposited in the institution on hand on any given day. If the American people made a run on a bank—as happened many times between 1929 and 1932—the institution would be unable to meet its customers' demands. To Roosevelt and his intelligentsia, the problem was not the banking system, or fractional reserve banking, but gold itself. There was not enough to go around and the price fluctuated, so the government came up with a way to rid itself of a hard money standard and inflate the money supply in one fell swoop. Roosevelt would use the power of the executive office to confiscate all privately held gold in the United States.

Less than one month after taking office, Roosevelt issued Executive Order 6102 "Requiring Gold Coin, Gold Bullion and Gold Certificates to Be Delivered to the Government." This was done to halt the "serious emergency" that had gripped the United States banking industry, namely the inability of American banks to meet demand deposit withdrawals. Some gold was excluded, mostly ornamental gold and rare coins, but anyone caught "hoarding" gold could be fined or sent to jail. Of course, the good people at the bank would redeem your gold in other currency, that is, paper money, and wish you on your way. In August Roosevelt followed up his initial order with another requiring Americans who still owned gold to fill out paperwork detailing how much they had and when they would return it and prohibiting them from acquiring more gold or exporting gold to another country.

The end result would be inflation and the ultimate demonetization of gold (and later silver through Executive Order 6814) in the United States. This was a dangerous time for the American worker. The little money that he did have would be devalued by inflation, and if he chose to "hoard" gold reserves he would become a criminal—all through the unilateral executive order of President Roosevelt. This move was unprecedented in American history. The best excuse for a constitutional argument that anyone could come up with in favor of Roosevelt's gold grab was the power to "coin Money" and "fix the Standard of Weights and Measures" in Article I, Section 8, of the Constitution. But even if that argument had merit, and it didn't, that power was granted to *Congress*, not the President. Roosevelt had usurped constitutional power from Congress and bullied the American people into giving up their hard assets for pieces of paper. King Midas would have been proud, except everything Roosevelt's Treasury touched turned to paper.

To make matters worse, the Supreme Court never challenged this unconstitutional abuse of power and in fact refused even to hear several cases concerning the issue. Lower federal courts upheld the government's power to seize private gold. Roosevelt had declared war on the Great Depression in 1933, and now American citizens were required to sacrifice for the cause. They probably had not anticipated that such a sacrifice would rob them and their posterity of the full value of a day's work. With prices being set in Washington, industry and agriculture under the heel of the central government, and now private wealth being forcibly turned over to the Treasury Department, Roosevelt had transformed the American economy almost singlehandedly, through the supposed implied presidential power of the executive order.

And the hits kept coming. Roosevelt used his pen to unilaterally create a federal agency tasked with handling labor relations, an Import-Export Bank, and boards and agencies designed to regulate industry and commerce and prisons; to set aside lands for migratory birds; to amend civil service rules and rules for immigration; and eventually, during World War II, to suppress civil liberties. Roosevelt issued more executive orders than the combined totals of all previous presidents. He had spoken of a willingness to act alone in his first inaugural address; he showed that willingness in the over twelve years he held office. Whereas George Washington thought he needed to display restraint to reassure the American public that the president was no elected king, Roosevelt went in the other direction and showed the American people that the Constitution could not contain the executive branch. Roosevelt was the founding generation's worst nightmare—at least up to that point in history.

PACKING THE COURT

By 1937, Roosevelt realized that the New Deal was on life support. Many of the programs did not work as intended, and the economy had taken a dip. But Roosevelt could not go before the American public and announce that billions of dollars worth of federal programs had produced only a sluggish economy or, even worse, another depression. So he simply changed the language. The economy, he said, was simply in a "recession." It would bounce back. (This was ingenious. Since 1937, no American politician has used the word "depression" to describe poor economic performance. A "recession" sounds softer, more palatable, and certainly more optimistic.) Roosevelt blamed the financial downturn on political enemies in Congress and on Wall Street. It could not have been poor policy or executive overreach.

Roosevelt and his fellow progressives threw the blame on congressional obstruction, claiming that had Congress continued to rubber stamp

New Deal initiatives the economy would have continued to grow. For Congress had finally grown a backbone. Led by Senator Josiah Bailey of North Carolina, a member of Roosevelt's own party, the Congress had crafted a philosophical answer to the New Deal and Roosevelt's out-of-control executive branch. Labeled the "Conservative Manifesto," the plan had bipartisan support and enough muscle to thwart new attempts to centralize power at Pennsylvania Avenue. It was neither an overt attack on Roosevelt nor an outright anti–New Deal program, but anyone who had lived through the past four years of frenetic government activity in America could see that the Conservative Manifesto was critical of the massive tax-and-spend policies of the administration. The ten-point manifesto mentioned a reduction of taxes two times and reduction of federal spending three and, most important, demanded that the government balance the budget. It insisted that the general government recognize state authority and adhere to the American economic model, that is, private enterprise. Since Roosevelt's first inaugural address, the general government had ignored or run roughshod over all semblances of checks and balances, federalism, and the free market economy. This was a reactionary move by men many of whom at one time enthusiastically supported the New Deal.

The New Deal certainly ruffled some feathers in Congress, but the issue that brought about the Conservative Manifesto was not the bad policies of the program but rather Roosevelt's naked usurpation of power. Frustrated by the Supreme Court's striking down some of the unconstitutional New Deal legislation, Roosevelt tried to pack the Supreme Court with political sycophants willing to do his bidding. Packing the Supreme Court would have reduced the power of Congress even further. Senator Bailey privately wrote about why he feared Roosevelt's bold move to pack the Court: "With a board here at Washington controlling hours and wages, and therefore industry, and a Court sooner or later compliant, [on what] can we base our hopes for the preservation of this Republic or this civilization?"[2]

The Supreme Court had been sporadically problematic for Roosevelt since he took office. Four men on the Court, dubbed "the Four Horsemen," disagreed with Roosevelt's progressive interpretation of constitutional executive and legislative power. They were often joined by one other member of the nine-justice court—typically Chief Justice Charles Evans Hughes, the Republican nominee for president in 1916, or Justice Owen J. Roberts—in striking down New Deal legislation. The "Four Horsemen" were opposed by three progressive justices, labeled "the Three Musketeers," who from time to time could also find support from one or sometimes two swing votes on the Court. Thus, during the 1930s, Court decisions were often split 5–4, with Roosevelt's agenda typically on the losing side. Hughes was generally not ideologically opposed to the New Deal, but he worried that much of the legislation was improperly crafted and gave too much power to the executive branch without proper congressional direction or oversight. Both Hughes and Roberts, however, upheld the government's power to confiscate gold, and Roberts favored an expansive interpretation of the General Welfare Clause, insisting that the general government had any powers needed to promote the general welfare of the American people.

Still, the New Deal took several blows from the Court late in Roosevelt's first term. On what was labeled "Black Monday" in 1935 the Court issued a series of anti–New Deal decisions, the most important of which was *Schechter Poultry Corp. v. United States*. This ruling declared the NIRA unconstitutional, thus undercutting the federal government's ability to regulate industry and control labor, wages, and prices. Roosevelt saw the justices' decision as a personal attack and publicly lambasted the Court. This was a break in protocol, an affront to the separation of powers; and Roosevelt took heat in the press for his openly challenging a Supreme Court decision. Public outrage over his comments caused the typically loquacious Roosevelt to refrain from further comment on the Court, at least for the time being.

The Court followed up one year later with another stinging assault on the New Deal. In a series of decisions, the Court found a revised AAA to be unconstitutional, a violation of the Tenth Amendment (though at the same time the Court found that the so-called General Welfare Clause was somehow magically unlimited by the enumerated powers in Article I, Section 8); declared a revised NIRA to be again unconstitutional; and struck down a minimum wage law in New York. All of the decisions were 5–4. Roosevelt's New Deal, and by analogy Roosevelt himself, had been pushed to the corner and pummeled with a series of legal uppercuts to the jaw. But Roosevelt was saved by the bell and, after a pep talk by his legal scholars, came out swinging in the next round. Unfortunately for Roosevelt, his wild roundhouses missed the mark and served to rally support for his political opponents.

Congress has the power to determine how many justices sit on the bench of the Supreme Court and to regulate the jurisdiction of all federal courts. As early as 1789, Congress had expanded federal court jurisdiction to a degree that would have ensured the defeat of the Constitution in the state ratifying conventions had such a plan been presented then. Congress had also restricted Court jurisdiction—most famously during Reconstruction when the Court had blocked congressional overreach on civil liberties. The number of Supreme Court justices had fluctuated since 1789, from six to ten, but it had remained stable at nine since 1869. Thus it was not unprecedented for the Congress to enlarge or reduce the number of justices or to regulate the federal courts.

Almost immediately after taking office, Roosevelt sensed that the Supreme Court could present problems for his sweeping (unconstitutional) legislative agenda. His predecessor, Herbert Hoover, certainly hoped the Court would provide such an obstacle. As a result, Roosevelt secretly had several members of the Justice Department draft a plan for removing the power of judicial review. This would have been a popular move in the early years of the Republic, but the American public had become accustomed to this undelegated and unpredictable power of the Court, which at least seemed to serve as a check on overreach by the other two branches of government. That plan was shelved for political reasons, but the desire to limit the influence of the Supreme Court was not, particularly after the series of stinging rulings in 1935 and 1936. Roosevelt again had his Ivy League scholars come up with a strategy to alter the traditional powers of the general government.

Roosevelt unveiled the infamous "court packing plan" to the general public on March 9, 1937, during one of his "fireside chats," the first of his second term. He began his address with a justification for the private gold grab of 1933 but lamented the fact that the Supreme Court had upheld his decision to act by only a 5–4 majority. The same held true for several pieces of New Deal legislation, and others that had been declared unconstitutional, again by slim 5–4 majorities. King Franklin's New Deal was being held hostage by the Supreme Court. That was unacceptable.

Roosevelt viewed the Court as a drag on the American political system. Two horses were plowing the field, but the third would not move, regardless of the will of the people. It could not be whipped or cajoled into action. The Constitution, he said, had given the government the power to act in national emergencies through the General Welfare Clause—and when one branch of government retarded that power, it was time to "save the Constitution from the Court and the Court from itself."

To this end, Roosevelt proposed a sweeping change in the process for appointing Supreme Court judges. According to the Constitution, federal judges have lifetime appointments. Roosevelt knew that he could not remove justices or force them to retire, but he could sign legislation authorizing the president to appoint a new judge for every judge over seventy and a half years old. The proposal would have allowed Roosevelt to add as many as six new judges to the Supreme Court and those judges to resume the practice of "riding the circuit," meaning they would have had the authority to handle the duties of lower federal courts if those courts faced a backlog of cases. The legislation would also have allowed these new judges to serve as "proctors" for lower courts. Translation: these new political appointees of the president would have virtually unlimited power over all federal courts. They would swing the balance of power on the Supreme

Court in favor of Roosevelt's judicial henchmen and make all efforts to stop his New Deal nugatory.

Many Americans today would agree with Roosevelt's sentiment that the Supreme Court justices should not legislate from the bench and should not bend or interpret the Constitution according to their will alone, but should defer to the Congress. Roosevelt was right in that judicial review can be problematic. (In fact, progressives have now used this power to create volumes of legislation without any input from the legislature.) And there was nothing constitutionally incorrect about the court packing bill. Congress has the authority to establish lower courts and set the rules for the federal court system. Roosevelt correctly pointed out that Congress had passed similar legislation before.

But the president's intention was to get around the Constitution by filling the federal judiciary with judges who would approve of unconstitutional acts. Roosevelt bristled at the assumption that he was trying to "pack the court" with like-minded judges who would do his bidding. But that was exactly what Roosevelt was trying to do. In fact in every instance before 1937 when the number of justices on the bench had been altered, it was for the same objective: the Court had blocked the agenda of the other two branches of government and thus needed to be stopped. Roosevelt had said as much in his opening statement during the fireside chat and in his few public outbursts against Court decisions. He was throwing a public tantrum, and the Court was put on notice. Do my bidding or I will emasculate the Court.

Roosevelt, however, made a major tactical mistake. He publicly unveiled his bill before presenting it to Congress. And Congress, at the direction of conservative Democrats like Bailey, immediately went to work hacking it to pieces. To make matters worse for the president, the public supported *Congress* in this constitutional crisis. Roosevelt's court packing bill went down in flames by a 70–20 margin in the Senate. An independent judiciary had been saved by the Senate—for the time being.

Roosevelt would eventually have his way. After his March 1937 fireside chat, not one piece of New Deal legislation was again declared unconstitutional, though the administration won many cases by only a 5–4 majority. Roosevelt may not have been able to pack the Court, but he had made a public mockery of the justices' decisions and thus put pressure on them to do his bidding. By 1941, the Supreme Court was as complicit in the unconstitutional New Deal as the Congress and the president. Only the states could serve as a hedge against federal overreach and they were, generally, unwilling to resist it. King Franklin had his government, and World War II provided the means for him to consolidate power. And by his third term in office, only two of the original nine judges who had been on the Supreme Court at the time of his first election remained on the bench.

THE WAR

World War II changed America, and there is no clearer example of the (largely unconstitutional) changes than in the powers of the executive branch. World War II was a conflict of intensity and scope never before seen in human history. It was the largest, costliest, and most destructive war on record. Almost immediately, that destruction engulfed American civil liberties and the Constitution. Wartime "emergencies" became the standard justification for massive power grabs by the central government, all at the behest of the executive branch. What Roosevelt could not accomplish through the New Deal he got done during the War. This was a more dramatic crisis than the Great Depression, and like a good progressive, Roosevelt did not let the crisis go to waste.

The war initially gave Roosevelt the opportunity to run for a third term. Germany's invasion of Poland in 1939 embroiled the world in war. Congress had granted Roosevelt the power to proclaim American neutrality, and he did so in November 1939. But the United States was inching closer to full involvement even before the Japanese attacked Pearl Harbor in December 1941. And Roosevelt insisted that consistent leadership was required during such a time and took the unprecedented step of standing for reelection in 1940.

This was not unconstitutional, but it broke an established tradition that dated to the Washington administration. Only two previous presidents—Ulysses Grant and Teddy Roosevelt—had ever contemplated a third term, and no one had ever pulled it off. FDR won another landslide victory in 1940 and therefore considered that he had secured a mandate from the American people to direct foreign and domestic policy as he saw fit. Roosevelt thought he was the new indispensable man, a president greater than Washington. America needed Roosevelt—or so he believed.

Even before the war began, Roosevelt had used the power of the executive branch in unprecedented ways to stifle growing American reluctance to enter the war. The most famous American in the world at the time, Charles Lindbergh, had publicly led a campaign—"America First"—to keep the United States out of the war. Lindbergh and other high-profile Americans were asking important questions about the costs and benefits of American involvement in the contest. This did not go unnoticed.

Lindbergh had been sent to Germany by the Roosevelt administration to assess German military strength, particularly its air power, and his report both lauded German military advancements and expressed fears about a lack of American preparedness to fight. The German government admired Lindbergh and presented him with a medal during his visit. Lindbergh had asked the several members of the Roosevelt administration who were accompanying him on his mission to Germany if he should accept the award, and they said yes. Nothing was made of it in the press at the time, but when Lindbergh returned home in 1939 a few short months prior to the German attack on Poland, Harold Ickes, one of the architects of the New Deal, used the full power of his position in the Roosevelt administration to roast Lindbergh. Ickes waged a very public war with the famous aviator in the press, tarring him as an anti-Semitic Nazi sympathizer, a charge that has stuck to Lindbergh to this day. It wasn't true, and it was unprecedented in American history for the sitting president or his administration to single out a private individual as an enemy of the state.

This bordered on an illegal writ of attainder, particularly when, after the war began, Lindbergh was denied the ability to serve in the army air force by the Roosevelt administration—he was forced to volunteer as a private citizen in the Pacific theater, where he ran bombing raids against the Japanese—but the Constitution had never stopped Roosevelt before, and World War II only strengthened his resolve to circumvent any prohibitions on executive power.

A "smoking gun" directly implicating Roosevelt in an insidious scheme to back door the United States into World War II does not exist, but historians have spent decades looking for one. The historian Charles Tansill, at great cost to his career, wrote a scathing critique of the Roosevelt administration's foreign policy titled *Back Door to War* in 1952. The circumstantial evidence, in his mind, pointed to a deliberate provocation of the Japanese, and more important, suggested that Roosevelt had advance knowledge of the December 7, 1941, attack on Pearl Harbor, an attack neither he nor his army chief of staff, George C. Marshall, did anything to stop. If true, this would be an impeachable offense, a dereliction of duty to protect and defend the United States, and the blood of three hundred thousand American soldiers would be on his hands. When war did reach America, Roosevelt asked the Congress for a declaration of war, which they provided quickly and unanimously. Congress had constitutionally declared war, but they followed up by allowing Roosevelt to unconstitutionally seize control of the American economy and wage war on American civil liberties, all under the umbrella of a wartime emergency.

Just one week after the declaration of war, Roosevelt convened a meeting of business and labor leaders at the White House. They agreed not to strike during the war, but Roosevelt took the matter a step further and through executive order created the National War Labor Board with the power to mediate strikes and prevent labor disputes. (Later the Board would fix prices and wages through the War Manpower Commission and the Office of Economic Stabilization, created by executive order.) Roosevelt had no constitutional authority for any of this, but the war and his role as commander in chief, he claimed, justified it all. Four days later, Roosevelt issued an executive order creating the War Production Board, an agency with full power to control all economic activity in the United States. Consumer industrial goods such as appliances were illegal to produce, and many common and essential household items, such as metal and paper, were rationed for the war effort. Americans had been used to scanty supplies during the Great Depression, but now the government was (unconstitutionally) forcing people to sacrifice even if they had enough disposable income.

Other executive orders would consolidate shipping and transportation under federal government direction, create a propaganda arm for the war effort (the Office of War Information, which, for example, used Donald Duck to urge people to pay their income tax), establish a National Housing Agency that allowed the federal government unprecedented control over the American real estate market, place the production and utilization of rubber and petroleum under the direct supervision of the executive branch, permit the federal government to control food supplies and food availability, and finally allow the government to seize the American coal industry, the railroads, steel mills, and even the retail corporation Montgomery Ward and Company. In essence, separation of powers ceased to exist during the war, as did American reliance on the free market. And the health of the American body politic has never recovered. Since World War II the United States has remained on a wartime footing, with government control and regulation of the economy. While Roosevelt's orders expired with the conclusion of the war, the belief that the U.S. government—and even the executive branch alone, acting by presidential order—may constitutionally seize control of the economy or strangle it with regulations has persisted. World War II and Roosevelt made the executive branch *the* federal government.

Perhaps the most glaring abuse of power during World War II, however, was the creation of concentration camps for Japanese Americans, both naturalized citizens and aliens, during the war. While American GIs were liberating Jewish concentration camps around Europe, American citizens of Japanese descent were herded into desert communities and forced into reeducation schools not only for the "good of America," but for their own benefit. The federal government promised that their property and businesses would be protected and returned after the war, but most never recovered what they had been forced to leave behind, and the stigma of relocation haunted the Japanese community for years.

The Office of War Information produced a series of films on the program designed to sell it to the American public. Japanese Americans were shown in good health and spirits, gleefully accepting their fate while turning the desert into an oasis and contributing to the war effort by constructing camouflage tents. The executive orders behind such a monstrous abuse of civil liberties were never questioned in Congress. One could make a constitutional case for the application of such laws to aliens on American soil, but when American citizens were rounded up en masse along with aliens, the federal government clearly violated every vestige of the Bill of Rights.

By 1944, Roosevelt had comfortably solidified his control of the federal government. Though in poor health, he accepted the nomination for an unprecedented fourth term. The war appeared to be in hand, but Roosevelt had larger plans, particularly on the domestic front. Winning the war in Europe and Asia would mean the resumption of a peacetime economy at home, one that Roosevelt hoped would include much of the policies of the New Deal, now repackaged as an "Economic Bill of Rights." The American civilian would be placed on the same footing as the American soldier. It was, as he said, "fair for one, fair for all."

Roosevelt unveiled his new agenda during his 1944 State of the Union address, and he continued to hammer the proposals in several speeches during the hectic 1944 campaign. At its core, the "Economic Bill of Rights," which Roosevelt also called a "Second Bill of Rights," sought to mitigate what progressives thought were the evils of the American system, particularly in regard to so-called economic inequality. After years of apparent pragmatism—which, judging by his policies during the war, was really only a mirage—Roosevelt moved hard left. The president called for a "realistic tax law," which would target "unreasonable profits." ("Unreasonable" was not defined.) Roosevelt also wanted an extension of the price controls on food and protection for labor unions, in what he called a "national service law."

These unconstitutional provisions all had precedents in the New Deal. Roosevelt, however, outlined the real meat of the plan a few paragraphs later. He believed that Americans in modern industrialized society had the need for new "rights," including the "right" to a job, food, clothing, recreation, a home, medical care, education, and freedom from the "fear" of unemployment, old age, sickness, and unfair competition. Roosevelt insisted, "Our fighting men abroad—and their families at home—expect such a program and have the right to insist upon it. It is to their demands that this Government should pay heed rather than to the whining demands of selfish pressure groups who seek to feather their nests while young Americans are dying."[3] Roosevelt's rhetoric was meant to be directed against a "rightist reaction" against the New Deal, the return to the "normalcy" of the 1920s, and the possibility of a fascist dictatorship in the United States. Of course the president didn't mention that his administration already smacked of policies that both Mussolini and Hitler made infamous in Europe, or that his own "selfish pressure groups" exerted tremendous influence on the administration.[4] These scare tactics were the origin of the phantom "vast right wing conspiracy" made famous during the Bill Clinton administration.

Roosevelt left implementation of his Economic Bill of Rights to Congress, but everyone knew that he would be pursuing the agenda with vigor in a fourth term and would possibly use the expanded powers of the office to roll out much of the plan. Fate intervened. Just over a year after he presented the "Second Bill of Rights," Roosevelt died, the war not yet won and his dream of a progressive utopia not realized. But both the "Second Bill of Rights" and the way that Roosevelt used executive powers during the war set a precedent for future administrations, notably those of his Democratic successors.

Roosevelt had created a new executive branch. Through crafty maneuvering, expert propaganda, and old-fashioned bully politics, Roosevelt persuaded the American public that an executive with wide-ranging powers was essential for the "preservation" of "democracy." His "Second Bill of Rights" became the basis of every progressive agenda of the twentieth century, and the American economy has never left a wartime footing. Next to Washington and Lincoln, Roosevelt is the most important president in American history. The modern executive branch is *Roosevelt's* executive branch, not the one crafted by the founding generation. That is no badge of honor.

CHAPTER 6

HARRY S. TRUMAN

Thirty-Third President, 1945–1953

I n many respects, Harry S. Truman represents what is both best and worst about American politics. He was truly the most middle class president in American history, a real man of the people, whose rise to the top of the executive branch was almost surreal. He did not become a real player in the national Democratic Party until his fifties, and he spent much of his life involved in local politics and running an unsuccessful small business. He never forgot his humble Missouri roots.

Yet Truman also perfected the art of the demagogue, used seedy and often corrupt machine politics to his advantage, and abused executive power in the same way his predecessor, Franklin Roosevelt, made famous. Truman was his own man, but it is difficult to divorce his administration from that of Roosevelt, largely because Truman's own domestic and foreign policy initiatives were, at times, indistinguishable from Roosevelt's. What Roosevelt imagined in 1944—"the Second Bill of Rights"—Truman attempted to put into practice during his almost eight years in office. By the end of his second term, Truman had become the most progressive president in American history to that point.

Like Roosevelt, Truman often couched his unconstitutional power grabs in language that would make his actions seem legal while in reality he was continuing the process of enlarging the scope of the executive branch at the expense of the original Constitution. Truman's political philosophy was simple: flatter voters when possible to gain public approval and then use that popular support to act "for the welfare of all of our people." Truman had once confided to his future wife, "If I were real rich, I'd just as soon spend my money buying votes and offices as yachts and autos."[1] Even without being rich, Truman figured out how to buy votes and how to win influence. His administration is a testament to the perils of democracy and the danger the founding generation feared most, an elected king.

WINNING THE WAR

Truman responded, "Jesus Christ and General Jackson!" when he heard that Roosevelt was dead on April 12, 1945. He had been kept in the dark in the brief time he served as vice president, meeting with Roosevelt only a handful of times. When he arrived to take the oath of office, he asked Eleanor Roosevelt what he could do for her. She famously responded, "Is there anything we can do for you, Harry? For you are the one in trouble now."

Truman was in an unenviable position. World War II was not yet over in either Europe or the Pacific; Truman did not know of the Manhattan Project; Joseph Stalin was attempting to flex his muscles in Eastern Europe; and in short order Winston Churchill would be removed from power in Great Britain. Truman had gone from a virtually unknown former United

States senator from Missouri to the lead player on the international stage. The American public gave him a long leash—more accurately a long noose—but Roosevelt's twelve years of executive overreach made it possible for Truman to form his own agenda as president. The buck stopped at Truman's desk, as he so famously asserted on his desk plate.

Truman handled the diplomatic and military situation in both Europe and Asia in a manner consistent with the war aims of the previous administration. The war ended in Europe three weeks after he assumed office, so his job was simply cleanup. That cleanup would involve an unprecedented and perhaps unconstitutional American activity in the years following the end of hostilities, but at the time Europe was simply signed, sealed, and delivered to the Allied powers, and Truman did nothing to hinder the foregone conclusion of the war against Germany.

Asia was a different matter. Truman's negotiations with both the Soviet Union and ultimately the Japanese were consistent with his constitutional responsibilities as head of state. His decision to use atomic weapons to bring Japan to the negotiation table and end the war was welcomed at the time by the vast majority of the American people, but it has come under fire in subsequent decades on account of humanitarian concerns and with the revelation that the Japanese were willing to surrender before the decision was made to use Little Boy and Fat Man. Certainly there was nothing unconstitutional about deploying the bomb in a time of war, and saving American lives made the move palatable. The Japanese had inflicted terrible mental and physical trauma on American soldiers, particularly as prisoners of war, so wiping out two industrial targets while showcasing American power to the world seemed to be a win-win situation, regardless of the cost in mostly innocent human lives. Once the United States had the bomb, the device was going to be used during the war. It was just a matter of where and when.

The Soviet Union also took notice, though Truman overestimated what Joseph Stalin's response would be. Truman had shown that the United States was willing to use "the big stuff," as he called it, but neither

Stalin nor Deputy Chairman Vyacheslav Molotov reacted with fear, at least publicly. Truman had played the hand he was dealt by Franklin Roosevelt—and added two aces from the deck. Atomic weapons would eventually play a significant role in the Cold War. But it was neither nuclear weapons nor diplomacy that raised constitutional issues for Truman or for subsequent presidents. It was the way the executive office handled the home front and intelligence operations that would make the Cold War a constitutional boondoggle.

While Truman enjoyed diplomatic success and deserves high ratings for his work in ending the war abroad, his actions on the home front showed a complete disregard for constitutional restraint. Within two months of taking office, Truman, by executive order, seized several private businesses for the war effort, including a coal mine, three oil refineries, an airport, cotton mills, a railroad, the Chicago cab industry, and a rubber plant. Like Roosevelt, Truman claimed his unconstitutional actions were legal because of the war emergency, and Congress passed several pieces of legislation granting the president wide ranging power over the economy. But the scope of government overreach under Truman was unprecedented in American history, and it has never been matched since. World War II is unparalleled in human history, in terms of both the number of lives lost and the property destruction. And it also led to unparalleled government control of citizens' lives. Even when the war ended, Truman simply moved much of the government control (regulation) to other agencies with softer titles.

For example, in August 1945, Truman rescinded every executive order issued since 1942 that had seized private property for the "national emergency." But he then began issuing executive orders transferring the various responsibilities of the unconstitutional wartime government agencies to newly minted peacetime government agencies or to existing government agencies. The Office of War Information was rolled into the Office of Inter-American Affairs. The functions of the Office of Economic Stabilization were transferred to the Office of War Mobilization and Reconversion. Same job, different title. The Civilian Production Administration took the place of the War Production Board, and the National Wage Stabilization Board replaced the National War Labor Board. Neither one of these wartime boards was completely abolished. Truman, like Roosevelt, feared what might happen should the United States revert to an antebellum or pre–New Deal economy. To progressives, World War II had validated government control of the economy, so the peace had to be won for the progressive state both at home and abroad. Throwing open the gates to private enterprise would undermine years of unconstitutional legislation and executive action. The public was clamoring for a return to normal economic freedoms, but Truman held the reins tightly and refused to let the market run free.

To Truman, World War II was only a pause in the effort to combat the Great Depression. He had suffered personally as a small businessman following World War I. Truman's haberdasher business went bankrupt during the 1920 depression, mostly as a result—in his mind anyway—of a sluggish economy following the war and the refusal of the government to help. Truman was determined not to let those conditions prevail again.

In a fifteen-thousand-word September 1945 special message to Congress, Truman outlined the policies that he believed would save the American economy from collapse. He lauded his own "demobilization" efforts immediately after the war (though any astute observer would have noted that Truman had really done very little to trim the size of government), but feared that the most probable effect would be unemployment. He therefore asked Congress to maintain price controls and increase unemployment compensation until at least 1946. The war "emergency" had turned into a great boon for government regulation and overreach, and Truman was eager to keep it all going. In fact, Truman, on the advice of his Attorney General Tom C. Clark, cautioned Congress not to consider the war over and reduce or revoke "emergency" powers. The president alone, he insisted, should have full discretion in declaring the end of hostilities; if Congress acted capriciously, it could throw the government into "chaos."

But Truman revealed his real intentions in his call for "full employment." He restated Roosevelt's "Second Bill of Rights," and firmly declared that national health insurance, "fair" housing, free education, a good job, and old age insurance would be the "essence of postwar American economic life." This declaration clearly put Truman far to the left on the political spectrum and made an unconstitutional expansion of government the stated goal of his administration. Congress dragged its feet in the implementation of Truman's aggressive domestic agenda, but over time these policies have in fact become the "essence of postwar American economic life." They were born out of a wartime "emergency" and have been fostered by a government that has refused to completely leave a wartime footing fully seventy years after the conclusion of hostilities. Truman's September message served as a springboard for the remainder of his time in office.

COMMIES, UNIONS, AND STRIKES

Historians have generally rated 1946 as the most difficult year for the Truman administration. The afterglow of victory in Europe and Asia had dimmed, and the president was now being sniped at from both the Left and the Right. He did nothing to show that he had recovered from his outright disregard for limited executive powers; in fact he was pressing for more government control of the economy. But this did not appease the hard Left in his own Party, men like former vice president Henry Wallace, who thought Truman was too attached to Southern conservatives and too anti-labor to be a real man of the people. Conservatives were frustrated by the Truman administration, too, for Truman never advanced a conservative agenda—the closest he came was half-heartedly suggesting that the United States needed to curb inflation, control spending, and fight communists both at home and abroad. Communist aggression did bother the president, but he would ultimately undermine the most ardent anti-communists in the United States even while waging war against communist expansion in Korea.

Truman had betrayed his aggressive approach to executive power in the September 1945 address, when he claimed that the president alone could declare the end of the war. Truman proclaimed World War II to be over on December 31, 1946, more than a year after the Japanese surrendered. This was clearly unconstitutional. The United States Senate had not ratified a peace treaty, and would not do so until 1947 with the former Axis powers and until 1951 with Japan. The president has no constitutional authority to unilaterally declare war or peace, but no one blinked when he alone decided when the war ended for the United States. In 1945 Truman had cautioned Congress not to act without his approval, and they complied. Their passivity worked to the president's advantage, for it allowed him great discretion in the use of "emergency" powers.

Some of Truman's actions had the full support of the American public despite their blatant unconstitutionality. But Truman's reluctance to end the war quickly and bring the troops home met swift resistance among the armed forces. Truman was playing with fire. Soldiers and their families were ready to resume a normal life, and with the fighting over they assumed they would be landing back on American soil in short order. Instead, Truman asked Congress in 1946 to extend the draft another ten months and suggested compulsory military training for all men of military age. Congress did pass another iteration of the Selective Service Act but refused to mandate universal military training. People had grown weary of war, and Truman's demands sparked protests at American military installations around the globe. Truman even threatened to punch a reporter who tried to hand him a stack of petitions from families demanding that he bring their men home. Congress was right to reject compulsory military training. That had long been (correctly) deemed a state issue under the Constitution. If a state wanted to make militia service mandatory, it could, but the general government could not, at least constitutionally, even after the Militia Act of 1903 supposedly nationalized the various state militias and placed all men between the ages of eighteen and forty-five in the Reserve Militia.

Executive action in regard to the armed forces could at least be defended under the president's responsibility as commander in chief, but when Truman attempted to use the artificially extended "emergency" of the war to quiet labor unrest, even conservative opponents of labor unions believed he was trampling the Constitution. Truman was frustrated that his advocacy of Roosevelt's "Second Bill of Rights" had not inspired swift legislation in Congress, and when eight hundred thousand steelworkers went on strike in early 1946, along with thousands of workers in other occupations, he blamed the strike on congressional reluctance to foster higher wages and better labor laws.

Then, when coal miners went on strike in the spring of 1946 and the railroad union supported them, Truman decided he had to act, particularly because he believed the public supported action and the strike disrupted the American coal supply. The president called on Congress to give him the power to draft every striking worker into the army so he could, as commander in chief, order them back to work under threat of court martial (he even privately remarked that he should hang a few in the railroad union). The House of Representatives passed a bill authorizing the move, but the Senate refused to concur, and Truman's heavy-handed plan for dealing with the strike died a humiliating death. Truman was playing both sides and like a good demagogue was courting public support. In the process, however, he alienated the Left and terrified many on the Right. And his failing bid to put the steel industry on a military footing was only a prelude to an even greater abuse of executive authority in regard to the American economy in his second term.

If Truman's disregard for labor "rights" frustrated the Left, his increasingly bellicose position in regard to the Soviet Union rattled their nerves. To Truman's credit, he was beginning to see the Soviet Union as a threat to American security both at home and abroad. The American diplomat George Kennan postulated that the United States needed to contain Soviet expansion. Truman agreed and privately accepted Winston Churchill's belief that an "iron curtain" had encircled Eastern Europe. Not everyone in his administration shared this view, in particular Henry Wallace.

Wallace had spent his political career expanding the power of the central government—particularly as Franklin Roosevelt's Secretary of Agriculture during the Great Depression—and there were whispers around Washington that he was a closet communist. Wallace's outright rejection of Christianity at one point and his flirtation with the occult tainted his reputation. Nevertheless, he was elected vice president for Roosevelt's third term but then dropped in favor of Truman in 1944, as Roosevelt bowed to political pressure from moderates and conservatives in his own party. Roosevelt then tapped Wallace to be the United States Secretary of Commerce. There was a well-known rift between the once powerful New Dealer and Truman, Wallace's successor as vice president. Their differences came to a head over foreign policy.

Near the end of 1946 Wallace made a speech that was highly critical of Truman's get-tough stance with the Soviet Union. Reportedly, before the speech, Truman said he agreed with everything in it, but afterwards he publicly rebuked Wallace and his foreign policy goals. This revealed more about Truman than just his foreign policy. Truman wrote to his daughter that a good president had to use two tools to be effective: dishonesty and deceit. Truman had played both Wallace and the Left, and Wallace resigned in disgrace. But the American public did not appreciate Truman's duplicity, and they sent a large number of Democrats packing in the 1946 congressional elections. Truman had become a backstabbing, waffling, untrustworthy figurehead, and everyone believed that his days as president were numbered. He would spend the next two years trying to salvage his administration and make a miraculous comeback in the 1948 presidential election. No one, not even his opponent or the opposition press, saw that coming.

THE COMEBACK

One reason for the improbable resurrection of Truman's political career was his foreign policy, much of which Americans, both then and today, have accepted as constitutional, but which has always been on shaky ground constitutionally. No one wanted to be called a "pinko" or a Soviet sympathizer, and opposing anti-communist foreign policy objectives could derail a political career. The Cold War cast a long shadow over American foreign policy decisions, and the 1950s witnessed a hypersensitive public reaction to anything deemed pro-Soviet. But the focus on international communist aggression and the search for potential communist sympathizers in the government deflected attention from the problems of real growth in government power in the United States, always at the expense of the Constitution, including policies that smacked of homegrown socialism. While American taxpayers ultimately dumped billions of dollars into foreign countries to combat communism, they were concurrently being bamboozled into dumping billions of dollars into domestic programs that brought much of the Marxist Utopia to American doorsteps. Eventually, Americans lost self-government in the name of democracy and liberty in the name of freedom. The Truman administration helped push the ball downfield.

Truman is often lauded for two landmark foreign policy decisions he made in the twilight of his first term in office, namely the Truman Doctrine and the Marshall Plan. Both policy objectives originated in the executive office and in both cases the president relied on Congress to cough up the dough to support long-standing commitments to foreign powers, including military aid. Early on, Truman did not have a stellar anti-communism track record. His move to publicly embarrass Wallace represented the high point, up to that time, of what was perceived as Truman's tepid opposition to the Soviet Union and communists in the United States. But 1947 changed everything.

Truman's newly confirmed Secretary of State, George C. Marshall, presented an alarming foreign policy brief shortly after taking office. The communists were making headway in Greece and Turkey, Marshall said, and only quick and decisive financial assistance would preclude a communist takeover of both countries. The Undersecretary of State, Dean Acheson, had been working behind the scenes for several months gathering data that supported Marshall's assertion. Acheson was the mastermind of both the Truman Doctrine and the Marshall Plan, though at first he had largely favored a policy of conciliation with the Soviet Union. George Kennan's 1946 assessment of communist aggression converted Acheson, and he became one of the more prominent Cold Warriors of the Truman administration.

On March 12, 1947, Truman addressed a joint session of Congress in an effort to sell a new foreign policy crisis to the American public. He claimed that the American way of life was under assault by a foreign power that relied on "terror and oppression, a controlled press and radio, fixed elections, and the suppression of personal freedom."[2] If Greece or Turkey did not receive $400 million in aid, the communists would sweep both countries. Truman did not publicly compare Joseph Stalin's Soviet Union to Adolf Hitler's Germany, but in private letters he consistently stated that he saw the two as indistinguishable. He hoped the American people, and most importantly the Congress, would concur. Truman warned, "If we falter in our leadership, we may endanger the peace of the world, and we shall surely endanger the welfare of this nation."[3] Thus the Truman Doctrine—the president's commitment of the United States to oppose Soviet expansionism, starting with Turkey and Greece—was born. The die had been cast. Truman had firmly planted his flag in Wilsonian internationalism.

While the president's critics on the Left were presumably coming from a pro-communist position, they were correct in asserting that the Truman Doctrine could involve the United States in an open-ended ideological crusade with a high cost in blood and money. The Cold War would eventually fracture the Right, with one camp standing firm against foreign adventurism and the other willing to lose a few battles against the unconstitutional expansion of government at home to win the war against the communist thugs in Europe. Constitutional restrictions didn't give Truman pause as he issued his call to action, but in hindsight it is clear that the commitment to stop communism in its tracks by any means necessary would later involve the United States in a series of futile wars on far away shores at great cost to both the American economy and American society. Truman's action was the culmination of American involvement in European affairs beginning with the war against Spain in 1898—a war that the great sociologist William Graham Sumner quipped resulted in the "Conquest of the United States by Spain." The United States won the battle, but European imperialism won the war. With the Truman Doctrine, the United States assumed the role of nineteenth-century Great Britain.

Additionally, Truman's call for economic assistance to war-devastated Europe presented constitutional problems. The Marshall Plan, including economic aid to foreign powers often made through a simple pledge by the executive office, would have been considered a dangerous scheme by the founding generation. The United States could through a treaty offer money or aid to a foreign government, but the Marshall Plan bypassed the treaty process, allocating money by a simple act of Congress. This created an expensive and unconstitutional precedent. By 1948, the United States had dedicated over $12 billion in foreign aid, with the largest sum going to Great Britain, an ally that had never been threatened by a communist insurgency. The Marshall Plan started with a $400 million request, which amounted to a subsidy for foreign powers to buy American consumer goods and helped prop up newly minted socialist and center left governments in Europe, many of which could not balance their books without American greenbacks. The United States was buying allies with taxpayer dollars—and fueling the expansion of leftist government across Europe, purportedly as a bulwark against communism.

Just a little over a week after his publicly acclaimed speech, Truman turned to another issue that had caused a public perception problem: communists in the U.S. government. The new Republican majority in Congress was determined to purge communist sympathizers from the government ranks. Leaks of American nuclear secrets had allowed the Soviet Union to develop nuclear weapons years ahead of schedule, and the race was on to develop more powerful hydrogen bombs. The House Un-American Activities Committee had made finding subversives a top priority, and J. Edgar Hoover's Federal Bureau of Investigation would be brought in for assistance. But Truman worried about potential abuses. Truman privately classified Hoover's FBI as little better than the Gestapo, and he worried about future domestic spying. Those fears were reasonable, and Truman himself added fuel to the fire with his Executive Order 9835 which created a "Loyalty Program" for the executive branch. Over four years the FBI collected data on millions of government employees in an effort to find communist spies. Two hundred and twelve would resign, but none was ever charged with a crime. There were spies in the government, notably Alger Hiss, but the Loyalty Program did not find them.

Truman, however, used his program to create political capital. Republicans admired him for his resolute action on the matter, and Americans began to favor his administration again. His poll numbers rebounded, though not to a level where reelection seemed certain. And he had given the communists a one-two punch to the gut. The Truman Doctrine and Marshall Plan changed the direction of American foreign policy, served as the foundation upon which future policy would be built, and ushered in the Cold War. By the end of Truman's second term, anti-communism would be the standard by which future candidates of both parties would be measured. These facts did not make either policy wise or constitutional. Containment would involve the United States in one undeclared hot war during Truman's tenure and several more in subsequent years, and the Marshall Plan would lead to further unconstitutional maneuvers by the executive branch and the development of dangerous foreign entanglements. Both initiatives would unconstitutionally grow the size and scope of the general government. But in the hysteria that became the Cold War that did not matter as much as beating the reds.

THE FAIR DEAL AND THE COLD WAR

Truman won an improbable victory over Republican Thomas Dewey in the 1948 presidential election by painting his very moderate opponent as a stooge for the ultra-conservative Republican element in Congress and by making a last minute "whistle-stop" campaign tour in the closing weeks of the election. He had positioned himself as the man who could best continue Franklin Roosevelt's dream for a new America. Truman would give the American people a "Fair Deal."

Truman had articulated what that would entail in his 1948 annual message, fully eleven months before the election. He did little more than expand on previous demands for legislation, but his call for a higher minimum wage, public support for housing and education, subsidies for farmers, national health insurance, more conservation and public power initiatives, and a tax cut for middle class Americans appealed to core Democrats, particularly those on the Left who believed Truman was too busy courting Republicans and conservative Democrats to dance with them. Truman knew that none of this legislation would move through the Republican-controlled Congress. (And of course, none of it was constitutional either.) But Truman also knew that these types of ideas found favor with a large segment of the American public and hoped they would win him votes. The man who privately complained of demagogues played one when it mattered, acting very much like the man who had admitted that he would rather buy votes and elections than cars and houses. While he never said it, either publicly or privately, Truman hoped to buy the election in 1948.

It still was a long shot. Truman was so far down in the polls going into November that one famous political cartoon showed a smug Dewey asking Truman, "What's the use of even going through with the election?" This is where Truman used artful demagoguery to prevail. During his last-minute whistle-stop campaign, he would call his wife "the boss" and appeared to be as middle class as his audience. In one case he made a speech in his bathrobe. This was very Jeffersonian, but while Jefferson was reported to have opened the door to the executive mansion himself in his robe, it is hard to image Jefferson making public speeches in his night-clothes. Truman interacted well with the crowds, and the people responded.

He handily won the election, tallying two million more popular votes than his opponent. Truman had won his second term, but getting his Fair Deal through Congress would be a monumental feat.

Truman doubled down on the Fair Deal in his 1949 State of the Union speech, the first of his second term. The address reads like a propaganda piece for the modern Left: "Our minimum wages are far too low.... Some of our natural resources are still being wasted.... Our health is far behind the progress of medical science. Proper medical care is so expensive that it is out of the reach of the great majority of our citizens.... Our schools, in many localities, are utterly inadequate.... Our democratic ideals are often thwarted by prejudice and intolerance." And like a good Keynesian, Truman opined, "The business cycle is man-made; and men of good will, working together, can smooth it out."[4] The solution to all of these problems, Truman insisted, could be found in government. Truman was hoping to wage a public and expensive war on poverty—nearly twenty years before Lyndon Johnson made that phrase famous. After the 1948 election, Truman hoped that the new Democratic majority in the Congress would work quickly to hammer through his legislative agenda. It wouldn't happen.

Southern Democrats balked at Truman's call for more government spending, and Truman could get very little of his agenda to the floor of the Senate for a vote. The Cold War compounded the problem for the administration, but also, at times, served as a nice diversionary tactic. The House Un-American Activities Commission, led by Richard Nixon, very publicly searched for communists in the Truman administration. They found one in Alger Hiss, and though he was not convicted of espionage, he was exposed as a communist. To many Americans, Hiss was indicative of a larger problem. Truman was still too soft on communism. To rectify the matter, Truman signed off on the creation of the North Atlantic Treaty Organization (NATO) in 1949. The public supported the move, and the Congress ratified the treaty, but the able diplomat George Kennan correctly saw the potential danger in such an agreement. It would, he insisted, militarize the Cold War. Within less than a year, he was proven correct.

Newly confirmed Secretary of State Dean Acheson was the mastermind behind the new Cold War urgency of the Truman administration. Acheson had crafted the Marshall Plan and the Truman Doctrine and was now in a position to guide American foreign policy. NATO was his first policy objective as Secretary of State. Acheson also effectively lobbied to increase military expenditures to fight the Cold War. This is where the generally frugal Republicans and their Southern Democratic allies went off the rails. While they rightfully opposed spending increases on constitutionally dubious ideas such as national health insurance and education, these fiscal conservatives gladly jumped at the prospect of expanding the budget to fight communism, even if the call to arms was open-ended and vague.

Acheson's famous NSC-68 report called for a massive increase in defense spending, from $14.3 billion to $50 billion. Defense spending passes the constitutional test without question. But plans were being made to increase the budgets of the recently created Central Intelligence Agency and National Security Council, and large chunks of money were being set aside for research and development, an often underappreciated realm of government waste and mismanagement. And while American taxpayers were forking over their money in an effort to combat communism abroad, they were surrendering their liberties to a government that eventually would rely on the same tactics communist regimes used to suppress dissent at home. Acheson insisted the money was needed to place the United States in a position of strength vis-à-vis the Soviet Union. It worked, but it also placed every international conflict in the context of the Cold War. America now had the means to fight the Cold War with money and muscle often procured at the expense of the United States Constitution.

This was made clear in the Korean War. The divided former Japanese colony had been jointly occupied by the United States and the Soviet Union following the conclusion of World War II. Korea had come under increasing influence from the recently proclaimed People's Republic of China and its communist premier Mao Tse-tung. Then, in 1950, the communist North Korean government launched an offensive against the pro-Western

South. Communist forces quickly surged through the peninsula, and the South Korean government appealed to the United States for assistance. The Truman administration had an opportunity to put the Truman Doctrine on Containment into action.

The United States approached the United Nations first in an effort to mask America's direct involvement in the Korean War. Obtaining a United Nations Security Council resolution against communist aggression in Korea, with a commitment to use military force to halt North Korean expansion, allowed Truman to say that he was acting in the name of the United Nations. He called it a "police action." This was the first time in American history that the United States had committed troops to a war without congressional authorization. Congress did not declare war, Korea had not attacked the United States, and finding any direct American interest short of a general commitment to stopping communist aggression in Asia was nearly impossible. But in the fall of 1950, American troops landed in Korea, and within two weeks they had pushed the North Koreans out of the South.

Truman, however, thought it necessary to prepare the United States for another major war, and he used the "police action" as a means of declaring another unconstitutional "national emergency." In a bizarre address, Truman declared that the United States would uphold "the principles of the United Nations," and advocated another round of price controls, wage controls, and production controls, along with higher taxes. He also, as "Commander in Chief," demanded that all the American people get back to work. This was necessary, Truman said, "for the defense of your homes and your way of life.... All of us will have to pay more taxes and do without things we like." But not to worry. Truman reassured Americans that this was not a sacrifice, but "an opportunity, an opportunity to defend the best kind of life that men have ever devised on this earth." Truman closed by reminding Americans that we were the "leaders of the free world." The "Commander in Chief" was essentially directing that the now militarized civilian population should act as such by sacrificing their money, their goods, and their freedom to defend their homes for "the principles of the United Nations" against non-existent North Korean bombers flying over American airspace. He followed up his address the next day with an unconstitutional proclamation declaring the "national emergency."[5]

The promising (but unconstitutional) military action quickly turned against the Truman administration. General Douglas MacArthur led the American military effort. It was no secret that he and Truman did not agree on the course of the war, but the public held MacArthur in high esteem and generally trusted his opinion on military matters over Truman's. He was, after all, the hero of the Pacific theater in World War II, and he was an ardent anti-communist. Because of the political ramifications, Truman gave MacArthur great discretion during the early phases of the war, even agreeing to direct confrontation with the Chinese, but when MacArthur insisted on invading China and disposing of the communist government there, potentially with nuclear weapons, and then publicly denounced the Truman administration for what in his mind amounted to unprecedented interference, Truman sacked him and forced MacArthur to retire. It was a highly unpopular move, and as the war went sour, Truman's approval ratings dipped to all-time lows.

By this point, Truman was despondent over the opposition he faced from those loyal to MacArthur, from a war-weary American public, and from labor unions who refused to live up to what he told them were their responsibilities during the "national emergency." The American steelworkers exemplified the latter problem. In 1951, steelworkers demanded a wage increase, which mill owners refused if they could not obtain permission from the federal government to raise steel prices. Remember, Truman had left much of the World War II economic apparatus in place following the war and now, because of the Koran War, ramped up government regulation of the economy even more. When neither side could come to a deal (even with federal intervention in the negotiations), Truman decided to unilaterally seize the steel mills and place them under direct government control.

This move had a precedent. Roosevelt had done essentially the same thing during World War II, and Truman continued the practice until the end of the war. Thus he was shocked when the public reacted negatively to this naked abuse of power. The press vilified him, and even some hard left leaders considered this a precarious move. One must ask where these same people were during World War II and the Great Depression when several major industries—and many minor ones—fell under federal control. It seems that the American public had an epiphany in 1952: the executive branch was out of control and needed to be reined in.

Of course Truman did not see it that way. He went on the offensive, with his administration claiming that the Constitution only limited the powers of the Congress and the Judicial Branch, not the executive, particularly in a "national emergency"—which Truman declared in December 1950. Truman had assumed the powers of a king, and though this transformation had not happened overnight, he was suddenly forced to defend his actions in a way that Roosevelt and all of his predecessors who had abused executive power had managed to avoid. He was the unlucky president who finally had to legally justify and defend unconstitutional executive overreach. The Supreme Court overturned Truman's decision in 1952, but it stopped short of declaring all such actions unconstitutional. The high court had now become complicit in the unconstitutional arrogation of power by the central government, and would continue to be so for the remainder of the twentieth century.

Truman greatly expanded the powers of the executive office during his nearly eight years as president. His Fair Deal, though it failed to pass into law, continued the tradition of progressive domestic "reform" and helped establish that the Left would never cease to advance a comprehensive agenda in domestic affairs (virtually every subsequent president had one). More important, however, was Truman's legacy with respect to executive authority. Truman built on what Roosevelt had done, but his use of executive power, particularly in relation to foreign policy, was unmatched in American history to that point. No longer would the president be bound to rely on Congress to authorize military action. "The principles of the United Nations" became a driving force behind executive overreach and open-ended, expensive wars.

Truman was a likable man who projected a Jeffersonian image, but he did not govern like Jefferson and did not view the powers of the central government in the same light. Truman left office in 1953 confident that the American public would see the wisdom of his domestic and foreign policies. The leftist historical profession has generally held Truman in high regard. His most important legacy is as the architect of the Cold War. Truman thought—and history proved him right on this score—that the United States would eventually win. But the cost for fighting the war with the methods Truman chose was too high: an out-of-control executive branch and a general government that has usurped powers never delegated to it by the Constitution.

LYNDON B. JOHNSON

Thirty-Sixth President, 1963–1969

The Lyndon Johnson administration can be viewed as a continuation of the Franklin Roosevelt and Truman administrations. Johnson cut his political teeth in both the House and the Senate from 1937 to 1961 and considered Roosevelt to be one of his political "fathers." The legislative philosophy of the two World War II presidents stuck. Johnson was an ardent New Dealer, supported Truman's Fair Deal legislative initiatives, was hawkish toward the Soviet Union in the early days of the Cold War, and like both Truman and Roosevelt reveled in personal politics. His tactics were the perfect blend of Truman's folksy style and Roosevelt's penchant for political kneecapping. And he was ambitious. Johnson wanted to be president and pursued that goal with unmatched energy. His turn finally arrived with John F. Kennedy's assassination in 1963. This was ironic because in 1956 one proposed Democratic ticket had had Johnson at the top with Kennedy as the vice presidential candidate, and Johnson had balked because he believed that Kennedy's powerful father, Joe Kennedy, simply wanted to use Johnson as a stepping stone for his son's rise to the Oval Office. He was right.

Johnson was never one to miss a political opportunity. Public mourning after Kennedy's assassination allowed Johnson to push his foreign and domestic policy goals forward without much opposition. This was, he said, what Kennedy would have wanted. But more than any president since Franklin Roosevelt (even Truman), Johnson unconstitutionally expanded the scope of the executive branch. His unconstitutional "war on poverty" nearly bankrupted the United States (it might still) and he used bully tactics ("the treatment") to throw his weight around in Congress. Johnson led from the Oval Office, but he might as well have been planted at the United States Capitol. His foreign policy initiatives involved the United States more deeply in Vietnam—through a lie and a request for congressional authorization to use force, not an honest request for a declaration of war. At every turn, Johnson used unprecedented and unconstitutional executive authority to force his vision on the American government, the states, and the people at large.

THE WAR ON POVERTY

Johnson grew up in a small Texas town riddled with poverty, and he believed that government should be used to alleviate financial distress. He toned down his populism while in the United States Senate, presumably to secure votes from the more conservative Texas voter base, but he always thought that Roosevelt's New Deal had been the proper course for the American economy. And once he was in the Oval Office, Johnson wasted little time in declaring "war on poverty."

The new president was pressed to make his first State of the Union address less than two months after Kennedy's assassination. He used the

platform to unveil his vision for America. Johnson said that his administration, "declares unconditional war on poverty in America. I urge this
Congress and all Americans to join with me in that effort." He then outlined a series of proposals that were intended to meet the "crisis," from
better unemployment compensation to "fair housing," food stamps, more
federal funding for public education, better mass transit systems, and more
libraries and hospitals. In short, Johnson proposed to provide federal
funding for virtually every aspect of American life. All these programs,
he argued, would alleviate and perhaps eliminate poverty in America.[1]

Curiously, Johnson suggested that part of the war on poverty would
be a *reduction* in income taxes in order to release "$11 billion" into the
private sector in order to create jobs: "We need a tax cut now to keep this
country moving." Such is not the mantra of the Left in 2015, but Johnson
at least understood one basic economic principle. Unfortunately, the price
tag for Johnson's "War on Poverty" would be substantial, and none of it
was remotely constitutional. In fact, the federal budget doubled during
Johnson's tenure in office. Some of the runaway spending could be blamed
on the war in Vietnam—another constitutional mess—but it was largely
because of greater federal spending on domestic programs.

Johnson immediately tapped Kennedy's brother-in-law Sargent
Shriver to head the war on poverty initiative. Like Roosevelt, Johnson
viewed his domestic initiatives as suitable for military organization and
regimentation. It was a national "emergency." Congress responded to
Johnson's declaration of war on poverty by passing the Economic Opportunities Act of 1964. The bill authorized the creation of several job programs and sent monies directly to local governments rather than in blocks
to the states. In essence, the states—often the road block to the expansion
of federal power—were cut out of the process. The jobs programs mirrored
those used during the Great Depression to "combat" poverty, and Shriver,
as the founder and head of the Peace Corps for five years, had the energy
and diligence to implement the bill. He created the Office of Economic
Opportunity (OEO) to serve as the central command for Johnson's "war"

effort. The way Johnson made use of the Kennedy legacy was genius. Johnson took a bill that Kennedy initially proposed, made it his own, and then used the Kennedy name and legacy to smooth its passage—and also its implementation.

Yet, the constitutional problems that had plagued the New Deal were also issues for what became known as the Great Society. Johnson was acting as chief legislator, and through his appointee Shriver the president had a personal hand in almost every regulation that would eventually trickle out of the OEO. This was certainly never intended by the founding generation. Additionally, the legislation that Johnson had pushed through Congress was itself constitutionally dubious. A case could be made for federal loans, but large blocks of money being applied directly to single individuals or even groups for economic assistance was a complete bastardization of the meaning of "the General Welfare Clause" of Article I, Section 8. And by eliminating the states from the equation, the Economic Opportunities Act distorted the Founders' understanding of the meaning of Union and expanded the powers of the general government beyond their original intent. The legislation reduced the states to mere provinces of the general government. Cities and towns which were incorporated by the states could directly apply to the general government for money without the approval of their creator. Both creations of the states were now usurping the powers of the states that had created them—from above and below at the same time. Neither the Congress nor Johnson even attempted to cloak their actions in the language of the Constitution. It was simply assumed, after over thirty years of patently unconstitutional federal legislation, that such moves *were* constitutional.

THE GREAT SOCIETY

Two well-known federal welfare programs originated in the Johnson administration, namely Medicare and Medicaid, but at Johnson's request (and often as a result of his badgering) several other federal programs were expanded to implement his "Great Society" agenda. Johnson believed that adequate food, shelter, education, and medical care were essential to ending poverty in America, but his Great Society agenda later also affected other areas of American life, such as "public safety" and the environment. His humanitarian concerns were laudable, but Johnson's belief that the general government could constitutionally undertake such grand schemes was a progressive delusion. To Johnson, the Great Society represented the culmination of Roosevelt's New Deal and his Second Bill of Rights. LBJ had attempted to hide his more Leftist inclinations while leading the Senate, but now that he was president, Johnson tossed aside any concerns about being seen as too liberal. His years bullying fellow senators as both Senate Democratic whip and, later, majority leader would pay huge dividends for a president intent on become chief legislator.

Food stamps did not originate in the Johnson administration. They were an outgrowth of early agricultural subsidies established in the 1920s and during the second New Deal in 1939. The war and a post-war conservative retrenchment ended the program, but it was revived (though not implemented) during the Eisenhower administration and later expanded by John F. Kennedy. The initial goal of the program was the reduction of surplus agricultural goods, mainly perishable food stores, by assisting farmers to sell unwanted products at a fair price.

Before becoming president, Kennedy had promised that he would increase the scope of the program, and after his death Johnson pushed the initiative forward, crafting the Food Stamp Act of 1964. His secretary of agriculture, Orville Freeman, presented the bill to Congress. Freeman was a hard-nosed former Marine Corps major with a populist streak, a law degree, and a willingness to battle Johnson on policy issues. But Johnson never bent. The president set the agenda, and anything that got his seal of approval was *his* bill. The Food Stamp Act was no different.

At first, the program targeted only the neediest Americans—with the first purchase under the program being a can of beans. But within three years expenditures had more than doubled, and by the early 1970s participation had far exceeded the original estimated four million targeted enrollments. Eventually food stamps became an entitlement used to prop up farm subsidies—and thus large farms—and funnel government money into American retail grocery stores. In effect, the federal government pays farmers to produce food, and then when they produce too much, it buys the food that it had already purchased again through food stamps, at a price higher than fair market value. If farmers had to sell products at the unsubsidized market value, the price of food would fall. Corn, wheat, and rice are three of the top four subsidized agricultural products in America, and all three are used not only to make foodstuffs but also to feed livestock. The prices of beef, chicken, pork, and milk are directly tied to the price of feed. A price floor means higher consumer prices for us all. The Food Stamp Act was never constitutional—nor was Johnson's full participation in drafting the legislation a constitutional role for the chief executive.

The most sweeping changes to the American economy as a result of Johnson's presidency, however, were effected by the Social Security Act of 1965. Progressives had been clamoring for a comprehensive national medical care system since Theodore Roosevelt had made it a component of his "Bull Moose" Party platform in 1912. Franklin Roosevelt addressed medical care in his "Second Bill of Rights," and Truman attempted to have national healthcare legislation passed as part of his failed "Fair Deal." Johnson finally had the ability to bully opponents into submission—and thus the votes. Nineteen-sixty-five was the year the American public was introduced to Medicare and Medicaid.

Medicare was sold as an extension of the Social Security program established during the New Deal. It provided medical coverage to retired Americans (over age sixty-five) regardless of income. Harry Truman and his wife Bess received the first issued Medicare cards at a signing ceremony in Missouri in 1965. The bill piggybacked on an already unconstitutional Social Security system and provided government health insurance through a payroll tax system. All Americans would be financing the few who collected Medicare. Like Social Security, Medicare is a Ponzi scheme doomed to fail. There is absolutely no authority for such a system in the Constitution, and by signing the bill Johnson abrogated his oath to defend our government's founding document.

Like Social Security, Medicare was defended under the Taxing and Spending Clause and General Welfare Clause. If the general government could levy taxes to provide old-age insurance, certainly it could levy more taxes to provide old-age medical insurance. Opponents pointed out that both taxes bastardized the meaning of the clauses and unconstitutionally expanded federal power. The Supreme Court disagreed—narrowly. It had upheld Social Security by slim majorities in the 1930s. Justice Benjamin Cardozo, a Herbert Hoover appointee and ardent advocate of a "living Constitution," suggested that if the Court interpreted the Constitution the way it was understood in the 1780s, the United States would be stuck in the 1780s. Surely America had progressed. Besides, Alexander Hamilton's Constitution of loosely implied powers had defeated James Madison's Constitution of expressly delegated powers. The war need not be fought again. This position, of course, was in sharp contrast to the position the proponents of the Constitution took when the Constitution was being debated in state ratifying conventions. If they had argued for Hamilton's loosely implied powers or Cardozo's living Constitution, the document would never have been ratified in the first place.

In practice, Medicare did not immediately spike medical costs, as the average life expectancy in the United States hovered around sixty-five for several years. In the early years of the program, most Americans never used the system for any period of time. That began to change in the 1980s. As Americans lived longer, the cost of their medical care after the age of sixty-five increased. Doctors and hospitals were provided an annually increasing price floor. When the elderly lived ten or more years on average past the enrollment age, the medical industry began pocketing more tax dollars for all types of medical procedures, from necessary surgery to unnecessary "hover chairs." The baby boomers compounded the problem.

A rapidly increasing retirement population coupled with a smaller tax base (baby boomers did not have many children) created an unsustainable fiscal nightmare. Older people need more medical procedures; more medical procedures require more money; pharmaceutical companies, doctors, and the healthcare industry are guaranteed to be paid; prices skyrocket. Knowing they would be compensated by a government-run health insurance industry flush with cash, the healthcare companies could raise prices and make higher profits. Government replaced the free market in healthcare for the elderly, and the consumer footed the bill, paying higher taxes and higher prices at the doctor's office.

Medicaid, the other insurance program created by the Social Security Act of 1965, exacerbated the problem. Medicaid was designed to provide health insurance for the poorest Americans regardless of age. The main beneficiaries were children and mothers without coverage. The federal government split the costs with the states but required each state to provide some type of Medicaid program. States would become addicted to the cash and unable to keep their budgets in balance without federal dollars. The federal government was now requiring states to do its bidding—the inverse of how things were in the Constitution as ratified and interpreted for much of American history. The Tenth Amendment had slipped into oblivion.

Funding for federally mandated programs—including Medicare, but others as well—would add billions to state balance sheets. With poor Americans of all ages now covered under some type of federal health insurance, those in the middle, the "forgotten man" who was paying the bill, began to feel the squeeze. Private insurance coverage softened the blow for some Americans, but those without insurance suffered the brunt of a medical industry on a federal cash drip—and the resulting inflated prices. And healthy people too young to receive Medicare and too "rich" to have Medicaid—even those with private insurance—were paying for sick people through higher taxes.

The sad truth is that had Lyndon Johnson not been interested in legislating from the executive branch and had faithfully defended his oath to uphold the Constitution by vetoing unconstitutional legislation, the American public would not be standing closer to the edge of a fiscal cliff by the day. Johnson, however, was at heart a legislator and a devoted acolyte of Roosevelt's New Deal and his belief in executive government, which is the real culprit behind the expansion of government in the last half of the twentieth century.

Besides medical care, Johnson also believed that every American had a right to a good education. His early life in impoverished rural Texas and limited access to quality educational opportunities—along with a dogmatic faith in the Second Bill of Rights—led him to pursue greater federal funding for public education. He was not really a pioneer in this field. Progressives had been calling for more centralization and more federal money in education for decades, but it took a president like Johnson to make it happen.

Almost immediately after taking office Johnson insisted that Congress tackle the education issue. But education had long been the exclusive realm of the state governments. This was (and is) the constitutionally correct position. Education is not an enumerated power, and while progressives had been pushing for a "national" education system for nearly a century, it had always been blocked by those dedicated to sound constitutional principles. Education was considered to be a basic component of local self-government. Certainly, education was deemed vital to the promotion of republicanism and prosperity, but the customs and traditions of the local community prevailed over concocted schemes for "national" standards. Jefferson once famously wrote that he wanted his University of Virginia to be a shield against the "dark Federalist mills" of the North. Until Johnson, provincialism had always won the day in American education.

But World War II, the Cold War, and the Civil Rights Movement changed the way many Americans thought about education. It was believed that winning an international struggle against communism required a "national" effort, and defeating communism at home could only be done by eliminating poverty and discrimination—because poor and disfranchised people make good pinkos. There was a lot of truth in this, but the methods used were unconstitutional. The Great Society usurped authority from state and local governments and destroyed federalism, the heart of the American political system. Practically, the Johnson agenda also led to exponentially increasing education costs for students and parents.

The Elementary and Secondary Education Act of 1965 (ESEA) radically changed the role of the federal government. ESEA was a billion-dollar federal program designed to increase funding for primary and secondary schools in the United States. Johnson insisted on its passage and held a high-profile signing ceremony with one of his childhood teachers. He believed, and every progressive to this day insists, that the money funneled to the states by federal grants would reduce the prevalence of poverty in schools and make better students. More dollars equals more success. In reality, it was little more than a Trojan horse.

ESEA increased state education budgets and eventually allowed the federal government to mandate specific outcomes for student success. If states and localities wanted the money, not only did school districts have to meet income guidelines—that is, have a high rate of poverty—but also students had to perform well; thus they were subjected to federal standards in all aspects of academic and social life. Students had truly become lab rats in government-funded laboratories. Johnson's push for a federal role in education did not begin that way, but once the federal government was so heavily involved in local schools, the writing was on the wall. His proper role as president would have been to veto such a blatantly unconstitutional bill. But Johnson was too ideologically driven to do so.

ESEA also created the much maligned Head Start program, a federal catastrophe that has dumped billions of dollars into state education budgets in the last fifty years with no measurable success, unless the call for more money from the federal government to fund the program or a cushion for fiscally stressed state education budgets (mostly from high salaries for school "administrators") is considered success. No one can question Johnson's desire to help poor Americans, but his unconstitutional methods extended the dangerous precedent of federal intervention through executive action in an area where the general government had no authority.

The Higher Education Act of 1965 (HEA) magnified unconstitutional federal involvement in American schools and jump-started an educational funding bubble that is just now showing signs of bursting. Following World War II, millions of returning GIs took advantage of the GI Bill to enroll in institutions of higher education. In the 1940s a college degree, particularly an advanced degree, ensured a better standard of living. Colleges and universities gobbled up the money and began raising tuition. They had guaranteed funds and an eager student population. The HEA created a financial system that provided direct funding to individuals seeking a college degree, thus bypassing the states, which had long been the gatekeeper in education funds. The subsidized loan program and low-income grants, later renamed Pell Grants after Rhode Island Senator Claiborne Pell, expanded student populations in colleges and universities across America, but there was a price.

More students had access to advanced degrees, but with a limitless supply of cash and federally backed default-proof student loans, higher education transitioned into a business that chased dollars. Tuition hikes became an annual rite of passage. Predictably, as higher education institutions raised prices, the Congress increased student loan caps and grant funding. The net result has been an almost four hundred percent increase in the cost of a four-year college degree at a public university since the early 1970s, a trillion dollars in non-dischargeable student loan debt, and—with more Americans obtaining degrees—diminishing returns on a college education. The system also led to federal dollars supplanting state and private investment in higher education. Now federal dollars comprise a large percentage—in some cases nearly 75 percent—of college and university budgets. Students, local school districts, and higher education institutions are addicted to the drug of the reckless unconstitutional federal spending on education. Johnson was the chief architect of it all, and he solidified permanent unconstitutional federal involvement in education by elevating the Department of Health, Education, and Welfare to a cabinet-level position in 1965.

The role the Great Society played in federal environmental regulation is often overlooked. "Conservation" had been a key component of progressivism since Teddy Roosevelt made it a federal responsibility during his first term in office. By the late 1960s, "environmentalism" had transitioned into a cult-like religion for the worshipers of "Mother Earth." Johnson and his ambitious Secretary of the Interior Stewart Udall had much to do with this development.

Udall was appointed secretary of the interior by John F. Kennedy in 1961. He had been an active proponent of "conservation" and now began pushing for more aggressive federal involvement in the environment. His book, *The Quiet Crisis*, was an alarmist look at environment in the United States. Udall insisted that the federal government should not only "conserve" natural resources but should regulate industry in an effort to protect the environment and thus man. That project has always been the key to environmentalism. "Saving the planet" simply translates to a mystical belief that man can save man from his own destruction. It is an anthropocentric religion.

Kennedy's assassination did little to slow Udall's quest to make the federal government the chief instrument in "environmental protection." Johnson kept Udall in his cabinet and adopted his heavy handed approach to government regulation. Virtually every current environmental regulation in the United States can be traced to Udall and Johnson. Between 1963 and 1965 Udall helped draft and Johnson signed eight comprehensive pieces of federal environmental legislation. Each created mountains of federal regulations targeted at curtailing pollution and protecting wildlife and natural resources. The impact on industry was almost immediate. Companies had to meet new federally enforced air quality and pollution standards while new factories faced mountains of red tape in increasingly burdensome environmental requirements before they could open shop. The resulting expensive upgrades to equipment forced businesses to either raise prices on industrial goods, shut down operations, or ship jobs to other countries without environmental controls.

All of this environmental legislation was and is unconstitutional, at least according to the Constitution as ratified. Neither the Congress nor the president is authorized by the Constitution to regulate either emissions or the requirements for opening a business. The states could, but Congress was purposely left powerless on these issues. Clean air and water are certainly laudable goals, but federal authority over these issues would require a constitutional amendment. This constitutional end-around was not unusual for progressives. They had been doing it since the first Roosevelt administration. By the Great Society and the 1960s, however, they were no longer even trying to cloak their moves in constitutional language. The federal government simply acted because it could, and Johnson, drunk with his own power and the realization that he finally achieved his dream of being president, encouraged such bad behavior.

To ensure that the American people supported the Great Society, Johnson and other progressives in the Congress knew that they had to win the propaganda and cultural war in America. If the public could be persuaded that Johnson's unconstitutional agenda was beneficial (and legal), his stamp on public policy would become permanent. As a result, Johnson signed three pieces of legislation in 1964 and 1967 that changed media and art in America. The goal—apparently—was to immerse the American people in progressive ideology one child and student at a time.

The National Endowment for the Humanities, the National Endowment for the Arts, and the Public Broadcasting Corporation all came into existence as part of the Great Society. Sold as public-private partnerships that relied on private support for their continued existence, these three bastions of liberal ideology allowed the federal government to have a direct role in the type of art, literature, and television Americans consume.

Programs like *Sesame Street* have a clearly leftist agenda, while the NEA has continually used taxpayer dollars to sponsor artwork that many Americans deem objectionable. It has even requested artwork that favors one candidate or political party over another.

Johnson, of course, wasn't the first president to propose federal aid for the arts. John Quincy Adams had made federal support for the arts one of his goals during his one term in office (Congress at that time had a backbone and said "No"), and Roosevelt's New Deal provided federal money for down-on-their-luck artists, actors, and writers. John F. Kennedy had pushed for some type of federal aid for the arts and humanities. But Johnson had the wind at his back and an agreeable Congress, and he sailed bill after bill through Congress without much opposition. And all these Great Society Programs, from Medicaid and Medicare to National Public Radio, have—to borrow the words of a more recent presidential candidate—fundamentally transformed America. Modern America is the Great Society.

CIVIL RIGHTS

During his first televised speech before Congress, Johnson looked squarely into the camera and demanded that all Americans be treated equally under the law. The camera then cut away to the Southern Democratic delegation who sat on their hands while the rest of the Congress applauded. Black Americans had been treated as second class citizens in the South. They had freedom, paid taxes, and in theory had the right to vote, but poll taxes and other restrictions on voting made achieving any political power nearly impossible, and their tax dollars did not ensure them equal access to public facilities. Johnson wanted to confront these issues head on.

The president determined that the only possible way to end legal segregation in the South was through a concerted federal effort. This idea did not originate in his administration. FDR, Truman, Dwight Eisenhower, and Kennedy had all pursued a civil rights agenda, but none had the legislative backing that Johnson enjoyed in both the Eighty-Eighth and Eighty-Ninth Congresses.

There were, however, serious constitutional questions raised by Johnson's civil rights agenda, not the least of which was the president's personal involvement in the legislative process—but that ship had sailed long before. In 1883, the Supreme Court had declared the Civil Rights Act of 1875 unconstitutional by an 8–1 vote. It had outlawed segregation in public facilities, generally defined as anything that allowed public access, such as transportation, inns, and theaters. The Court at the time was composed of eight Republicans and one nominal Democrat, all appointed no earlier than the Lincoln administration. The majority opinion, written by Grant-appointed Justice Joseph Bradley, stated that when black Americans were being discriminated against by private individuals rather than by state law, neither the Thirteenth nor the Fourteenth Amendment applied. Congress had no authority to regulate the actions of private individuals.

Justice John Harlan dissented, arguing that rail transportation should be considered a "public road" and therefore subject to public regulation, and that innkeepers, while they were private businessmen, served the public and thus were "agents or instrumentalities of the State" subject to "governmental regulation." He applied this line of thinking to any person who worked for any private enterprise that could be subjected to government regulation. That would mean every citizen of every state because the states can lawfully regulate the people of the states. Because the Fourteenth Amendment applied to the states, Harlan concluded that the federal government could regulate every person in the states. This expansive interpretation of the Fourteenth Amendment found virtually no support at the time, but the times were a changin' in the 1960s.

The Great Society civil rights initiatives were an outgrowth of previous attempts by the federal government to curtail legal segregation. The Civil Rights Act of 1957, met with a twenty-four hour one-man filibuster by Strom Thurman of South Carolina, still passed by a vote of 72 to 18 in the Senate and a similar margin in the House of Representatives. The bill was weak on enforcement mechanisms, so the Congress passed the Civil Rights Act of 1960 to combat discrimination in voting practices. But like the 1957 bill—both were signed into law by President Eisenhower—the 1960 law was mostly bark and no bite.

Civil rights activists noted that still very little had changed in the South. There were only around 3 percent more registered black voters in 1960 than there were in 1954 after the landmark *Brown v. Board of Education* decision, and Jim Crow laws remained firmly in place. Shortly before his assassination, John F. Kennedy demanded that Congress act, and Johnson continued that push when he assumed office in November 1963.

The ghost of Judge Harlan would finally have his say in the matter (his grandson was now an associate justice). The Civil Rights Act of 1964 formally codified his interpretation of the Fourteenth Amendment. The 1964 Act was a sweeping piece of legislation designed to end both *de facto* and *de jure* segregation. Two parts of the bill came under fire. The first of these, Title II, was essentially the Civil Rights Act of 1875. The Supreme Court had already declared that law unconstitutional, but Congress was going to give it another shot. The second, Title VII, prohibited discrimination in hiring practices. The constitutional question centered on the ability of the general government to regulate the private activities of American citizens, the same issue that Harlan and the Supreme Court had tackled in 1883. In his dissent in the case striking down the 1875 Civil Rights Act, Harlan had said anyone who had a "public" job could be subject to government regulation through the Fourteenth Amendment.

But defenders of the 1964 Act went a step further. They relied on an expanded interpretation of the Commerce Clause of Article I, Section 8 ("To regulate Commerce with foreign Nations, and among the several States, and with the Indian Tribes"), to justify the regulation of obviously private economic activity. Proponents of the bill considered individuals who could cross state lines to be commercial agents engaged in interstate commerce. So just a few individuals or even a single person could be a "State" for the purposes of regulating commerce "among the several

States." Thus all economic activity could be regulated by the federal government, including hiring by private companies and any "commercial" activity by non–state owned companies or individuals that catered to the public, such as inns and restaurants.

The Supreme Court quickly took up a case challenging the law. In 1964, in the landmark unanimous decision of *Heart of Atlanta Motel, Inc. v. United States*, the Court held that because the business in question (a hotel) was situated between two interstate highways and because 75 percent of its clientele came from out of state, the hotel was engaged in and affected "interstate commerce" and thus had to be racially integrated. Note that the Court considered hotel patrons "States." One of Robert F. Kennedy's advisors said that, "There is not a self-respecting lawyer who would have written you an opinion that the bill would be anything but constitutional right from the beginning."[2] Perhaps not among proponents of the bill, but there were many "self-respecting" people who did disagree with the decision.

The ruling was a departure from the founding generation's interpretation of the Commerce Clause when the Constitution was ratified. At that time, the main concern was to prevent states from erecting prohibitive tariffs against other states. Roger Sherman of Connecticut maintained that the sole purpose of the Commerce Clause was to keep commerce "free" by establishing what amounted to a large free trade zone in North America. Chief Justice John Marshall, no friend of strict construction of the Constitution, opined in the famous *Gibbons v. Ogden* case of 1824 that only commerce "between the States" could be regulated by the general government. Individuals were not states.

The 1964 Republican presidential nominee, Barry Goldwater, voted against the Civil Rights Act because of Title II and Title VII. Even after the Court upheld Title II, Goldwater insisted that it was unconstitutional. He had voted for both the Civil Rights Act of 1957 and the Civil Rights Act of 1960 but thought that the issues addressed in the 1964 law should be handled at the state level first. He took a lot of political heat for this decision. Goldwater, however, stated that this was a matter of law versus politics. In his mind, it would have been sound politics to vote for the bill, particularly considering his run for president, but bad law.

There is no question that the aim of the Civil Rights Act of 1964 was morally just. But that was not the only issue. As Goldwater pointed out, it was also a question of law. During a long series of hearings on the bill, Senator Sam Ervin of North Carolina and Attorney General Robert Kennedy verbally sparred on the issue of moral right vs. legal right. Ervin forced Kennedy to concede that a Fourteenth Amendment defense of the Act would fall flat, but Kennedy concluded that the Commerce Clause made the bill constitutional. Ervin then rattled off several Supreme Court decisions that refuted Kennedy's claim, only to have the attorney general counter with an equal number of post–New Deal decisions that buttressed his argument. And to the public, Kennedy stood on the moral high ground, even when Ervin ardently defended his record on racial justice and that of his home state.

This is the inherent problem with judicial review. The 1883 Supreme Court—all appointed by Republicans (including two of the justices by Lincoln)—would have declared the 1964 Civil Rights Act unconstitutional. The 1964 Supreme Court, reflecting the moral values of its time, decided otherwise. The Constitution had not changed in eighty years, but public opinion had. The only anchor, then, is the Constitution *as ratified* by the founding generation. This is the position that is often called originalism. Even the ardent progressive Supreme Court Justice Hugo Black cautioned against creating new rights out of thin air through the expansion of the meaning of the Fourteenth Amendment when a challenge to poll taxes was overturned by the Court in 1966. The post–New Deal Supreme Court often did just that.

The Johnson administration and the Congress could have pursued a Constitutional amendment codifying the 1964 Act. They had the requisite votes in the Congress, and judging by the support in the states for the Twenty-Fourth Amendment (1964) which outlawed poll taxes (in federal elections), a Civil Rights Amendment would almost assuredly have been ratified. But instead Johnson skirted the Constitution and relied on nine politically appointed justices to uphold the law. This is a recipe for disaster. Eighty years from now, the Court could reverse the 1964 decision because of the values and opinions of the time. An amendment to the Constitution could ensure that would not happen. Johnson and the Congress were right in history but wrong in law.

Other legislation followed, all morally correct but with constitutional flaws. Johnson signed it all. For example, the landmark Voting Rights Act of 1965 was constitutionally dubious because it directly violated Article I, Section 2, which allows the states to determine voter qualifications. The founding generation considered state control of elections as an essential protection against federal encroachment. The Selma riots of 1965 stimulated interest in the bill, with both Johnson and the Congress concluding that swift action was necessary to prevent further violence. The Act passed by crushing majorities in the House and Senate, which leaves open the question as to why such a sweeping change to the power of the federal government vis-à-vis the states was not subjected to the amendment process. Like the Civil Rights Act of 1964, there is little doubt a Voting Rights Amendment would have been ratified.

Johnson's reputation as a civil rights crusader has been challenged by recent artistic interpretations of the 1960s, and various Republican partisans have attempted to place the Republican Party at the forefront of the Civil Rights Movement. In fact both Johnson and the Republican Party contributed to the moral triumphs—and the constitutional abuses. It is incontrovertible that Johnson supported the aims of every piece of civil rights legislation he signed into law and that Republican support was instrumental in the passage of every bill. It is also certain that the entire Great Society legislative program had serious legal and constitutional flaws; these laws were passed, signed and enforced, and upheld on judicial review by a Congress, a president, and a Supreme Court that were all willing to find new federal powers between the lines of the Constitution.

According to his oath, Johnson had a legal responsibility to veto all unconstitutional legislation that crossed his desk. Instead he was a willing and
active accomplice in its passage and implementation.

VIETNAM

President Johnson inherited a mess in Vietnam. He made it worse. By
1963, the Kennedy administration had involved the United States in a
tangled web of diplomatic intrigue that had finally led to the assassination
of South Vietnamese Prime Minister Ngo Dinh Diem. As vice president,
Johnson had called Diem the "Winston Churchill of Asia" and adopted a
strong anti-communist position. He advocated more American money
and training for South Vietnam, to support the struggle against the communists in the North. This stand was not uncharacteristic of Johnson. He
had been an ardent Cold Warrior during the Truman administration, and
the situation in Vietnam was being compared to that in Korea a decade
before. Johnson saw this as a containment problem. Like many other
Americans, he was determined to stop communist aggression by any
means necessary.

After he assumed office in November 1963, Johnson pressed for a
greater American role in Southeast Asia. The new South Vietnamese government was little more than an organized crime syndicate, and it was
quickly losing ground to the better prepared and more determined communist opposition, particularly among groups in South Vietnam who were
committed to repelling the "imperialist invaders."

In 1964 Johnson seized a chance to escalate American involvement in
Southeast Asia when the USS *Maddox* was apparently attacked by North
Vietnamese forces in the Gulf of Tonkin in August 1964. The torpedo boats
that attacked the *Maddox* may really have been nothing more than "radar
ghosts," but Johnson believed he had enough evidence to ask Congress for
broad-ranging powers in a great military commitment to Vietnam. Congress complied with the Gulf of Tonkin Resolution, which authorized the

president to send ground troops into Vietnam and use whatever means necessary to defend American allies in the region.

This resolution was not, however, a declaration of war. Congress had abrogated its constitutional responsibility by giving the president wide-ranging war powers without any legislative check save for military appropriations. The founding generation would have been aghast. One of the most important debates of the ratification period centered on presidential war powers. Proponents of the Constitution insisted that the president would not have the power to "make war" and that the congressional check on the issue would ensure that the American people would not be subjected to long-standing open-ended conflicts for the glory of the executive or the "nation." Vietnam was certainly neither a glorious crusade for Johnson nor an attempt to create a Pacific empire, but the cost, both in blood and money, was staggering.

Over thirty thousand American soldiers were killed in Vietnam. At home, Johnson's massive spending initiatives coupled with the need for greater military spending ("guns and butter") led to higher taxes, inflation, and ultimately the removal of a precious metals standard for the American currency. The United States was on a path to financial insolvency, speeded exponentially by the Vietnam War.

By 1968, LBJ realized that the American people would not support another four years of a Johnson administration. The Left had soured on the war in Vietnam, and the Right was chipping away at the massive expansion of the federal government by the Great Society. Even Richard Nixon, the ardent cold warrior, had declared that if elected he would end the war in Vietnam. Johnson bowed out gracefully and returned to Texas, but his administration had a lasting impact on the American economy, the American legal system, and the powers of the executive branch. Johnson had radically transformed America.

CHAPTER 8

RICHARD M. NIXON

Thirty-Seventh President, 1969–1974

Nixon has an undeserved reputation as an admirer of "limited government"—not to be confused with originalism. His fight for "executive privilege" during the Watergate scandal betrayed his firm commitment to a more substantial role for the executive branch. Nixon's administration expanded federal regulatory agencies (OSHA, EPA), endorsed a greater role for the general government in healthcare, and supported unconstitutional federal social engineering schemes (busing and affirmative action). Even his foreign policy—he is credited with a period of détente due to the "Nixon Doctrine"—involved unconstitutional covert operations around the globe. Far from being an intellectual heir of the founding generation, Nixon sought to make the executive branch the overwhelmingly dominant force in government. Though he failed during his administration, successive presidents have used Nixon's blueprint to great effect.

Nixon had a bumpy road to the White House. He was the presumed front-runner in 1960 against upstart Democratic candidate John F. Kennedy because it was thought that President Eisenhower's long coattails would drag Vice President Nixon into the White House. They didn't, but the results were not without controversy. Nixon's lackluster performance in a televised debate against the "bronzed warrior" Kennedy did much to undermine his electoral prospects. Nixon looked tired and much older than Kennedy (he wasn't really), and he was not well prepared for the debate. A large lead in early polling evaporated, and, while Nixon performed much better in the three remaining debates, not as many Americans tuned in to watch.

"Landslide" Lyndon Johnson and dead voters in Chicago complicated things for Nixon. Kennedy polled less than a quarter of a percentage point more in the popular vote, the closest result in the twentieth century—but won the Electoral College tally easily, or at least so it seemed. But Nixon barely lost Texas and Illinois, and immediately there were accusations of voter fraud in both states. Johnson had a track record of such shenanigans. He had defeated Coke Stevenson in the 1948 Democratic Primary by less than one hundred votes, all of which were secured by a crooked judge at the last minute. Johnson's political machine still held sway in Texas, and the presumptive vice president undoubtedly put the screws to influential Democratic operatives in the state. In Illinois, Chicago mayor Richard Daley's political machine went to work digging up dead voters. If Nixon had carried both states, he would have won the election. Nixon refused to challenge the results and graciously accepted defeat.

His 1968 victory over liberal vice president Hubert Humphrey and independent candidate George Wallace did not go much more smoothly. Nixon edged Humphrey in the popular vote by less than a percentage point; his election had appeared in doubt as late as October 1968. Nixon never forgot these close calls, and when 1972 rolled around he and his campaign team were determined not to have a repeat performance.

NEW FEDERALISM?

Nixon's primary focus both before and after becoming president was foreign policy. He inherited a grueling war in Vietnam, heightened tension between the United States and the Soviet Union, and brewing problems in the Middle East. Nixon also faced increasing inflation and questions about the stability and health of the American economy. The Great Society and the war in Vietnam had created massive deficits and strained the precious metals standard backing the dollar. The Federal Reserve Bank could print money, but it had to be tied to gold and silver reserves. To his credit, Nixon realized that something had to be done to right the ship.

His first budget proposal to Congress immediately balanced the budget through spending cuts. Nixon did not care for the top-down approach to federal spending that Roosevelt and Johnson had made infamous during their administrations. Instead, Nixon proposed directly involving the states in the spending process through block grants—in what he called the "New Federalism." To Nixon, the problem was not the money or the unconstitutional federal programs, but the process. States could better handle the distribution of large sums of money and therefore should be trusted with the implementation of federal programs. (His idea stalled in Congress throughout the 1970s and was only revived long after he left office in the 1990s.) Most of the block "grants" attached federal mandates to the money. States often failed to comply with the mandates because of the mountains of red tape and unreasonable requirements. Nixon the micromanager still wanted to have a say in the money the federal government "gave" to the states.

This was a half-cocked solution to an enormous problem, namely unconstitutional federal programs. Nixon had no problem with the programs, only with the way the federal government administered them. Nixon had grown up during the Great Depression and cut his political teeth during the Truman and Eisenhower administrations. Neither of those former presidents favored reductions in government spending. The New Deal had become the model for American government, and Nixon was not going to rock the boat. He remembered the suffering of the Great Depression and believed in federal intervention in the economy. Nixon expanded several Great Society programs and initiatives; in fact, Nixon was responsible for more of the growth in unconstitutional federal regulation than Johnson himself.

Nixon is not regarded as a conservation crusader. No one would confuse him with Teddy Roosevelt, Gifford Pinchot, or Stewart Udall. But Nixon signed several unconstitutional "conservation" bills and was behind the creation of one of the most glaringly unconstitutional regulatory agencies in American history, the Environmental Protection Agency (EPA). Biographer Jonathan Aitken wrote that Nixon "delivered more results to it [environmentalism] than any other president before or since."[1] Though suspicious of the first Earth Day events in April 1970, Nixon believed that the public favored greater federal regulation of the environment. Thus he made a political decision to support clearly unconstitutional legislation— perhaps in an effort to score points with the progressive Left, but more likely because Nixon envisioned himself as a hands-on administrator who had to "swim with the stream."[2] That was not his constitutional duty as executive.

Nixon had already signed the National Environmental Policy Act of 1969, a bill that required environmental impact studies for future federal projects and created the Council on Environmental Quality to enforce the law. But he did not stop there. In an effort to consolidate environmental policy in one agency, Nixon created the EPA in December 1970 through executive order. His 1970 State of the Union address had foreshadowed this move: "Clean air, clean water, open spaces—these should once again be the birthright of every American." No one could disagree (though one could question if these things had ever ceased to be Americans' "birthright"), but this was an unprecedented seizure of power by the executive office.[3]

Like other federal regulatory agencies, the EPA had legislative, executive, and judicial functions. The EPA could make rules concerning the environment, enforce those rules, and then adjudicate when they decided the rules had been broken, thus combining all three branches of government into one agency under little or no oversight by the American people. The power to create such an agency does not exist in Article II of the Constitution (nor in Article I, for that matter), but Nixon disregarded his oath to defend the Constitution and saddled future generations with expensive environmental regulations that, otherwise justifiable or not, are blatantly unconstitutional.

Nixon followed up by signing the Clean Air Act into law in 1970. The EPA would be responsible for enforcing the requirements of the Clean Air Act, most of which were targeted at American industry, fossil fuel–burning power plants, and automobile emissions. The Act created four federal regulatory policies— all unconstitutional—and would eventually serve as a deterrent to new American industrial projects, including new power-generation facilities. Some states adopted their own stringent air quality regulations, which were entirely constitutional, but Nixon's move for federal control of air quality could not be defended by any language in the Constitution.

Several other pieces of environmental legislation followed, including the Oil Spill Act, the Noise Control Act, the Ocean Dumping Act, and the one bill that Nixon vetoed, the Clean Water Act of 1972. Nixon vetoed the Clean Water Act not because it violated the Constitution—it did—but because Nixon deemed the money Congress set aside for its implementation excessive. After a congressional override of his veto put the law into effect, Nixon unilaterally impounded the funds, a move that did little to slow the implementation of the law. Nixon also issued an order directing the Department of the Interior to take excess federal land and create national parks. A whopping 642 were established during his administration. Forget selling unneeded public land back into private hands. No. Nixon decided that this land needed to be kept in the hands of the government for "conservation" purposes.

Another great federal regulatory boondoggle that Nixon helped craft during his administration was the Occupational Safety and Health

Administration (OSHA). Like the EPA, OSHA, charged with ensuring "workplace safety," acted as a multi-branch regulatory agency combining the functions of all three branches of government. Finding constitutional authorization for such a federal entity is tricky (non-existent, actually), and Nixon's role in the process made him chief legislator, a role not granted to him by Article II of the Constitution. Nixon's top-down consolidated approach to "national" problems, typical of the times, stemmed from a belief in national solutions to local problems. OSHA has done little to improve workplace safety; instead it justifies its half-a-billion-dollar budget by the number of inspectors it hires. Nixon had simply created another layer of federal oversight by signing another unconstitutional "Great Society" bill into law.

Nixon and his advisors bristled at accusations that they had done little to improve American society. Nixon's Chief of Staff Bob Haldeman, made infamous by the Watergate scandal, once lamented that though they were "doing as much or more than Johnson or Kennedy" in passing "good proposals for significant reform," the Left continued to criticize the administration for its "illiberality…and lack of concern for the less fortunate."[4] This remark is instructive. Nixon was not concerned about the Constitution or his duty to block unconstitutional legislation. Nixon was a politician involved in a high stakes game of public perceptions. He wanted to out-progressive the progressives, the Constitution and his oath to defend it be damned.

There is no better example of Nixon's position vis-à-vis the Constitution than his civil rights agenda. The 1954 *Brown v. Board of Education* decision had mandated that public schools (in Kansas) integrate "with all deliberate speed." Southern states dragged their feet, insisting that the ruling applied only to schools in Kansas. But in the ensuing years efforts were made to apply the decision to every state in the Union. Still, by 1970, most schools in the United States remained segregated, not by law but because of the racial composition of neighborhoods and school district boundaries. Civil Rights leaders complained that school segregation was as alive in 1970 as it had been in 1954, and they demanded federal action.

In 1971, the Supreme Court, now led by Nixon appointee Chief Justice Warren Burger, unanimously ruled in the *Swann v. Charlotte-Mecklenburg Board of Education* decision that the school district in question had to either redraw school district lines or "bus" students across district lines to achieve "racial balance." This policy became known as "forced busing." The Court was relying on the *Brown v. Board of Education* ruling—itself constitutionally problematic—to create a new federally mandated program that was also constitutionally problematic. It would not be a stretch to say that with this decision the Court was legislating from the bench in a clear violation of the separation of powers in the Constitution.[5]

Nixon had a constitutional obligation to defend the Constitution by refusing to enforce the unconstitutional decision. Instead, while he opposed the busing mandate—even liberal Georgia Democratic Governor Jimmy Carter said it unfairly burdened the South—Nixon decided to enforce court-ordered busing to the letter of the law "and nothing more," as he often said. Not enforcing busing would have placed Nixon in the crosshairs of Civil Rights groups, who would have accused him of kowtowing to the South for political advantage. Enforcing the decision, however, created a firestorm of opposition not only in the South but in places like Boston, where riots broke out over court-ordered busing to integrate schools. Northerners were shocked when the decision applied to their schools, none of which had ever been organized under legal segregation. But that was not the point of the court decision. The Burger Court determined to attack *de facto* segregation with unconstitutional proactive federal policies that the majority of Americans, both black and white, thought problematic. Nixon violated his oath in a vain attempt to win support from those who opposed his administration—that is, liberals, whom Haldeman knew would never breath a kind word in support of the president's programs or initiatives. He was right.

Nixon also expanded on a Kennedy civil rights initiative called "affirmative action." Through Executive Order 11478, Nixon mandated that the federal government "shall establish and maintain an affirmative program of equal employment opportunity for all civilian employees and applicants for employment" consistent with the policy of providing "equal opportunity in Federal employment for all persons, to prohibit discrimination in employment because of race, color, religion, sex, or national origin...."[6] This has often been labeled the "Philadelphia Plan" because its initial targets were Philadelphia-based skilled trade unions that had restricted membership for black construction workers. The historian Stephen Ambrose contends that Nixon's strong anti-union streak influenced his decision to issue the order.[7]

Nixon was following already established precedents in issuing the order, but the constitutionality of this move was immediately challenged. As in the case of busing, opponents of affirmative action pointed to the Civil Rights Act of 1964 for defense. That law, constitutionally problematic as it was, prohibited any federal law that used quotas (as busing did) to achieve racial balance. In other words, the entire court-ordered and executive-driven federal agenda was in clear violation of the law. No matter. The courts simply rewrote the law from the bench. Once the Constitution has been openly disregarded, constitutional arguments fall flat.

In 1971 the United States Court of Appeals for the Third Circuit heard a challenge to the Philadelphia Plan. Philadelphia labor unions argued that because "affirmative action" used race as a determining factor in *not* hiring *white* workers, it was clearly a violation of Title VII of the Civil Rights Act. The Court of Appeals rejected this position, not out of deference to the Constitution or the law, but because Philadelphia labor unions had to that point used employment practices that had "fostered and perpetuated a system that...effectively maintained a segregated class." The opinion, written by Nixon appointee Judge John J. Gibbons, stated "That concept, if I may use the strong language it deserves, is repugnant, unworthy, and contrary to present national policy. The Philadelphia Plan will provide an unpolluted breath of fresh air to ventilate this unpalatable situation."[8] In other words, "present national policy," whatever that might be, trumped the law and the Constitution. The Supreme Court refused to hear an appeal of the Third Circuit opinion.

The Supreme Court, however, did take an affirmative action case in 1971, *Griggs v. Duke Power Co.* The case involved thirteen black employees of the Duke Power Company in North Carolina seeking a promotion from custodial staff to coal miners. Following the 1964 Civil Rights Act, the company had adopted a policy mandating an employee had to either have a high school degree or pass an aptitude test (used in other companies and developed by an outside organization) for employment. The thirteen workers, none of whom had a high school diploma, could not pass the test. The Burger Court in a unanimous decision declared the use of the test to be unconstitutional because it created a situation hostile to minority hiring. Regardless of the fact that the test was given to all applicants, white and black, most black applicants (and many white applicants) could not pass the test, and the Supreme Court could not ascertain how the test was essential for employment.

With this decision in hand, affirmative action quickly spread to other cities and was applied to every aspect of federal hiring. Racial quotas, while technically illegal, were not defined. Nixon's Philadelphia Plan established "racial goals and timetables." When the Nixon administration was dragged before Congress to defend the Plan, Sam Ervin of North Carolina read several definitions of the word "quota" and bluntly asked how establishing "ranges" or "percentages" for minority hires was anything but a quota. George P. Schultz, Nixon's Secretary of Labor, defined a quota as "a limitation" and said that race had no bearing on affirmative action or the Philadelphia Plan. He then engaged in a personal attack, stating that Ervin paid "attention to race" and that that was not the goal of Nixon's agenda. If you can't defeat their arguments, call your opponents names. Schultz's spin-doctoring left Ervin befuddled and the American people perplexed about what affirmative action actually meant.[9] Race was certainly the basis of the plan. Everyone, it seems, but the Nixon administration knew it.

Ultimately, Nixon's determination to court civil rights leaders and undercut the power of labor unions led to an unconstitutional policy. Ervin said it best during the subcommittee hearings on the Philadelphia Plan, calling it "an invalid attempt by the secretary of labor to engage in legislation—not merely in an area where Congress has not spoken, but in an area where Congress has specifically prohibited the action which the Secretary desires to take..." resulting in "a blatant case of usurpation of the legislative functions by the executive branch of the Government."[10]

Nixon's other actions on civil rights legislation are a mixed bag. Though he did not actively campaign for it, Nixon supported the Equal Rights Amendment—the proper method for altering the powers of the federal government. It went down in defeat after Nixon was out of office, but in this case, for once, Nixon and the progressive Left had abandoned unconstitutional methods for effecting change. It would be the only time they chose to do so.

By 1972, the public storm over forced busing made Nixon reconsider his stance on enforcement. The pressure to end the practice had been unrelenting, so when Congress passed the Education Amendments of 1972, Nixon jumped at the opportunity to end busing. The bill was a compromise measure that allowed existing busing for "racial balance" to continue while prohibiting its future use. Nixon issued a signing statement in June 1972—an unconstitutional action—complaining that the act did not go far enough to end busing. But that was not the only part of the bill that would have longstanding implications. Title IX of the bill addressed discrimination in higher education.

Title IX reads, "No person in the United States shall, on the basis of sex, be excluded from participation in, be denied the benefits of, or be subjected to discrimination under any education program or activity receiving federal financial assistance." The legislation cast a wide net because virtually every public education institution in the United States received "federal financial assistance." As a result, the federal government could now micromanage college programs to ensure "equality" between the sexes. Large public university athletic programs immediately felt the pinch. For example, Paul

"Bear" Bryant's University of Alabama football team was forced to make dramatic cuts in scholarships, with the main beneficiary being the women's gymnastics team, a program that made little financial contribution to the University. Many men's athletic programs met the axe and were replaced with women's individual and team sports. Men's wrestling programs suffered the most from Title IX, though one journalist has recently applauded Title IX for bringing back the sport it killed, this time with *women's* wrestling.[11]

The real problem with Title IX, however, is not the outcome of the program but its legal—or rather illegal—underpinnings. The general government has no constitutional role in education, in either funding or policy direction. Title IX would not have been effective if not for the enormous amount of unconstitutional federal aid to colleges and universities. Schools wanted the money because it allowed them to build new buildings; pay administration, faculty, and staff higher wages; create academic programs that would not have had funding before federal education expansion (gender studies, for example); and inflate the price of college tuition. By signing the bill into law, the president continued on the path of an unconstitutional federal takeover of education in America. If Nixon had remained true to his oath, he would have vetoed the bill.

Nixon's domestic policy differed very little from Johnson's "Great Society." The "New Federalism" was an ingenious smoke screen for continued unconstitutional expansion of the federal government into areas where it had no legal authority. Nixon relished his role as a "hands-on" president, and in many cases he had direct input into the legislative process. When scandal finally derailed his administration, it was simply the culmination of several years of unconstitutional executive overreach.

THE NIXON SHOCK

Following World War II, the United States and its industrial Western allies had signed an agreement known as Bretton-Woods. It created the International Monetary Fund (IMF) and what eventually became the

World Bank. The agreement also pegged international exchange rates to the United States dollar, which in turn was redeemable for gold and silver at a rate set by Congress. The United States promised not to devalue (inflate) its currency, and the other countries promised not to speculate in dollars or manipulate their currencies to gain a favorable exchange rate on the open market. The United States had the strongest economy in the world and as a result became the lender of first and last resort for industrial powers looking to rebuild after the most destructive war in human history.

But the United States quickly abandoned fiscal responsibility and began printing more greenbacks than it could redeem at the congressionally set price of gold and silver. The Marshall Plan dumped billions of dollars into Europe; the bursts of spending under the New Deal, Fair Deal, New Frontier, and Great Society doubled the federal budget, with the most dramatic expansion occurring under Lyndon Johnson; the Cold War ramped up American military spending; and the Vietnam War in particular forced the United States government to print more money to satisfy military contracts and foreign commitments to halt communist aggression in Asia and elsewhere. Employment was up, but a government-mandated minimum wage forced employers to pay higher wages and thus necessitated the need for more dollars. All this, coupled with government subsidies for agriculture, higher prices for oil and energy, and government money pumped into education and healthcare, created a currency crunch—or, more accurately, an inflation problem. Foreign powers soon realized that the United States might not be able to redeem their dollars, and so began demanding gold.

The situation became acute in the administration of John Kennedy, but neither he nor Johnson could see that cutting spending both at home and abroad might force dollars out of circulation and thus reduce the crisis. By 1971, Nixon realized that something had to be done to solve the problem, but his answer to the crisis, like many other actions during his administration, was an unconstitutional one.

In August 1971 Nixon summoned his top economic advisors to Camp David to discuss the situation. The course of action he decided on involved tax cuts and spending cuts and a price-and-wage freeze for ninety days, along with a suspension of the dollar-to-gold convertibility—in essence a unilateral dissolution of the Bretton-Woods agreement. Nixon presented his "New Economic Policy" to the American people on August 15, 1971, in a televised address. Nixon argued that he had the legal authority to act independently because of the Economic Stabilization Act of 1970, a bill he had signed into law. In that Act, Congress had given the president wide-ranging authority to "stabilize" the economy in the event of a crisis. But they had no constitutional authority to do so. The Congress cannot delegate legislative functions to the executive office. Thus Nixon had no legal authority to direct the Secretary of the Treasury to "suspend temporarily the convertibility of the dollar into gold."[12] That could only be done by Congress.

The net result of Nixon's series of unconstitutional moves was the end of the gold standard and the establishment of a commodity-based financial system with a floating dollar tied to nothing. The dollar had once been "as good as gold." Now it was as good as paper. Yet the real threat to the American economic system—out-of-control spending on both "guns and butter"—had not been addressed. The United States government continued to spend and, with the Federal Reserve printing greenbacks at an unprecedented rate, inflation quickly followed. It was no surprise that Gerald Ford had to run for president in 1976 on a promise to "Whip Inflation Now." In the early 1970s the American people, and for that matter American economists, had become convinced that gold was the culprit behind a stagnant economy in the early 1970s—when the real problem was government spending. Nixon's Leninist approach to the problem (Lenin had called his centralized command–communist economic system the "New Economic Policy") not only violated the Constitution, it led to perpetual inflation and government-created economic bubbles.

WAR POWERS

In 1968 Nixon had campaigned on a promise to scale back the war in Vietnam. The American public had grown weary of body bags, the draft, and a seemingly endless military commitment in Southeast Asia. After Nixon took office, he quickly scaled back military operations and brought tens of thousands of American soldiers home. But he did not end the war. Nixon *expanded* the conflict by beginning a new bombing campaign dubbed Operation Linebacker and by widening the conflict into Cambodia. American boots were still on the ground, and American bombs were being used in an effort to bring the North Vietnamese to the negotiating table. It didn't work.

Still, Nixon had made good on one of his campaign pledges, even while continuing the war. Yet when he unilaterally expanded the war into Cambodia, Congress took notice and quickly banned operations by United States ground troops. They ignored air combat missions, however, which continued unabated. Nixon bristled at congressional interference in his "constitutional" role as commander in chief. Tension between Congress and the president finally boiled over in 1973, when Congress finally "realized" that Nixon's secret war in Cambodia had continued and passed the War Powers Resolution, allowing the president to begin military operations but requiring that he notify Congress within forty-eight hours of the opening of the conflict. The resolution also capped military involvement at sixty days without congressional authorization or a declaration of war and allowed for a thirty-day drawdown period.

Nixon vetoed the bill. In his veto message, he argued that the resolution was unconstitutional because it illegally curtailed the powers of the executive branch. The president did not cite any contextual defense for his claim—he couldn't—and the crux of his argument was not that the resolution was unconstitutional, but that it would have a "dangerous" impact on American foreign policy. Roughly two-thirds of his veto message was dedicated to a justification of previous unilateral executive military operations, all done in the name of "defense," "diplomacy," and "humanitarian aid." Congress was unmoved and overrode his veto.

Did Nixon have a constitutional point? After all, he wrote in his veto message, "I firmly believe that a veto of House Joint Resolution 542 is warranted solely on constitutional grounds." Nixon was correct about the resolution being unconstitutional, but not on the legal grounds he relied on.[13]

The War Powers Resolution was and is unconstitutional because it allows the president wide "war making" discretion for sixty days without congressional authorization, something that would have been shocking to the men who drafted and ratified the Constitution. The founding generation had debated the role of the president in making war both at the 1787 Philadelphia Convention and in the state ratifying conventions. And the general consensus had deemed unilateral executive action for any length of time to be an unconstitutional abuse of power. Certainly, many proponents of the Constitution had thought that the president should be able to "repel sudden attacks," but that does not constitute legal authority for sending troops into combat in remote regions of the globe where American soldiers had not been attacked or where no clear threat to American public safety existed.

James Iredell of North Carolina argued that the president "has not the power of declaring war by his own authority, nor that of raising fleets and armies.... The power of declaring war is expressly given to Congress, that is, to the two branches of the legislature.... They have also expressly delegated to them the powers of raising and supporting armies, and of providing and maintaining a navy."[14] Nixon vetoed the War Powers Resolution because he believed it unconstitutionally limited his role as commander in chief. He should have vetoed it because it unconstitutionally enlarged his role as commander in chief. Military operations in Vietnam, Korea, Southeast Asia, the Middle East, South America, and Africa in the post–World War II period have been conducted without congressional oversight, even in the years following the War Powers Resolution, which has amounted to a blank check for the executive branch to involve American armed forces in conflicts for at least two months without congressional approval. According to the Constitution, Congress has the sole responsibility of making war, as proponents of the Constitution in 1787 and 1788 argued repeatedly. Nixon should be given credit for vetoing the Resolution, but his message made it clear that he did so for the wrong reasons. The end result has been an unabated string of unconstitutional military operations directed by the executive branch while Congress watches on television with the rest of America.

WATERGATE

Watergate was the defining moment of the Nixon administration, not because of the leftist reaction to it or the public calls for Nixon's impeachment, but because it exposed the damage that the executive branch had inflicted on the Constitution. Nixon, along with virtually every successive president, is a symptom of the larger problem, the unconstitutional expansion of executive power.

The eminent legal historian Raoul Berger wrote, "Executive privilege—the President's claim of constitutional authority to withhold information from Congress—is a myth."[15] Watergate was a legal and ethical problem that became a constitutional problem when Nixon attempted to dodge, obfuscate, and deflect congressional inquiry into his role in the cover-up of a politically motivated burglary. Did the president by nature of his office have a right to hide documents from both the Congress and the general public? The answer is clearly no.

As we have seen, the roots of the Watergate scandal were back in Nixon's close presidential races in 1960 and 1968. Nixon had received barely 43 percent of the popular vote in 1968, and he and his campaign team were not willing to squeak by again. They wanted a mandate. Early polling data suggested that Nixon could be defeated by at least one of the potential

Democratic nominees in the 1972 election, Edmund Muskie, so, without Nixon's consent, several political operatives broke into the Democratic National Committee headquarters at the Watergate hotel in Washington, D.C., to establish wiretaps and photograph sensitive documents related to the Democratic campaign. They were caught.

News of the arrest of the five "burglars" reached the White House within hours. Long before he made any public acknowledgment of the break in, Nixon knew about it, and—realizing that it would potentially damage his reelection bid—tried feverishly to cover up any connection to the White House or his administration. But evidence soon materialized that some of Nixon's most trusted advisors, including Chief of Staff Haldeman, knew of the break-in and may in fact have been part of the plan. Haldeman at least helped create the cover-up.

The cover-up worked beautifully. Nixon was reelected in 1972 by crushing majorities in both the popular vote and the Electoral College. But his landslide election would soon unravel after the United States Senate created a special committee to investigate the Watergate affair. Senator Sam Ervin of North Carolina was appointed chairman of the committee.

Ervin was a Democrat and no fan of the Republican administration, but he had long been considered an independent voice in the Senate, a man who would vote his convictions and principles regardless of the way the political wind blew. He had even broken ranks and voted with the administration several times during Nixon's first term, particularly on issues relating to civil liberties. He was also, however, a staunch defender of the Constitution and regarded any violation, particularly from the executive branch, as the greatest threat to American liberty.

Ervin became an American icon during the televised hearings. The man who had at one time been vilified for his opposition to Civil Rights legislation now found himself on the cover of *Time* magazine while his folksy homespun tales of life in Burke County, North Carolina, made headlines. Everyone had a favorite Senator Sam story. His penchant for weaving humorous tales about North Carolina farmers and dramatic quotes from Shakespeare into political discussions belied a keen constitutional mind. Nixon never stood a chance.

Before the Watergate Committee met, Nixon went on the offensive, claiming "executive privilege" shielded his administration from congressional inquiry. He then challenged the committee to prove that "executive privilege" was unconstitutional, something that Ervin admitted would take more time than the committee had allotted for the investigation. Nixon blocked the committee from receiving information about the Watergate scandal, all the while claiming that it would exonerate him. He cited "executive privilege" again. He fired the special prosecutor assigned to work on the case. When he finally produced tape recordings of conversations held at the White House about the break-in, it turned out that sections of the tapes had been mysteriously erased. Nixon was conducting the most opaque administration in American history.[16]

None of it was constitutional. The founding generation made clear that their establishment of a "vigorous" single executive did not shield that individual from congressional oversight. Perhaps the most ardent proponent of executive power in the Philadelphia Convention, James Wilson, said that "not a single privilege is annexed" to the president's character.[17] More important, under the Constitution the president must faithfully execute the laws of Congress. It logically follows, then, that Congress has the right to receive any and all information from the president detailing how he executed (or failed to execute) the law. Chief Justice Warren Burger summed up this principle nicely: "… there is not a scintilla of evidence in the constitutional records of a design to curtail the historical scope of legislative inquiry or to authorize executive withholding of *any* information from Congress."[18]

Nixon, of course, was not the first to claim "executive privilege"—that doctrine had been developed by (unconstitutional) precedents long before he took office—but according to the original Constitution, Nixon was violating his oath to defend the Constitution. Therefore impeachment proceedings, which made it out of committee but were never voted on in the House, were justified by the Watergate scandal. They were justified for many other reasons as well, but unfortunately Nixon, like other twentieth-century presidents, avoided impeachment because of a too-narrow understanding of "high crimes and misdemeanors." Violating the presidential oath, in whatever fashion, constitutes a "high crime and misdemeanor"— according to the founding generation's definition. Nixon's six years in office can best be described as an unbridled romp over the Constitution. That alone places him among the ranks of the worst presidents in American history. Watergate just sealed his fate.

CHAPTER 9

BARACK OBAMA

Forty-Fourth President, 2009–2017

onservatives have been clamoring for Barack Obama's impeachment nearly since he was elected. It's very unlikely that he will ever be impeached. And yet during his tenure in office, the forty-fourth president has continually violated the Constitution, piling illegal act on illegal act—signing the patently unconstitutional "Obamacare" law, unilaterally delaying its implementation for political gain, refusing to enforce immigration laws on the excuse of "prosecutorial discretion," waging war without a vote in Congress, and even making appointments without the advice and consent of the Senate. The executive branch of our government is so obviously out of control that America is being called a banana republic. When the president engages in such blatantly unconstitutional behavior, clearly breaking his oath of office to "preserve, protect and defend the Constitution of the United States," why is it unrealistic to think of holding him to account by the method that the Constitution specifies—namely, impeachment for "high Crimes and Misdemeanors"? The history that we have reviewed in the first eight chapters of this book goes a long way toward elucidating that mystery.

The truth is, the slow trend toward an American elected monarchy began in earnest long before the twenty-first century. Benjamin Franklin predicted it in 1787—and in the past two centuries plus, his prediction has come true. Recent presidents' blatant disregard for the original Constitution, both in foreign and domestic policy, has been observable on a daily occurrence. But these presidents are the symptoms of the disease, not the disease itself. Americans need to understand that executive usurpation of power is a non-partisan problem, and the erosion of constitutional checks on the executive branch has been a gradual process, like waves lapping at the beach. There's not much sand left.

Obama has followed the established precedents of the executive office in the modern age—and pushed them even further. He has disregarded his charge to execute the laws and has unilaterally created, altered, or suspended legislation at will (e.g. Obamacare, immigration). His non-recess "recess" appointments were a clear violation of the Constitution, and his use of the executive branch to target political opponents is both unethical and unconstitutional. Obama is the end result of more than a hundred years of unconstitutional executive abuse, the culmination of practices that began with Lincoln, gained steam with Teddy Roosevelt, were codified by custom through the presidencies of Wilson and Franklin Roosevelt, and gave rise to the imperial presidency in the twentieth century. Obama's executive is not the Founders' executive. He admitted as much when he promised that his election would result in "fundamentally transforming the United States of America." His various threats to use executive orders and executive action to implement his agenda in defiance of Congress betray an utter disregard for constitutional government. But he has been simply more open about his disdain for the Constitution than most of his predecessors.

FROM FORTY-ONE TO FORTY-FOUR

George Herbert Walker Bush took office in 1989 on the heels of arguably the most popular administration in the twentieth century. He had big shoes to fill, and his campaign continually referenced the Ronald Reagan revolution in an attempt to attach Vice President Bush to the popular Reagan. It worked well. Bush won in a landslide over liberal Michael Dukakis, but there were signs that not all Republicans bought the newly crafted image of Bush as a conservative crusader for limited government and the original Constitution.

Bush had been Reagan's principal opponent in the 1980 Republican primary. He had long been considered an establishment Republican beholden to the more moderate element of the Party. In the 1988 campaign, Bush brushed off those charges, promising to continue Reagan's hard-nosed foreign policy objectives in relation to the Cold War—he also had to shake off the "wimp factor" that had dogged his earlier run for the White House—and not to raise taxes.

His no-tax pledge was indicative of the twentieth-century distortion of the executive office. Bush could no more raise taxes than he could lower them. This was simply pandering to the electorate in the face of a Congress controlled by the other party, which had been itching for taxes hikes since Reagan took office in 1981. Bush could veto legislation, and his promise to say "No" to new taxes could be construed as referring to that presidential prerogative, but the executive office was not created to be the final referee on public policy. If the Congress wished to hike taxes, so long as they were constitutional, according to the original Constitution the president had a constitutional obligation to sign the bill.

But by 1988 Americans, it seemed, had come to the conclusion that the president was the "chief legislator" of the United States and that battles between the legislative and executive branches over purely legislative matters were part of the "checks and balances" system they had been taught in school. This is not how the founding generation conceived of the powers of the executive branch, but Bush was simply following twentieth-century precedent in this matter.

Very early in his administration, Bush battled with congressional Democrats over the federal budget. By 1990 ballooning deficits had created a political mess that was putting pressure on the president to abandon his no-new-taxes pledge. Congress had passed the Gramm-Rudman Act in 1985 as a means to achieve a balanced budget within five years. The bill established deficit targets that had to be met, and if the budget deficit exceeded those targets, the General Accounting Office (GAO) could implement spending cuts, tax hikes, or a combination of both to meet the target. If nothing could be worked out, both defense and domestic spending would be slashed to meet a balanced budget by 1991.

There was one problem. In the case of *Bowsher v. Synar* (1986), the Supreme Court had declared a portion of the bill unconstitutional. The Court opined that because part of the bill lodged executive tasks in the legislature (the GAO is part of the legislative branch) it unconstitutionally blended the two branches of government. Ironically, the Court had never had a problem with this blending in other regulatory agencies, all of which were more egregiously unconstitutional than Gramm-Rudman. Justice Byron White's was the lone voice of dissent. He correctly argued that spending was a legislative function and thus Congress should have control over the purse strings. In response to the Supreme Court decision, in 1987 Congress amended the law to give the (executive branch) Office of Management and Budget complete control of the process. The results were not good.

A projected near-$300 billion deficit in 1990 led President Bush to call for spending cuts to meet Gramm-Rudman targets. The Congress balked, and a battle ensued over spending cuts and tax hikes. The battle deteriorated into a political standoff, with Bush ultimately agreeing to minor spending cuts coupled with tax increases. This compromise broke his campaign pledge and led to severe political backlash, but the real devil was in the details.

To his credit, Bush pursued the proper course in advocating spending cuts, but most of the federal budget could not be cut. Entitlement spending, interest on the national debt, and deposit insurance were off limits, and with the implementation of "baseline budgeting"—a budgeting method established by the Congressional Budget and Impoundment Control Act of 1974 (another Richard Nixon gift that keeps on giving)—spending was guaranteed to increase no matter what "cuts" were proposed. Under baseline budgeting, "cuts" simply meant trimming the growth in spending, not the spending itself. The massive growth of the executive branch had finally overwhelmed Congress, so they kicked the can down the road and unconstitutionally placed the burden of budgeting on the executive branch. Gramm-Rudman sought to fix that problem partly by returning some of the authority to a legislative agency. But the Supreme Court wouldn't allow that, and now the president is unconstitutionally required by Supreme Court precedent to partake in the budgeting process. That is a true violation of "separation of powers."

Bush followed in Lyndon Johnson's footsteps by signing the Americans with Disabilities Act (ADA) into law in 1990. Like the Civil Rights Act of 1964, the ADA relied on an expansive interpretation of the Commerce Clause for constitutional justification and expanded federal regulation of employment, transportation, communication, and education. The Commerce Clause defense of the 1964 Civil Rights Act was weak, and the ADA faced the same problem. Nowhere does the Constitution as ratified give the federal government the power to mandate how many handicapped parking spaces are available at a local retailer or what educational "accommodations" should be given to a college student, but the ADA did just that and more. As with the Civil Rights Act, a moral argument can be made for such regulations, and the states can pass legislation to that effect, but at the time the Constitution was ratified, the people and the states delegated to the central government only the powers that document enumerated. Clearly, the ADA does not comport with an originalist interpretation of our founding document. Bush should have vetoed the bill.

Bush's other glaringly unconstitutional move involved firearms regulation. The Constitution is clear on the issue. The Congress can organize, arm, and discipline the "Militia," but the Second Amendment prohibits the general government from disarming it. By "Militia," the founding generation meant every able-bodied male citizen. In 1989, Bush signed off on a Treasury Department request (made at the urging of Drug "czar" Bill Bennett) to ban the importation of semi-automatic "assault rifles." Congress had passed no legislation to that effect, so Bush simply accomplished this policy objective by executive decree. Additionally, Bush began pushing for restrictions on large-capacity magazines and an eventual ban on the manufacture of all "assault rifles" in the United States. He may have had good motives, but any federal "gun control" legislation fails the constitutional litmus test. The First Congress, in fact, *required* all able-bodied Americans to possess a musket or rifle, powder, and ammunition—the "assault weapons" of the time.

While these actions were imprudent, Bush's most flagrant assault on the Constitution was in foreign policy. In 1989, Bush unilaterally launched "Operation Just Cause" in Panama with the goal of removing Panamanian dictator—and long-time American ally—Manuel Noriega from power. The United States had not declared war on Panama; American security interests that supposedly necessitated the military operation were vague; and Bush defended his swift action with the unconstitutional War Powers Resolution of 1973. Bush was making war on Panama without any congressional oversight. The American people cheered when Noriega was brought to "justice," but the Constitution wept.

Realizing that Congress would not be an obstacle to further foreign adventurism, Bush sent half a million troops into Saudi Arabia in 1990. "Operation Desert Shield" was in response to Iraqi dictator Saddam Hussein's invasion of Kuwait. Hussein had been an ally of the United States during the Iran-Iraq War from 1980 to 1988, and he claimed that Kuwait had illegally seceded from Iraq. He did not believe the United States would respond with force to what he considered to be a re-occupation.

Bush began making plans for a full-scale invasion of Iraq during the five months combat troops were in Saudi Arabia. In January 1991 Bush approached Congress and requested a resolution authorizing military force in Iraq in accordance with a United Nations Security Council resolution mandating that Iraqi forces withdraw from Kuwait. Bush additionally suggested that action against Hussein's Iraq would usher in a "New World Order," with the United States at the head of a unified world coalition dedicated to the rule of law, peace, and security. The constitutional problem, of course, was Bush's request for a simple "authorization of force" resolution. He did not ask Congress to declare war on Iraq. That would have been the responsible move constitutionally. But Bush did not believe he even needed to go to Congress to seek approval for the use of military force; he requested it as a courtesy to Congress.

His January 8, 1991, letter to congressional leaders asked for "support" but not "approval" for military action in Kuwait. When asked about the issue the following day in a press conference, Bush responded, "I don't think I need it [congressional authorization].... I feel I have the authority to fully implement the United Nations resolutions." Bush then added that his attorneys believed that he had the "constitutional authority" to act without congressional approval.[1]

Truman had established the precedent that American presidents could act unilaterally without congressional approval with the backing of the United Nations. Bush took it one step further—the United States had, in essence, become the military force of the United Nations. The "New World Order" would place UN resolutions above American law and the Constitution. Bush broke every constitutional check on executive power during the lead-up to the First Gulf War. Successive presidents would use his actions as a justification for even greater American military involvement around the world. More than anything else, George H. W. Bush should be remembered as the president who succeeded in codifying the power of the executive branch to make war unilaterally. The American people would pay the price for his recklessness.

SLICK WILLIE

William Jefferson (Bill) Clinton took office in 1993 without the support of the majority of the American people. He had run as a "New Democrat" against an unpopular president and a billionaire political upstart (H. Ross Perot), continually chiding the Bush administration over the sagging economy. There were questions about Clinton's character, but his ability to connect with voters—"I feel your pain"—coupled with Bush's unpopularity and Perot's third-party campaign catapulted him into the White House. In 1996 Clinton became the first president since Woodrow Wilson to be elected twice without receiving more than 50 percent of the total popular vote. This is no great honor.

Bill Clinton was only the second president to be impeached in American history. The charges brought against him were justified, but his record in regard to the Constitution should have led Congress to include a much longer list of charges against him. They missed the boat, perhaps because they spent too much time on his character and too little time on his policies—or perhaps because Congress had become complicit in the unconstitutional growth of the executive office. They are part and parcel of the problem and would be as much affected by a reduction in federal power as the president.

Clinton, like virtually every president from Teddy Roosevelt forward, acted without regard to the Constitution. Clinton's first two years in office exposed his limited understanding of the Constitution's original meaning and of its restraints on executive power. Virtually all of the legislation Clinton signed in his first two years in office should have been vetoed for violating the Constitution. The 1993 Family Medical Leave Act, a popular bill, particularly with women, relied on an expansive interpretation of the Fourteenth Amendment and a gross misunderstanding of the Commerce Clause for a constitutional defense. Congress, of course, never questioned whether the bill was constitutional when it was being debated, and Clinton gladly signed the bill into law less than one month after taking office in 1993. The Supreme Court has never declared the bill to be unconstitutional, but it has restricted the ability of individuals to sue the states in federal court over violations of the law. If Clinton had followed his oath to defend the Constitution, the bill would have never received his signature.

Later in 1993, Clinton signed the Religious Freedom Restoration Act, which did little to restore "religious freedom" and was later declared unconstitutional by the Supreme Court. The bill attempted another round of "incorporation" of the First Amendment to the states through the Fourteenth Amendment. Incorporation was rejected by the founding generation at the time of the adoption of the Bill of Rights in 1791; it was imposed by Supreme Court precedent only in the twentieth century, long after the Fourteenth Amendment was ratified in 1868. Moreover, the authors of the Fourteenth Amendment had never suggested that it would incorporate the Bill of Rights to the separate states. According to the original Constitution, states had wide leeway in regard to religion. Three states had state-established churches in 1791 when the Bill of Rights was ratified. There would have been substantial opposition to the First Amendment had the people of these states believed that it would ever control state law on religion. This is another bill that should have met the veto pen on constitutional grounds.

Clinton also signed the most sweeping "gun control" legislation into law since the 1960s. The Brady Handgun Violence Prevention Act (1993) and the Violent Crime Control and Law Enforcement Act (1994) placed federal restrictions on gun purchases and banned the manufacture, distribution, and sale of certain types of firearms, most famously semi-automatic "assault rifles." Both laws violated the Second and Tenth Amendments to the Constitution.

The Supreme Court invalidated the "Brady Bill" in the 1997 decision *Printz v. the United States*. States, the Court said, would be free to continue to conduct background checks if they chose to do so, but the federal government could not unilaterally infringe on state powers in regard to firearms. This was the correct originalist position. States have always been able to regulate firearm possession as long as such legislation comported with their own constitutions, but under the Second Amendment the federal government cannot.

The federal ban on "assault rifles" and high-capacity magazines as outlined in the Violent Crime Control and Law Enforcement Act clearly violated an originalist interpretation of the Second Amendment. For ten years, American citizens could not purchase any post-ban "assault rifles" or magazines. (Rifles and magazines manufactured before 1994 and sold through private transactions were still available, but the bill made it more difficult to obtain these types of weapons.) This, in effect, was a bill that disarmed American citizens, the militia. Again, states have the power to enact similar legislation, but the federal government, through the Second Amendment, is prohibited from disarming the people.

The Violent Crime Control and Law Enforcement Act also increased federal spending on local law enforcement through the COPS program and federal spending on prisons. While these provisions are popular even among conservatives, the Constitution does not grant the general government any power in regard to local police or the establishment of jails. This point was made by Constitution proponent Tench Coxe in 1788 when he wrote that the Federal Government would not be able to build "county gaols [jails] ... or other public buildings" and that all police activities would be exclusively the domain of the states.[2] Clinton later regretted signing the bill, but not because he had pangs of guilt about its unconstitutionality. Clinton did not want to be regarded as the liberal who threw everyone in jail. He should have vetoed the bill because it violated the Constitution.

These bills are just the tip of the iceberg. Most of the legislation that Clinton signed in his first two years in office was unconstitutional, and his healthcare task force, chaired by wife Hillary Clinton, met stiff opposition when it was learned that the administration wanted to implement a "single-payer" healthcare system in the United States. This led to the Republican takeover of Congress following the 1994 congressional elections. Clinton then moved to the center and co-opted much of the Republican agenda in an attempt to take credit for reform initiatives. This was an ingenious political move. Clinton was a great politician, but honesty and integrity were not his strengths.

In 1998, Clinton issued an executive order that in essence nullified the Tenth Amendment to the Constitution. Congress had not paid much attention to Clinton's previous two-hundred-forty-plus executive orders, but with one stroke of Clinton's pen, the president finally got Congress's attention, and they reversed course. Clinton's Executive Order 13083, cynically titled "Federalism," used vague language that claimed new authority for the executive branch to enact rules and regulations where the states were deemed incompetent to do so. One of Clinton's advisors quipped that fundamentally altering the nature of the United States government through executive fiat was "cool."

But it didn't last long. Once Congress and the public caught on, Clinton quickly suspended the order and explained that he had issued it simply to protect individual liberty. The following year, Clinton issued Executive Order 13132, which revoked Executive Order 13083 and greatly curtailed the power of the central government to wreak havoc on the states. Clinton may have backpedaled, but the intent and philosophical underpinnings of the original order were clear. Clinton believed, as did virtually every man who had occupied the executive office since 1901, that the states and the Congress presented an obstacle to "national" reform and must be checked. Clinton had probably hoped that the first of the two executive orders, like every one before it, would slip by unnoticed. When he was caught with his hand in the cookie jar, Clinton simply lied his way out and "triangulated" to agree with popular sentiment.

For all of the barbs thrown at the Clinton administration for his reckless and unconstitutional domestic policies, the Republican Party remained virtually silent on the subject of his reckless and unconstitutional foreign policy. Clinton was accused of using the military to deflect attention from his more infamous problems in the White House, namely the personal scandals that ultimately got him impeached, but there was little Republican criticism of Clinton's unilateral deployment of the military in overseas adventurism—over forty times in his eight years in office.

To put that in perspective, from 1948 to 1993, United States armed forces had been deployed overseas only eight times.[3] Under Clinton the military became an international peacekeeping force often (and illegally) under the direct control of the United Nations. He unilaterally expanded Operation Restore Hope in Somalia, launched during the George H. W. Bush administration with a restricted mission to provide humanitarian supplies and then pull out. Clinton involved American forces in nation building and the capture of Somali warlords. This led to the infamous "Blackhawk Down" incident and over eighty American casualties, including eighteen killed.

Clinton ordered a prolonged bombing campaign in Serbia in 1999 to prevent "ethnic cleansing" in the region. The Balkans war was another long-term bad result of Woodrow Wilson's failed nation building in Europe following World War I. Yugoslavia began splitting up into separate states beginning in 1991. By the time Clinton took office in 1993, civil war had erupted in the region, with horrific crimes against humanity perpetrated by all parties in the conflict, namely Serbs, Croats, and Muslims. Clinton decided to side with the Muslim extremists in the region, supported the importation of jihadists from the Middle East, and then went on a massive propaganda campaign to gain public support for American involvement in the war. There was just one problem. Congress *refused* to authorize any military role for the United States. Clinton ignored Congress and bombed away. This was the first time in American history that a sitting president openly defied Congress in regard to a military campaign. Congress alone has the power to declare war, and while they had shirked that responsibility countless times since World War II, they still had to be consulted—at least until 1999. Clinton tore a page from George H. W. Bush's book, except Clinton didn't even give Congress a courtesy call.

The House of Representatives impeached Clinton in 1998, making him the only president besides Andrew Johnson to have been called to account by the method prescribed in the Constitution. Clinton had lied under oath in regard to the nature of his relationship with White House intern Monica Lewinsky, and the Republican Party considered perjury to be enough of a criminal offense to bring the president up on charges. Did they have a case? According to James Madison, yes.

During the Philadelphia Convention in 1787, Madison said that "incapacity," "negligence," "perfidy," "peculation," "oppression," and betraying "his trust to a foreign power" were the most relevant reasons for impeachment and conviction. "Perfidy," defined as deceitfulness, fit Clinton perfectly. He had lied under oath and deceived both the Congress and the American public in regard to his personal conduct. If he would be willing to lie under oath about an affair (that Hillary Clinton probably knew about), what would stop him from lying to the American people about any other issue? The Senate, however, did not concur with Madison's standards and acquitted him in 1999. Clinton, like other presidents before and after him, could have been impeached for so much more.

TAKING THE IMPERIAL PRESIDENCY TO A NEW LEVEL

George W. Bush took office in 2001 under less than ideal circumstances. He had won the 2000 election over Al Gore in the Electoral College, but lost the popular vote. This had happened before, but legal challenges to his election—"hanging chads" in Florida and a split Supreme Court decision—did not bode well for the incoming president. He had run on a platform of tax cuts, limited government, and American strength abroad. Like Presidents Bush and Clinton before him, Bush forty-three would unconstitutionally expand the powers of the executive branch—something that actually became an issue in the 2008 presidential campaign.

Candidate Bush promised to cut spending. President Bush did the opposite. With the Congress and the executive branch under the control of the same party for the first time since 1995, virtually all caution was thrown to the wind. President Bush signed scores of unconstitutional bills, and the fiscal restraint that Republicans promised they would bring to the central government evaporated like a puddle in the Texas panhandle summer. Bush supporters would claim that the president had no choice. The September 11 attacks and subsequent War on Terror necessitated bloated federal budgets. This is only partly true. Bush's foreign adventures were expensive, but domestic spending never slowed down during the Bush administration, which ran the highest deficits in American history—that is until his successor assumed office in 2009.

Bush signed several high-profile unconstitutional bills into law. Much of the legislation can be traced to earlier federal initiatives, such as the New Deal and the Great Society. Admittedly, Bush had never promised to undo nearly six decades of bad federal policy, but he should have been more reluctant to sign laws that reinforced the unconstitutional programs of the past. He signed the Medicare Act of 2003, a Republican-led initiative to reform medical benefits for the elderly. It amounted to an expansion of an unconstitutional entitlement program that added thousands of pages of regulations to a bloated federal register and put the stressed federal budget on the hook for more spending that it could not afford.

Bush's decision to sign the Troubled Asset Relief Program (TARP) and the Housing and Economic Recovery Act in 2008 also reflected a willingness to support the failed and unconstitutional policies of the past. These programs were nothing more than twenty-first-century New Deal initiatives. TARP pumped billions of dollars into the American banking system in an effort to "bail out" struggling banks deemed "too big to fail." The problem with the program, as with every federal economic intervention initiative since Alexander Hamilton's First Bank of the United States, is that it was unconstitutional. Proponents would argue that TARP funds were simple loans and had to be repaid, but the "loans" were not guaranteed a return and thus American taxpayers would be on the hook if the banks collapsed. Additionally, Article I, Section 8, does not grant Congress the power to lend money to ailing private institutions.

In reality these weren't loans. The Congress was acquiring more debt. Hamilton had met resistance when he wanted the federal government to assume the debts of the state governments in 1790. He eventually got his way through the infamous "Washington D.C. Compromise," but at least that debt was "sovereign debt," meaning debt owed by a government entity. In 2008 the government was assuming dubious mortgage securities and mal-investments by automobile companies and banks.

The Housing and Economic Recovery Act allowed the unconstitutional Federal Housing Administration to unconstitutionally take over two already unconstitutional "government-sponsored enterprises," Fannie Mae and Freddie Mac. That was an unconstitutional mess. Both Fannie Mae and Freddie Mac had been accused of corruption, and yet the takeover by the Treasury Department resulted in large executive bonuses and government assumption of billions of dollars worth of risky debt, all at the expense of the American taxpayer. According to the Constitution as ratified in 1788, the Congress cannot constitutionally charter "enterprises," a softer term for corporations, nor can it seize corporations and run them as a component of the federal government. No matter. The Constitution has become whatever the government wants it to be. Add General Motors to the list of government takeovers, and the Bush administration, through the cover of "loans," accomplished what Franklin Roosevelt could not: government control of a large sector of the American economy. The executive branch had long since failed to serve as a check on unconstitutional legislation.

Bush signed legislation increasing funding for the unconstitutional National Science Foundation (NSF) and National Institutes of Health (NIH) and enlarged federal control of American education. A moral argument can be made for the NSF and the NIH, but the Constitution does not grant the federal government the power to establish federal public health and educational organizations. These functions could be undertaken by the states. Bush also signed the No Child Left Behind Act (NCLB) into law in 2001. The bill renewed the Great Society–established Elementary and Secondary Education Act (ESEA) and enhanced a national, one-size-fits-all policy in regard to American education. Schools were required to administer federally approved standardized tests, and prospective teachers had to meet newly created federal guidelines in education, particularly in science and math, regardless of their major field of study. NCLB added another unconstitutional layer to an unconstitutional federal program and piled more regulations on an already overregulated American education system—with few positive results.

Bush's greatest contribution to unconstitutional government, however, was his extensive use of executive "signing statements." Bush did not, as critics have often charged, invent the signing statement. The practice went back to the James Monroe administration. But before 1981, all the presidents had issued only a total of 101 signing statements.[4] Ronald Reagan increased the practice and argued that such a move could result in an effective line-item veto of legislation. He was right, but this was not the constitutional way to achieve that type of veto power. Congress had unconstitutionally given Bill Clinton the line-item veto in 1996—he used it eighty-two times before the Supreme Court correctly declared it unconstitutional—but signing statements had never been challenged. By the time Bush took office in 2001, presidents had issued around six hundred signing statements, with Reagan issuing the most in history to that point. Yet Bush put even him to shame. The forty-third president issued nearly twelve hundred signing statements in his eight years in office.[5] This, more than anything else, is the Bush legacy.

Many of these statements were intended to expand executive powers by carving out exclusive jurisdiction for the president. In some cases Bush may have in fact had legitimate constitutional reservations about the bills that inspired his signing statements, but he should have used the veto rather than unconstitutional means to object to their unconstitutionality. Most of the time, however, Bush implied that he could simply ignore provisions of laws that he did not like even if those laws were perfectly constitutional. This is a direct violation of the presidential oath of office.[6]

A case can certainly be made that a line-item veto would be an effective check against legislative incompetence and maleficence. Virtually every president since the Ulysses S. Grant administration has called for one. But to change the powers of the president would require a constitutional amendment. This is an important point. Congress cannot legally change the constitutional authority of the executive branch—for example, it cannot give legislative responsibilities to the president—without an amendment to the Constitution. Similarly, the president cannot unilaterally expand the powers of the executive branch. Both are examples of lawless abuses of power. The Constitution does not exist to make life comfortable for the government or cater to the political whims of the ruling party or the political class. The Constitution exists to render government abuse difficult if not impossible.

However flagrant Bush's abuse of signing statements may have been, he is better known for his foreign policy initiatives during the War on Terror. The Democrats quickly pounced on every faulty move Bush made during his eight years in office, while the Republicans typically sat on their hands. Their man was in power. This dynamic is precisely why George Washington cautioned against political parties. Partisanship quickly led Republicans to dismiss Democrat claims of abuse of power. But did the Democrats have a point? Absolutely, at least according to the Constitution as ratified.

The Congress overwhelmingly supported Bush's plan for the invasion of Afghanistan in 2002. While he did not receive a constitutional declaration of war, Bush nevertheless had a use-of-force authorization from the Congress to find and kill or capture the parties responsible for the September 11, 2001, attacks. Most of them were believed to be hiding in Afghanistan, shielded by the corrupt Taliban government. No one blinked at what was tantamount to a declared war in the Middle East. Americans wanted justice, and the Bush administration at least had congressional support for an armed conflict. But this is where Bush's limited adherence to the Constitution ended.

In response to the fear that gripped the United States in the weeks after September 11, Congress passed the USA PATRIOT Act on October 26, 2001. It was one of the more sweeping pieces of legislation in American history, and, to make matters worse, very few congressmen either read or debated the bill. Critics correctly charged that the PATRIOT Act undermined the Fourth Amendment to the Constitution. It opened the door to unconstitutional warrantless domestic surveillance—which has now been exposed by recent National Security Administration leaks—allowed the federal government to examine American reading habits by seeing what books they checked out from a public library, and authorized the FBI to collect personal information on thousands of American citizens simply because they opposed the war in Iraq.

When the Congress attempted to revoke various illegal provisions of the law in 2005 and 2006, Bush issued signing statements that basically vetoed certain portions of the laws. Bush refused to enforce the legislation, explaining that the provisions in question—having to do with harsh interrogation techniques and congressional oversight, among other things—challenged the authority of the "Commander in Chief." The Commander in Chief clause of the Constitution, however, does not give the president the authority to ignore legislation, particularly once it is signed into law by the president himself, and the executive branch is never shielded from congressional oversight. (Bush would periodically dust off Nixon's claim of "executive privilege" when threatened with congressional inquiries into the conduct of the administration.)

Nor does the Commander in Chief clause grant the president unlimited war making powers. According to Article I, Section 8, Congress can set limits on presidential powers in a time of war—and it has. The legislative branch has the exclusive authority to "raise and support Armies," "make rules concerning Captures on Land and Water," and "make Rules for the Government and Regulation of the land and naval forces."

In the months leading up to war in Iraq in 2003, Bush had his own "Gulf of Tonkin" moment. The Bush administration claimed that it had irrefutable evidence that the Saddam Hussein regime was producing and hiding weapons of mass destruction. Hussein denied these charges, and United Nations weapons inspectors—admittedly stalled and blocked by Hussein—reported they had no evidence that any existed. Secretary of State Colin Powell testified before Congress that Hussein was lying and that the United States needed to take quick action to ensure that these weapons were never used against American troops in the Middle East. It turns out that the evidence was not so indisputable and that Powell did not even believe his own testimony, but the Congress took action and authorized a full-scale invasion of Iraq in March 2003. Bush declared "Mission Accomplished" in April.

Again, even though this was another clear case of war against a sovereign state, Bush did not have a formal declaration of war, just a basic authorization-of-force resolution. Like his father before him, Bush did not believe he needed congressional approval to begin hostilities in Iraq because the 1973 War Powers Resolution allowed unilateral action. Unfortunately, after Hussein's ouster, the conflict turned into a costly war of attrition with American soldiers bogged down in Iraq as an occupation force charged with peacekeeping. The United States government spent billions on foreign aid to Iraq, all without a formal treaty ratified by the Senate, and in the years since the "Mission Accomplished" speech we have seen American military involvement expand to other regions of the Middle East and North Africa. The War on Terror has become the new Cold War, with endless American military commitments, all justified by the geopolitical necessity of fighting the "Axis of Evil," as Bush labeled it during his 2002 State of the Union address. The War on Terror presumably gave the executive branch a blank check to violate the Constitution.

FUNDAMENTALLY TRANSFORMING AMERICA

As the Bush administration came to a close in 2009, the incoming president, Barack Obama, promised to scale back Bush's abuse of the Commander in Chief clause, signing statements, and unconstitutional domestic spying. But like presidents forty-one to forty-three, Obama continued the unconstitutional actions of his predecessors. In fact, he has become the most powerful, lawless, and the worst president in American history—according to the Constitution as ratified.

Obama still has time left in his administration to roll back years of unconstitutional usurpations of power. He won't. His track record proves that President Obama is as committed to the imperial executive as anyone who preceded him in office—if not more so. Obama made Bush's abuse of the Constitution one of his central themes in the months leading to the 2008 presidential campaign. He said in 2007, "I will provide our intelligence and law enforcement agencies with the tools they need to track and take out the terrorists without undermining our Constitution and our freedom. That means no more illegal wiretapping of American citizens. No more national security letters to spy on citizens who are not suspected of a crime. No more tracking citizens who do nothing more than protest a misguided war. No more ignoring the law when it is inconvenient...."[7] Obama claimed that Bush's handling of the national debt was "un-American," and in 2008 he said, "The biggest problems that we're facing right now have to do with George Bush trying to bring more and more power into the executive branch and not go through Congress at all, and that's what I intend to reverse when I'm President of the United States of America."[8]

Attacking Bush was convenient and popular on the campaign trail. Bush had one of the lowest approval ratings of any president in American history in 2008. And in all fairness, Obama was *correct* about the Bush administration. But once Obama was elected, rather than reverse Bush's policies, he *expanded* the unconstitutional actions of his predecessor, all the while pandering to his core constituencies by blaming Bush for every problem facing his own administration. Though it is still incomplete, the Obama regime will undoubtedly be remembered for several deliberate violations of the president's oath to "defend the Constitution" in both foreign and domestic policy.

Obama promised healthcare "reform" during the 2008 election. Once in office, he was not going to let Republicans block what has become his signature legislative initiative, the Patient Protection and Affordable Care Act of 2010 (ACA). Of course, simply by involving himself in the legislative process, Obama violated the original Constitution; and by signing a patently unconstitutional law, he abrogated his duty to "defend the Constitution," though his actions in this regard were nothing new in the modern era.

The Supreme Court upheld the law in the 2012 decision of *National Federation of Independent Business v. Sebelius,* but not because it believed the Congress had the power to force people to buy insurance under the Commerce Clause or the Necessary and Proper Clause. Congress, the 5–4 majority decided, had the power to mandate that people buy health insurance because the fine for failing to do so could be regarded as a tax. This particular argument was buried in the legal defense of the law and was only teased out in the final day of arguments by the Court itself. This proves that the Court cannot be trusted to block unconstitutional legislation. Obama had a "constitutional" victory, but he quickly realized that in order to ensure that his unconstitutional monstrosity survived, he had to unconstitutionally legislate from the executive branch.

Over a two-year period, the Obama administration delayed the implementation of the Affordable Care Act twenty-eight times, ostensibly to give employers time to comply with the law.[9] This was a blatantly unconstitutional power grab by the executive office. Congress alone has the power to legislate, and once a law is passed and signed by the president, the executive branch has a constitutional responsibility to enforce that law. Obama had no legal authority to issue such delays, particularly in regard to employer and individual mandates. These mandates would have been (and are) painful and probably would have resulted in even larger losses for the Democrats in the 2014 election cycle. Representative government means that the people can remove their representatives if those representatives pass legislation the people disapprove of. In this case, the executive was protecting legislators from the just anger of the people by delaying the enforcement of a law whose effects were predicted to be highly unpopular.

Obama also decided to dust off a legal mechanism called "prosecutorial discretion" in regard to a host of issues during his administration. In some cases, this was the proper course of action. In others, it was a blatant abuse of power and a violation of his oath.

The Obama administration decided not to enforce the Defense of Marriage Act and the federal marijuana laws in states that had decriminalized possession, even for recreational use. This was the proper legal course. The Defense of Marriage Act had created unconstitutional federal qualifications for a marriage. No such power exists in Article I, Section 8. By ignoring the law, Obama was doing his job to "defend the Constitution." Only constitutional laws are subject to enforcement. The Supreme Court later found the first provision in DOMA to be unconstitutional, but not the second, allowing states to avoid recognizing same-sex marriages from other states. In fact, this was already an inherent power of the states, codified in the Tenth Amendment to the Constitution. Typically the federal courts have ignored this legal roadblock to same-sex marriage through "incorporation" of the Fourteenth Amendment to the states. But neither the Fourteenth Amendment nor any federal statute supersedes the Tenth Amendment, no matter what a federal judge claims.

The same holds true for federal marijuana laws. The federal government can regulate the sale of marijuana between states, but all *intrastate* commerce, including what people grow and consume, falls outside of federal regulation and control. The general government has not properly adhered to this constitutional principle since at least the New Deal in the 1930s, but in the case of marijuana, the Obama administration is taking the proper legal course. This is another Tenth Amendment issue. The problem, of course, is that the Obama administration has chosen to take positions consistent with the original federal nature of the government only selectively. For the majority of his actions as president, Obama has followed a different path.

Obama's use of prosecutorial discretion hit a stumbling block in respect to immigration. The Constitution grants the Congress the power to "establish an uniform Rule of Naturalization," which, as Madison suggested in Philadelphia, covered the ability to restrict immigration. He did not wish to do so, but there were men both in Philadelphia and at the state ratifying conventions who cautioned against "foreign influence" in the government and the harmful effects of too many non-native peoples. The First Congress established a naturalization law in 1790, and subsequent congresses followed suit. The states also could regulate citizenship within their own borders and prevent foreigners from establishing residency, but federal regulation of immigration had rarely been contested—until the Obama administration, that is.

The 2012 Deferred Action for Childhood Arrivals Program, an unconstitutional arrogation of power by the executive branch with the sole purpose of undermining legally passed immigration statutes, allowed the executive branch to grant "children" two-year reprieves from deportation as long as they applied to the program. These "children" could be thirty-one years old. The program potentially halted the deportation of five million illegal immigrants. The rule of law never stopped the administration before, and it would not prove a hindrance in this case. Obama had essentially chosen not to enforce immigration law—a decision that, according to the Constitution as ratified, violated his oath. Federal immigration statutes are perfectly constitutional and thus are required to be enforced by the executive branch. Refusing to do so, and claiming that "prosecutorial discretion" somehow shielded the administration from enforcing the law not only violated Obama's oath of office, it was an impeachable offense.

Also in 2012, Obama decided to appoint several members to the National Labor Relations Board without the advice and consent of the

Senate. He claimed that the Senate was in recess and thus he was authorized by the Constitution to make these appointments. The Senate, however, denied that it was in recess and immediately challenged the move. The Supreme Court unanimously struck down the "recess" appointments because the Senate was clearly not in recess when Obama decided to unconstitutionally circumvent the appointment process. This was one of the few times in the modern era when the Supreme Court struck down an expansion of executive powers. They almost had no choice. The case was clear-cut, and still five members of the Court tried to add wiggle room by crafting artificial rules out of thin air.

Obama's shredding of the Constitution has not been confined to domestic policy or the constitutional separation of powers. In 2011, the Obama administration began air strikes in Libya; the president said he would continue to drop bombs in the North African country even when Congress threatened to pass a law against continued military involvement in the region. Obama then claimed that he had the authority to ignore Congress and rejected his own Office of Legal Council in choosing to continue the effort. His message to the Justice Department and the Congress in this case was clear: I am the law.

Obama's position, however, had already been advanced by a Republican legal expert, John Yoo, during the Bush administration. Yoo in fact excoriated Republicans for opposing Obama's strikes in Libya, stating, "Sadly, they've fallen victim to the siren song of short-term political gain against a president who continues to stumble in national-security matters."[10] Yoo argued that the only recourse the Congress had in this matter was to cut off funding for the operation. Of course, that would require a presidential signature, something they would not get. Absent the supermajority the Constitution requires to overturn a presidential veto—and that it does not require for the Congress to decide whether or not to go to war—the Yoo Doctrine would leave war making in the hands of the executive branch, unconstitutionally removing a congressional check on the president's foreign adventurism.

Taken as a whole, the last four administrations represent the culmination of a century of executive abuse. With each successive president from forty-one to forty-four the disease grew worse. By the time Obama leaves office in 2017, Americans will have suffered under twenty-eight consecutive years of unconstitutional executive usurpation of power. An elected king? The British taxpayer spends around $50 million annually to support the entire royal family. With an annual budget that exceeds $1 billion for expenses, including travel, the American president supplanted the British monarch in everything but a title long ago.

PART II

THE FOUR WHO TRIED TO SAVE HER

CHAPTER 10

THOMAS JEFFERSON

Third President, 1801–1809

Thomas Jefferson called his election in 1800 a political revolution. Jefferson's Republicans swept both the executive and legislative branches after twelve years of Federalist control. The Federalists had unconstitutionally enlarged the powers of the executive branch and the general government, and John Adams, Jefferson's predecessor, who had presided over four years of miserable relations between the executive and both the Congress and the American people, became the scapegoat. Jefferson brought a new vision of America to the executive branch, a reserved version of executive authority that jibed with his belief in republican principles and limited government. His first term is a model in executive restraint; it turned around an American political system that had deviated widely from the promises that the proponents of the Constitution had made when it was ratified in 1788. Jefferson was not perfect—his second term was a disaster constitutionally—but he set the stage for twenty-four years of executive authority that generally coincided with the way the friends of the Constitution had sold the office to a reluctant population during the state ratifying conventions.

The Jefferson presidency almost didn't happen. The 1800 election resulted in a tie between Jefferson and the other Republican candidate, Aaron Burr of New York. Before the Twelfth Amendment to the Constitution, the man finishing with the most votes won the presidency and the runner-up became vice president. In 1800 Jefferson and Burr tied with the most votes, and Adams, the incumbent, finished third. As per the Constitution, the election was thrown to the House of Representatives where the lame duck Federalists still held power. Voting was by state, not member, and it became apparent early in the balloting that Jefferson faced a rocky road to victory.

The more partisan Federalists in the Congress, who later became known as the "Essex Junto," favored throwing the election to Burr. To them, Jefferson personified the "terrorists" of the Republican Party. He was, after all, the head of the other political faction, the man who paid for newspaper editors to fillet the Federalists in the press, who supported the "Whiskey Rebellion" and the dreaded French and denounced every move the Federalists made as a step toward monarchy. Denying him the office made perfect sense. Burr complicated matters by not stepping aside. He was politically ambitious and aware of the hatred his fellow Northerners had for Jefferson. There was even talk of secession among the Northern congressional delegation. If they couldn't keep Jefferson out of the executive mansion, they might simply leave the Union.

Two important Federalists had broached this subject long before 1800. In 1794 Rufus King of New York and Oliver Ellsworth of Connecticut, who had both been members of the 1787 Philadelphia Convention, cornered then Senator John Taylor of Virginia in a cloak room and pressed him about a potential parting of the sections. They argued that it had become crystal clear that the North and the South would never be able to reconcile their political and economic differences and thus a negotiated separation was more desirable than continuing in a bad marriage. This was only six years after the Constitution was ratified and five after the First Congress opened for business.

Taylor was shocked. He was considered to be the leading spokesman for what became known as "Jeffersonianism"—in fact, he was more Jeffersonian than Jefferson himself, but he did not see secession as desirable or practical at that moment. Taylor would later change his mind, but meanwhile the spirit of extreme Northern sectionalism, which would never subside during Jefferson's two terms in office, almost cost him the presidency in 1800. It was the North, not the South, that first considered secession and that pressed the issue for nearly two decades in the formative stages of the federal Republic.

Cooler minds prevailed. Federalist James A. Bayard Sr., the lone representative from Delaware, gained assurances through a proxy that, if elected, Jefferson would not axe every Federalist from the general government. This would be a revolution, but a mild one in regard to the "spoils of office." Bayard was important. His vote was *the* vote from Delaware, and as a well-respected man with political connections, he could also persuade other Federalists to vote his way. Alexander Hamilton also helped. Hamilton and Jefferson were diametrically opposed on almost every issue, but Hamilton feared a Burr presidency. In several private letters, Hamilton insisted that his colleagues vote for Jefferson: Jefferson could be trusted to be reasonable. Burr was a wildcard. On the thirty-sixth ballot, Jefferson was elected president by one vote. Bayard's blank ballot made the difference.

THE SMALL-R REPUBLICAN PRESIDENT

When it came to executive powers, Jefferson's symbolism was as important as his policies. Jefferson rejected the precedent of a formal coach ride to his inaugural and instead chose to walk. Carriages were the trappings of monarchy. Walking placed him among the people and immediately reduced the status of the office. Throughout his administration, Jefferson found ways to trim the trappings of office. He abolished the Washington and Adams practices of official state dinners, wore his slippers and robe around the mansion, and sometimes opened the front door himself. The executive mansion was not only his home but the people's home in the people's city. Jefferson was no king. To many Americans, his administration was a refreshing departure from the previous four years of heavy-handed executive government. Jefferson would not always maintain such a minimalist approach to executive authority, but aesthetically, Jefferson had transformed the American presidency.

Politically, Jefferson's first inaugural address set the tone for the early years of his administration. According to the Constitution as ratified, the legislature was to be the most powerful and important branch of government. Jefferson echoed this theme in the opening paragraph of his speech. "To you, then, gentlemen, who are charged with the sovereign functions of legislation, and to those associated with you, I look with encouragement for that guidance and support which may enable us to steer with safety the vessel in which we are all embarked amidst the conflicting elements of a troubled world." Notice that Jefferson was not setting policy; he was looking for "guidance and support" from the "sovereign" men who served in the legislative branch. He would not be "chief legislator." Jefferson's job, as he saw it, was to make recommendations and then execute the laws of Congress, nothing more. And in a subtle though important change, Jefferson's "recommendations" would arrive as a written message to Congress rather than in person—the executive was not to encroach on legislative matters. Every successive president continued Jefferson's practice until Woodrow Wilson took office in 1913.

Jefferson was acutely aware of the political tensions that had nearly torpedoed his election. He had been an active participant in the political instability. Now, Jefferson wanted to calm the waters. In the most famous line of the inaugural address, Jefferson insisted, "We are all Republicans, we are all Federalists." But Jefferson qualified that statement with the next sentence. "If there be any among us who would wish to dissolve this Union or to change its republican form, let them stand undisturbed as monuments of the safety with which error of opinion may be tolerated where reason is left free to combat it." This was a direct message to the Federalists who had supported secession for the last several years. Jefferson did not believe secession to be the rightful remedy to the political squabbles of the day, but he would not persecute those who favored this position. They were not "enemies of the state" or "terrorists" but Americans with a difference of opinion. "The minority," Jefferson said, "possess their equal rights, which equal law must protect, and to violate would be oppression."

Jefferson outlined his belief in "Federal and Republican principles" in the next two paragraphs of the address. These included a belief in a "wise and frugal" representative government "which shall restrain men from injuring one another, shall leave them otherwise free to regulate their own pursuits of industry and improvement, and shall not take from the mouth of labor the bread it has earned." Jefferson reaffirmed his dedication to core American principles: the even application of justice regardless of religious or political persuasion; "peace, commerce, and honest friendship with all nations, entangling alliances with none"; respect for the states' powers as "the surest bulwarks against antirepublican tendencies"; support for the delegated, constitutional powers of the "General Government"; reliance on elections to correct government abuses; a well-regulated citizen militia and civil control of the military; economy in government, including light taxes and low debt; civil liberties and "freedom of person under the protection of the *habeas corpus*"; and the promotion of an agriculture-based society. An executive with such core values would faithfully adhere to his oath to defend the Constitution and protect the citizens of the federal Republic. Jefferson knew he would make mistakes, but he regarded office as a public trust, a duty rather than a station, and therefore asked for forgiveness in advance for any errors of judgment.[1]

THE CONGRESS

Jefferson had a luxury few presidents in American history have enjoyed. When he assumed office the Congress was dominated by like-minded men as determined to uphold republican principles as Jefferson himself, maybe more so. The Federalists had spent twelve years pushing legislation through Congress that to Jefferson and other Republicans undermined the Constitution and the "spirit of '76." The government had become too centralized, too British in character; and it needed swift reform. Jefferson did not have to cajole the Congress to act, nor would he have insisted had the need presented itself. That was not in his character. He led by staying aloof from the political fray. Jefferson believed the president should remain disengaged from the legislature and stay clean from the mudslinging in the trenches. Congress legislated and the president executed. Congress responded to this hands-off approach with a slew of solid republican legislation. Jefferson never issued a veto.

Jefferson did have several recommendations for Congress: reduce the debt; eliminate as many taxes as possible; reign in the federal judiciary; repeal, replace, or let expire odious Federalist legislation; and authorize appropriations only for specific purposes. Congress immediately went to work in 1801. In a spirit that would rival the Seventy-Third Congress (1933–35) in zeal though not in unconstitutional legislation, the Seventh Congress took aim at every piece of Federalist legislation that they believed had violated the original intent of the Constitution.

First up were the infamous Alien and Sedition Acts of 1798. These laws had been passed as a reaction to public outrage over a potential war with France in 1798. Several Republican-leaning newspapers had printed editorials disparaging both the leaders of Congress and President Adams. Though he was vice president at the time, Jefferson financially backed some of the attacks through payments to partisan newspaper editors. Federalists worried that this criticism—and the fact that the fresh-faced immigrants who were arriving in America in this period tended to vote Republican—would make them a political minority. So the Alien and Sedition Acts were passed with the sole purpose of rigging elections and crushing political dissent. They had the opposite effect.

Jefferson and James Madison worked secretly through the states of Virginia and Kentucky to obstruct the implementation of the Acts. Jefferson correctly viewed the Sedition Act as a violation of both the First and Tenth Amendments to the Constitution. It was a blatant suppression of a free press, and Congress had no authority to pass such a law. As we have seen, Jefferson's Kentucky Resolutions and Madison's Virginia Resolutions advanced a political idea known as nullification or state interposition. The principle was that no state was obligated to follow an unconstitutional law—a point that had been made clear during the ratification process of the Constitution. No other state supported the Resolutions, but after several Republican newspaper editors and one congressman were thrown in jail for violating the Sedition Act, the American public reacted by booting the Federalists from power. Rather than securing a perpetual majority in the general government, as the Federalists hoped, the Acts nailed shut the lid on their political coffin.

Jefferson urged Congress to repeal the laws or let them expire. The Sedition Act expired in 1801, and the more outrageous elements of the Alien Acts were repealed in the first session of Congress. Jefferson followed up by pardoning all ten men still incarcerated for violating the law, and Congress voted to pay all of the fines levied by the unconstitutional act back with interest. This was the even-handed justice Jefferson had referred to in his inaugural address. Political opinion should not be subject to a fine, imprisonment, or censorship. Jefferson helped ensure that the general government would respect free speech and a free press.

Congress then sought to reform the tax and appropriations systems of the previously Federalist-dominated government. Direct property taxes, excise taxes, and carriage taxes were all repealed. Within the first year of the Republican-dominated government, 90 percent of federal revenue came from a small revenue-collecting tariff alone. Jefferson's genius secretary of the treasury, Albert Gallatin, thought that if Americans were not saddled with excessive taxes in peacetime, they could be counted on to ante up should the government need the revenue in a time of war. More money in the pockets of average Americans also equated to a more robust economy. People had capital to invest and money to spend.

Gallatin also insisted that appropriations be made for specific purposes. Targeted appropriations are often derided as "earmarks" today. Jefferson and Gallatin believed they were the mainstays of honest, frugal government. The Federalists had often appropriated money in blocks with little or no accountability as to how or when the money would be spent. In some cases, Congress passed appropriations bills *after* the money had already been withdrawn from the treasury. Jefferson and Gallatin considered this practice to be immoral and illegal. Throughout the Jefferson, Madison, and even into the Monroe administrations, Congress presented appropriations bills with "earmarked" spending so that the public could both see how and where the public money was being spent and the government could be held accountable to the American taxpayer.

The real cutbacks in appropriations occurred in military spending. Even under the Federalists, domestic spending had never reached substantial levels. Treasury Secretary Hamilton, for example, had worked out of a one-room office with one single clerk for an assistant—this was not the modern bureaucracy. The Federalists did, however, spend on defense. Jefferson and other Republicans considered a standing army to be a danger to American liberty. Gallatin went to work dismantling as much of it as possible, with the net result being the smallest peacetime army in the history of the United States.

Jefferson insisted in his first inaugural address that the militia should be the backbone of the American military, but he did believe in the necessity of a small but well-trained professional army. To that end, Jefferson signed into law an 1802 bill that established the Army Corps of Engineers and the United States Military Academy at West Point. West Point became the source of most of the best generals in American history, and the Army Corps of Engineers has counted among its ranks several leading members of the American military. Jefferson had the foresight to understand that a modern military required skilled professionals to lead it. The militia, if well-trained, could serve as an initial line of defense if the United States were invaded, but a regular army would be needed to win a war. The House concurred with Jefferson's requests for the professional army but rejected more investment in the militia. A twentieth-century president would probably have vetoed such an affront to his recommendation. Instead, Jefferson signed a scaled-down military spending bill because the Congress controlled the purse strings and none of the bill was unconstitutional even if it did not meet Jefferson's recommendations.

Jefferson likewise signed bills that gutted the United States Navy. All appropriations for new warships were scrapped, the existing fleet was cut in half, and spending for the Department of the Navy—created during the John Adams administration—was reduced by two-thirds. Jefferson agreed with the moves on the basis of economy, though Federalists howled that these reductions left the United States vulnerable to attack. The Congress, with Jefferson's approval, did supplement the Navy with smaller and cheaper "gunboats," which did not have the firepower to defend American commerce on the open ocean. These ships amounted to a naval militia.

To the Jeffersonians, defense meant protecting the United States from invasion. The militia and gunboats, they believed, would be able to repulse sudden attacks on land and sea, and the thousands of miles of ocean that separated the United States from other land would act as a natural line of defense. This system would be tested during the War of 1812 nearly four years after Jefferson left office. It proved to be inadequate, at least initially, though some of the most spectacular victories for the United States were won by militia, particularly in the South.

Jefferson's hands-off (meaning constitutional) style of governance in regard to legislation would be deemed weak by modern critics. But it worked. The reductions in spending cut the United States debt in half, and the government ran large budget surpluses for several years. Jefferson let Congress legislate even when their ideas did not match his own. Treasury

Secretary Gallatin and Secretary of State Madison did wade into the leg-islative process, but Jefferson stayed out, believing that the chief executive's involvement in legislation would have rendered the presidency too close to an elected monarchy.

THE COURT

Chief Justice John Marshall swore Jefferson in as the third president on March 4, 1801. Marshall had been Chief Justice for only a shade over a month. He had been appointed in the waning days of the Adams admin-istration for the express purpose of impeding the oncoming Republican revolution. The lame duck Federalist-controlled Congress had passed the Judiciary Act of 1801 after Jefferson secured victory in the House of Rep-resentatives. The bill expanded the federal court system, allowed Supreme Court justices to "ride the circuit," meaning that they also presided over Federal Circuit courts in addition to the Supreme Court, and established several new federal district courts. Adams spent his last month in office making nominations, right up to the point when he left office.

Marshall was not Adams's first choice for chief justice, but he proved to be a more dedicated anti-Republican nationalist Federalist than any of the men who had previously sat on the Supreme Court. Marshall had been secretary of state and he remained in that position until Adams left office. He had called the Republicans "absolute terrorists" and spent most of his career on a crusade to maintain a strong "national" government. Adams later claimed Marshall's appointment to the Supreme Court to be one of the most important decisions of his life. Adams's judicial appointments made under the Judiciary Act set up an early battle with the Jefferson administration and led to one of the most famous decisions in American legal history, *Marbury v. Madison* of 1803.

Marshall spent his final days as secretary of state delivering judicial appointments to the throngs of Federalists whom Adams had appointed to the expanded federal court system. By March 4, 1801, the day of Jefferson's inauguration, he had simply run out of time to get every notice into the hands of the new judges. So Marshall left a stack of undelivered commissions on Jefferson's desk when he assumed office. Jefferson argued that because the appointments were not delivered and still sealed, they were invalid and void. In fact, Jefferson argued that any appointment made after his election in 1801 was illegal and immoral.

On March 3, 1801, Adams had appointed William Marbury the Justice of the Peace for the District of Columbia. When Jefferson refused to honor the undelivered appointment, Marbury applied to the Supreme Court for a mandamus—a legal demand for action—for Jefferson to deliver the appointment. By the time the case worked its way to a hearing, Madison had been confirmed as secretary of state, thus making him the legal party to the suit. Obviously, Marshall should have recused himself from the case. After all, he was secretary of state when Marbury had been appointed. Instead Marshall issued the majority opinion in the first instance of "judicial review" in the history of the United States general government under the Constitution.

The Court called Madison's actions illegal but stopped short of ordering him to deliver the commission. Instead, the Court declared one part of the Judicial Act of 1801 unconstitutional and denied Marbury the right to sue for his appointment. It was technically a victory for the Jefferson administration, but neither Jefferson nor Madison was happy with the result. They concluded that Marshall had unconstitutionally enlarged the powers of the Court and by doing so threatened the fabric of the federal Republic.

In his defense, in the Virginia Ratifying Convention of 1788 Marshall had hinted at the possibility of "judicial review"—an idea that had received a mixed reaction in the Philadelphia Convention, with those delegates from states that already had the procedure in agreement and those without it against its use. Oliver Ellsworth of Connecticut had put his faith in judicial review as a way of avoiding using the military as the "coercive principle" of the Constitution. But "judicial review" was by no means a settled policy when the Constitution was ratified. The very fact that it took fifteen years from the ratification of the Constitution for the idea to be dusted off, all while Federalists controlled the Supreme Court, shows that not everyone believed it was within the powers delegated to the Court in the Constitution. Jefferson wrote later in life, "This practice of Judge Marshall, of travelling out of his case to prescribe what the law would be in a moot case not before the court, is very irregular and very censurable," and lamented that "this case of Marbury and Madison is continually cited by bench and bar, as if it were settled law, without any animadversion on its being merely an *obiter* dissertation of the Chief Justice."[2] Jefferson saw the danger of a politically appointed justice's making decisions in line with his personal political philosophy and without regard to the original Constitution.

The Republicans had a chance to stop the Federalists and Marshall during Jefferson's first term. On Jefferson's recommendation, the Republican-controlled Congress went to work attempting to undo the Federalist takeover of the judicial branch. They started by repealing the Judiciary Act of 1801 and then replaced it with a scaled-down version that reorganized the federal court system without adding a multitude of new judges and new courts. By repealing the 1801 Act, the Congress abolished dozens of federal judgeships and replaced them with nothing. How inspirational. The Supreme Court remained intact, though the Congress decided to dust off one of the arrows in their quiver by impeaching Associate Justice Samuel Chase and Federal District Judge John Pickering.

Just like the president, Supreme Court justices are subject to impeachment for "high crimes and misdemeanors," but no federal office holder had been impeached since the Constitution was ratified. Pickering's case was a slam dunk. The man was insane and could not even attend his own trial. The Senate convicted and removed Pickering from the bench in 1803.

Chase's crimes were less obvious. In his youth, he had supported Jeffersonian principles and was a signatory to the Declaration of Independence, but after the bloodshed of the French Revolution, Chase pivoted to the right and became an outspoken opponent of "mobocracy."

His rulings reflected his partisan shift, as did the way he handled his cases. Chase spent years making political statements from the bench—lecturing juries and Republican prosecutors—and exercised blatant partisanship in allowing (or not) evidence at trial. Republican defendants, notably during the 1798 crisis over the Sedition Act, did not face a fair hearing with Chase on the bench. The Republicans considered excessive partisanship to be an abuse of power and a "high crime and misdemeanor," particularly when it resulted in a miscarriage of justice. If Chase could be removed from the federal bench, it would put other federal judges, namely Marshall, on notice that excessive partisanship would not be tolerated.

Chase decried *Republican* partisanship in this matter, warning that it would obliterate the independence of the judicial branch. But Republicans knew that impeachment was the only way to check an abusive and excessively partisan federal court system. They were constitutionally correct. Congress had legal authority to define the jurisdiction of the judicial branch and set the number of federal judges as well as the number of "inferior courts." Congress could make the Supreme Court virtually impotent through legislation, and impeaching a federal judge for abuse of his office was clearly within the powers delegated to them by the Constitution.

Senator William B. Giles from Virginia, Jefferson's most trusted ally in the upper chamber, lambasted not only Chase but the entire slate of Federalist judges appointed by the infamous 1801 Judiciary Act. In fact Giles believed that every Federalist member of the Supreme Court should be removed. It was imperative, he argued, that should "a federal judge declare an Act of Congress unconstitutional, or to send a mandamus to the Secretary of State..." the House impeach him and the Senate convict him for his "dangerous opinions."[3] Jefferson concurred and watched the proceedings carefully—though at a distance, so as not to taint Chase's trial in the Senate.

It became clear during the trial that Chase would not be convicted. He had already reassumed his seat on the bench. The prosecution's case rested on the facts that Chase was an outspoken Federalist, that the Judiciary Act was a political move designed to achieve partisan ends, and that rabid partisanship had traditionally been considered an impeachable offense. These things were all true, but the Republicans did not have close to the required two-thirds majority on any of the eight articles of impeachment. Members of their own party balked. When Jefferson received the news, he hurled invectives against the entire impeachment process, calling it, "a bungling way of removing Judges," "a farce which will not be tried again," "an impracticable thing—a mere scarecrow."⁴ The House responded by passing two constitutional amendments that would have made federal judges removable by a simple majority vote in the Senate and that would have allowed states to recall their senators. Predictably, neither made it through the Senate.

Jefferson lost the war against the judiciary. Marshall had been genuinely scared that a Chase conviction would mean the end of his tenure as chief justice, and Chase's acquittal emboldened him. For the next thirty years Marshall placed his stamp on the Constitution—the end result being the codification of the nationalist or "loose construction" reading of the general government's founding document. Federalists rejoiced that the independency of the judicial branch had been maintained. But the triumph of the nationalist understanding of the Constitution did not remove politics from the bench. And it did not make Jefferson's crusade any less noble, nor did it alter the fact that there had been two distinct visions for the judicial branch even during the ratification process.

"Independency" of federal judges is an ambiguous term. Federalists interpreted independency to mean that federal judges would not be beholden to the whims of the legislative branch or the politics of the day. The Republicans, on the other hand, regarded independency to mean judicial neutrality, as Jefferson himself had said in his first inaugural address. In retrospect it's clear that Jefferson and the Republicans were prescient to view the judicial branch as a potential roadblock to republican government. Jefferson wrote only three weeks after his inauguration that "the Federalists have retired into the Judiciary as a stronghold ...and from that battery all the works of republicanism are to be beaten down and erased."[5] By republican government, Jefferson and his political allies meant the supremacy of the people's representatives in the legislature and the maintenance of real decentralized federalism. The current Congress could take inspiration from their predecessors in the Seventh and Eight Congresses and scrap a federal court system that since the mid-twentieth century has operated without regard to the original Constitution. Jeffersonians succeeded in at least reducing the number of federal justices. For that alone they should be applauded.

LOUISIANA

The most famous accomplishment of Jefferson's first term was also the most controversial constitutionally. The 1783 Treaty of Paris had ceded a large swath of territory that stretched to the Mississippi River to the state governments (principally Virginia). Over time, the state governments had given this land to the central government so that it could be partitioned and sold to raise revenue. Jefferson had been the driving force behind the Virginia land cession and was the principal author of the Land Ordinance of 1784. This legislation divided the western territory into townships, and each township was then sub-divided into lots to be sold at $1 an acre. By 1785, Americans had begun purchasing the land and moving into the region.

Jefferson also authored the Northwest Ordinance of 1787, often considered to be the crown jewel of the general government under the Articles of Confederation. The Ordinance prohibited the introduction of slavery into the territory and provided the framework for new states, with each state being on "equal footing" with the existing states. Jefferson had a vision for the west. He believed that eventually an "Empire of Liberty" would stretch from coast to coast in North America—but it was not to be a consolidated empire under the direction of a benevolent king. Jefferson thought that the new states would eventually form confederacies of their own, remaining on a friendly basis with the United States. To Jefferson, a state was a sovereign political entity, and if each western state was on "equal footing" with the existing states, it had the same rights, powers, and privileges as Virginia or Massachusetts. These states would be agrarian allies with the South—a prospect that gave the Northeast pause.

In 1802, through a treaty with Great Britain, France gained a large chunk of North America from Spain. Napoleon Bonaparte, soon to be crowned emperor of France, had designs on a North American conquest. Jefferson feared the results and worried that he would have to establish a permanent alliance with Great Britain to protect the United States from the ambitious Bonaparte. Thus Jefferson sent James Monroe to France to purchase the city of New Orleans and any surrounding territory from the French. When Monroe arrived, Napoleon's foreign minister, Talleyrand, dropped a bombshell. Talleyrand was willing to sell the entire Louisiana Territory to the United States for $15 million. Monroe wasn't certain that either the Jefferson administration or the Congress would ratify such a treaty, but he worked out the details and sailed home with an opportunity to grab a third of the American continent for less than three cents an acre.

Jefferson was intrigued. He had long been a proponent of western expansion, and the Louisiana Purchase would free North America from a potentially hostile European power. But he wasn't sure that the Purchase was constitutional, and he was concerned about the fact that it would have to be financed by the Bank of the United States by adding 20 percent to the United States debt. Jefferson believed admitting Louisiana to the Union set a dangerous precedent for the future. "Our peculiar security," he wrote, "is in the possession of a written Constitution. Let us not make it a blank paper by construction. I say the same as to the opinion of those who consider the grant of the treatymaking power as boundless. If it is, then we have no Constitution."[6] At Jefferson's insistence, Madison began drafting a series of constitutional amendments to be submitted with the treaty in order to ward off any questions about its constitutionality.

But Secretary of the Treasury Gallatin told Jefferson amendments were unnecessary. The purchase fell under the treaty making power of the general government, a power that was exclusively contained within the executive branch. Under a treaty, Gallatin argued, the United States could purchase and acquire territory regardless of whether that particular power was specifically enumerated in the Constitution. Madison probably thought it was constitutional as well. Even John Randolph of Roanoke, perhaps the most strident strict constructionist in the Congress, agreed with this assessment at the time—though he would later change his tune. Jefferson reluctantly concurred (perhaps prodded by the fact that France had realized it had made a mistake), dropped the amendments, and submitted the treaty to the Senate for ratification.

New England Federalists immediately balked at the deal. They claimed that Jefferson did not have the constitutional authority to negotiate the treaty, that the treaty belied his commitment to "strict construction" of the Constitution, and that France had acquired the land from Spain illegally and thus had no right to sell it to the United States. These arguments were just a smokescreen for the real issue—political power. Northern Federalists feared that the Louisiana Purchase would render them a permanent political minority in a government dominated by Southern and Western farmers. Timothy Pickering of Massachusetts, former secretary of state, secretary of war, and postmaster general, issued a call for Northern secession that continued to resonate until the conclusion of the War of 1812. But Jefferson remained undaunted, the Senate quickly ratified the treaty with only seven votes against it, and the House followed up by providing the funding. All seven negative votes in the Senate came from New England and Delaware, its tiny ally in the early federal period.

The Louisiana Purchase represented a watershed in American constitutional history. The historian Henry Adams argued that it "gave a fatal wound to 'strict construction.'"[7] Gallatin, however, had assessed the situation correctly. Jefferson did not make the treaty by decree; it was not an executive agreement with France with little to no congressional oversight.

Jefferson submitted a negotiated treaty with a foreign power to the Congress for "advice and consent." The Senate could have rejected the treaty, and the House could have refused to fund the purchase. Jefferson had no control over either result. It is true that the Constitution is silent on the matter of admitting foreign states—Jefferson had expressed a fear that the precedent established by the Louisiana Purchase might mean that the United States could, in the future, admit Ireland if it wished. But in the Constitution the states had delegated foreign diplomacy to the general government, and treaties had long been written and ratified without the direct input of the people. The people had had their say via their representatives in the House, and the states had had theirs via the Senate. While a treaty without congressional acquiescence would be tyrannical, the Louisiana Purchase is not comparable with unconstitutional modern diplomatic agreements with foreign powers, many of which are sealed with a simple handshake by the president—with Congress cut out of that process until funding is required. Jefferson followed the proper constitutional protocols, and while the Louisiana Purchase may not have been popular in one section of the country, it was neither illegal nor unconstitutional.

TERM TWO

Unfortunately, Jefferson's role as a president who "tried to save" the United States from unconstitutional government ends with his reelection. Jefferson's second term was a constitutional and political minefield—culminating in his advocacy for an unconstitutional trade embargo with all of Europe. Inept diplomacy in Jefferson's second term led to increased tensions with both the French and the British that ultimately spilled over into a war that was justified at the time—but that perhaps could have been avoided with defter diplomacy early on.

Still, Jefferson's first term set a standard for executive restraint, particularly in regard to domestic policy. He made his wishes known to the Congress through written messages and private letters but did not wade into the political trenches. He was not a prime minister. The successive presidents in the Virginia Dynasty—Madison and Monroe—generally followed Jefferson's path, though like Jefferson both deviated from their core principles in their second term in office. The period from 1801 to 1825 was the Age of Jefferson, and the men in the chief executive office who were most like Jefferson adhered more closely to the Constitution as ratified than any other presidents in American history. None was perfect, but as Jefferson wrote in his first inaugural address, none could be expected to be perfect. "Sometimes it is said that man cannot be trusted with the government of himself. Can he then be trusted with the government of others? Or have we found angels, in the form of kings, to govern him? Let history answer that question."[8]

Jefferson was no king, and during his first term, at least, he allowed the states and the people to dictate his course. This restraint has been perceived, both then and now, as a lack of leadership. But Jefferson was attempting to remain true to his republican principles and reduce the presidency to its rightful place as a co-equal rather than dominant branch in relation to the legislature. A strong executive had its place—particularly when Congress attempted to subvert the Constitution. Resistance to that kind of tyranny was the sort of leadership Jefferson aspired to. As Jefferson wrote in 1799, when the American public was turning against the Federalist Congress that had overstepped its constitutional bounds to pass the Alien and Sedition Acts, "The spirit of '76 is not dead. It has only been slumbering. The body of the American people is substantially republican. But their virtuous feelings have been played on by some fact with more fiction; they have been the dupes of artful maneuvers, and made for a moment to be willing instruments in forging chains for themselves. But time and truth have dissipated the delusion, and opened their eyes."[9] At least in his first term, Jefferson worked to save America from unconstitutional government; in doing so, he provided a truly republican blueprint for future administrations.

JOHN TYLER

Tenth President, 1841–1845

John Tyler is not a household name, but he should be; perhaps he should even be given a spot on some denomination of American currency. He was arguably the best president in American history—according to the Constitution as ratified. Tyler's life and administration almost always come in near the bottom of presidential rankings because of his staunch defense of states' rights both before and after he occupied the presidency, including his support for secession and the Confederate States of America. He is also known for his marriage to a much younger woman while president (after his first wife died) and for fathering fifteen children. His opponents called him "His Accidency"—even those in the Whig Party, on whose ticket he had been elected to the vice presidency, from which he succeeded to the presidency when William Henry Harrison died—and booted him from the party when he failed to toe the party line, and he is generally ranked in the bottom of all presidential polls. But this ranking is unjust.

Tyler, more than any other president, took his oath of office seriously. He came closer to representing the proper mix of executive energy and Jeffersonian restraint that the ratifiers had argued the presidency required than any other man who held the office, either before or after his administration. Tyler quickly turned around a general government that was moving in the wrong direction—and in the process saved the presidency and the Constitution. Tyler became a man without a party, ostracized by the people who had placed him on the Whig ticket in 1840 and shunned by his former colleagues in the Democratic Party. Tyler reveled in the moment, renaming his plantation "Sherwood Forest." He was the Robin Hood protecting the American people from the abuses of the general government, an outlaw from the political class who had abandoned his former colleagues—to protect the people, and defend his oath of office.

Tyler vetoed several unconstitutional bills (for central banks, "internal improvements," and so forth), using the veto power exactly the way the founding generation had intended. He worked through Congress to bring Texas into the Union, all within the limits of the Constitution. Though Congress refused to confirm several of his appointments, he eventually packed the cabinet with fellow states' rights supporters and generally remained independent from the legislative branch. Such a man deserves our highest esteem rather than a throwaway question in some trivia contest.

A REPUBLICAN PEDIGREE

Tyler had been bred for this role. His father, John Tyler Sr., was a Republican ally of Thomas Jefferson who had roomed with Thomas Jefferson at William and Mary. Tyler Sr. voted against ratifying the Constitution in the Virginia Ratifying Convention of 1788, served in the Virginia House of Delegates and as governor of Virginia, and later was appointed to the federal court system by James Madison. Jefferson spent many an evening at the Tylers' supper table, and John Tyler Jr. cut his political teeth on the philosophy of the Sage of Monticello.

Tyler Jr. was elected to the Virginia House of Delegates when he was twenty-one and the United States House of Representatives when he was twenty-eight. In 1825 he was elected governor of Virginia and two years later was sent by the Virginia legislature to the United States Senate, where he served until 1836. The Whig Party picked Tyler to be their vice presidential candidate in 1840 in order to gain the support of the states' rights faction of the South. Their plan worked, and in a twist of fate that left Whig leaders like Henry Clay distraught but seemed to give proof of Divine intervention for the American people and the Constitution, Tyler assumed the presidency after William Henry Harrison died only a month into his term in 1841. Tyler was at his home playing marbles with his children when he heard the news. At that point, Washington city had lost its appeal to Tyler—no one considered the vice presidency to be much more than a ceremonial position with few responsibilities.

Tyler became the first vice president to assume the presidency. No one knew how this would work. Article II, Section 1, of the Constitution states that, "In Case of the Removal of the President from Office, or of his Death, Resignation, or Inability to discharge the Powers and Duties of the said Office, the Same shall devolve on the Vice President." Tyler considered this to mean that upon Harrison's death "he was by the Constitution, by election, and by the act of God, President of the United States."[1] The Congress quickly solved the problem by passing a resolution conferring not only the title of president but also the powers of the office of the presidency to Tyler. Tyler's reading of the Constitution became the standard procedure for presidential succession until the Twenty-Fifth Amendment was ratified in 1967.

The Cabinet and other members of Congress did not necessarily agree with this outcome. Secretary of State Daniel Webster believed that Tyler should be considered a figurehead and that all executive tasks should be handled by consensus among the Cabinet, with the president having only an equal vote with the rest. Former President John Quincy Adams suggested that Tyler was nothing more than an "Acting President" and hoped for another election to place a new man in office. Senator Henry Clay, who didn't think Tyler had a backbone, believed that the arrangement the Congress and the Cabinet had with Harrison would carry over into the new administration: Clay wrote the legislation and the president and his rubber stamp cabinet would approve it. But all the politicians who were counting on Tyler to be weak were gravely disappointed. Tyler was the ideal Southern gentleman, and Clay was mistaking congeniality for weakness.

Tyler dispelled any hopes for government by cabinet and Congress with no real chief executive when he informed the Cabinet at its first meeting: "I beg your pardon, gentlemen; I am very glad to have in my Cabinet such able statesmen as you have proved yourselves to be. And I shall be pleased to avail myself of your counsel and advice. But I can never consent to being dictated to as to what I shall or shall not do. I, as President, shall be responsible for my administration. I hope to have your hearty cooperation in carrying out its measures. So long as you see fit to do this, I shall be glad to have you with me. When you think otherwise, your resignations will be accepted."[2]

No one had been more independent or principled than John Tyler in his various government positions. While in the Virginia legislature, he had voted to censure the state's two United States senators for refusing to comply with the state legislature's directions. He was the lone man to speak and vote against Andrew Jackson's Force Bill, giving the administration extraordinary powers to collect the tariff. He resigned his seat in the Senate after the Democrats expunged Jackson's censure from the record. When he was inaugurated as vice president in 1841, Tyler's brief speech emphasized his adherence to Jeffersonian principles and states' rights. That created friction. Clay was counting on Harrison to be a one-term placeholder until Clay himself could run for president in 1844. The feeble and aged Harrison was not going to block the nationalist Whig legislative agenda.

Tyler's assumption of the office muddied the picture and forced Clay to reconsider his political strategy.

Tyler was a worthy opponent for the powerful Whig politician. Former Virginia Governor Thomas Walker Gilmer, a staunch ally of Tyler's, said that Tyler would "regard his own and every other office under the government as a sacred trust, created for the public good, and not for party or for private emolument."[3] Tyler was a statesman who placed principle above party, position, or accolades—an independent man who could not be corralled. Clay, on the other hand, was the consummate politician, ambitious, politically astute, the "Great Compromiser." Tyler eventually came to believe that Clay was trying to undermine him to gain the nomination for president in 1844. He was correct. Clay's obvious ambition and his advocacy for unconstitutional legislation eventually resulted in a clash between the two men. Tyler had finally had enough. In May 1841, he told Clay forcefully, "Then, sir, I wish you to understand this—that you and I were born in the same district; that we have fed upon the same food, and breathed the same natal air. Go you now, then, Mr. Clay, to your end of the avenue, where stands the Capitol, and there perform your duty to the county as you shall think proper. So help me God, I shall do mine at this end of it as I think proper."[4] The two men never spoke again, and Tyler became a consistent burr under Clay's saddle. That alone made him great.

JEFFERSONIAN

Tyler delivered his first address to the Congress in April 1841. It was pure Jeffersonianism. In his opening paragraph the new president said, "My earnest prayer shall be constantly addressed to the all-wise and all-powerful Being who made me, and by whose dispensation I am called to the high office of President of this Confederacy, understandingly to carry out the principles of that Constitution which I have sworn 'to protect, preserve, and defend.'" Notice that Tyler called the United States a "Confederacy" and that he was dedicated to the "principles of the Constitution" and his oath of office. He made it clear that he would not abandon his Jeffersonian beliefs in a limited central government with defined powers and a federal Republic of independent states.

In the same speech, Tyler outlined his foreign policy objectives, which included peaceful neutrality and bolstering the American army and navy. He then addressed a problem that had become increasingly problematic in the "Age of Jackson"—patronage. As early as the Washington administration, patronage had been used to gain loyalty to the general government. Alexander Hamilton knew that federal money and jobs would ensure obedience to the new central authority and reduce the natural American disposition to independence. As the government began to hire more people and segments of society became wealthier through federal economic policies, loyalty to the government increased.

Then Andrew Jackson took the "spoils system" to another level. In the first year of his administration alone Jackson removed over nine hundred bureaucrats from federal appointments and replaced them with political sycophants. Tyler viewed this as dangerous because it removed the "complete separation...between the sword and the purse." A president who could skirt the boundaries of the law by appointing and firing people at will for differences about public policy created a concentration of power "in the hands of a single man." An "army of officeholders spread over the land" would reduce the liberty of the people and leave them at the mercy of a bureaucracy beholden to the executive for their subsistence and subject "the course of State legislation to the dictation of the chief executive officer and making the will of that officer absolute and supreme."

In other words, Tyler feared a despotic demagogue wielding an army of unelected administrators to do his partisan bidding. Tyler urged Congress to implement civil service reform—something that would not happen for another four decades—and promised to be a vigilant guardian of the public trust by removing overtly partisan political operatives from their positions in government. This did not sit well with the political class, but it aligned perfectly with Tyler's conception of government service and political statesmanship. The Constitution cannot be defended by politically ambitious or corrupt rent-seekers. Tyler was ahead of his time.

Tyler emphasized economy in government in order to reduce the public debt, particularly in peacetime, and forcefully recommended the elimination of sinecures. All spending, he argued, should be for specific purposes and "explicit, so as to leave as limited a share of discretion to the disbursing agents as may be found compatible with the public service." Tyler also considered fraud to be a grave offence, and insisted that, "A strict responsibility on the part of all the agents of the Government should be maintained and peculation or defalcation visited with immediate expulsion from office and the most condign punishment." No $700 toilet seats, $450 hammers, expensive off-the-books booze-filled parties, or multi-million-dollar presidential vacations allowed.[5]

THE BANK, THE TARIFF, AND "INTERNAL IMPROVEMENTS"

Tyler then went to work defending the Constitution. No issue was causing more excitement, controversy, or comment than the attempt to re-charter a Bank of the United States. The Second Bank of the United States had died a slow and painful death in 1836. Jackson had ultimately won his war with the "Monster Bank." The Bank War had caused instability in the American financial sector and it was partly blamed for the severe economic downturn of 1837. Jackson's successor, the Democrat Martin Van Buren, floated a "subtreasury" plan (for U.S. government agents, rather than either national or state banks, to hold federal deposits) that was adopted by Congress and signed into law in 1840, but not without a protracted legislative fight that lasted for most of his administration.

A preference for a central banking system had been a core element of the Whig Party almost since its inception. But not all Whigs were economic nationalists. Many of the leading Whigs from the South, including Tyler, differed with Henry Clay's "American System." Clay believed that an active central government could ensure the economic prosperity of the American people through protective tariffs, federally funded "internal improvements," and a central bank. This economic nationalism was nothing more than a repackaging and rebranding of Alexander Hamilton's financial system, made infamous during the Washington administration. Jeffersonians had always considered every element of the Hamiltonian system to be unconstitutional. That hadn't changed in 1841.

Clay and the Whigs controlled the Congress when Tyler assumed the presidency. Their rise to power had been a slow process, but two "panics"—1837 and 1839—had inspired the American public to put the Whigs in control of both the executive and legislative branches with a charge to "fix" the American economy. Whig propaganda had been very effective. During the 1840 campaign, Van Buren was portrayed as a pseudo-king, a man who ate with golden spoons and rode in fancy carriages and whose unchecked executive authority had destroyed the Constitution. The 1840 presidential race was the first modern campaign in American history, featuring amusing slogans, songs, and badges that attempted to sway the public to vote for Harrison and Tyler over the "aristocrat" Van Buren. One jingle quipped, "In English coaches he's [Harrison] no rider but he can fight and drink hard cider." In fact neither Harrison nor Tyler was a "log cabin" frontiersman. Both came from prominent American families that traced their lineage to the earliest settlements in Virginia, but the folksy, homespun, and frankly disingenuous messages worked. The Whigs' focus on image over substance hid their real agenda, but Tyler was not willing to violate his oath or his principles to support an unconstitutional economic model.

Clay was drunk with power in 1841. This was his moment, and he was not going to let an "accidental" president deny his legislative accomplishments. Tyler was willing to compromise supporting an initial plan that would have chartered a central bank in the city of Washington but permitted the states to refuse to allow branches of the bank within their jurisdictions without their consent. The Congress controlled Washington, D.C., and thus could legislate for the capital city, but this did not mean that

Congress could constitutionally incorporate a bank within its limits. Such a power was not delegated to the legislative branch in the Constitution. Still, this compromise muted the constitutional objection to a central bank because the states did not have to subscribe to the institution. But still Tyler wasn't going far enough for Clay, who balked and refused to support a banking system that allowed the states to reject any part of the plan.

Congress was therefore at a deadlock, and Tyler remained firm in his opposition to a revitalization of a Bank of the United States on the Hamiltonian model. Tyler had made clear his opposition to a central banking system during the 1840 campaign, but one longtime friend, John Minor Botts of Virginia, insisted that Tyler had told him while the two bunked together at a hotel in 1840 that he would support a national bank. Botts thought he could forge a compromise between the president and the Congress, and so he ventured to the White House and, according to his account, gained a verbal commitment to an amendment he offered in Congress just days later. It would create a national bank and would allow the states to reject branches within their borders but only if they did so within the first session after the new bank was chartered. Otherwise, silence would be read as consent.

Congress passed a bank bill with Botts's amendment by only three votes in the Senate. It satisfied neither Clay's national Whigs nor the states' rights faction of the Party, including Tyler. For years historians have argued that Tyler led the Whigs astray at this critical moment—but that assessment depends on believing Botts's story over Tyler's. The president had no reason to lie, and vetoing a bill he had supported would have been political suicide—not to mention, a sign of clinical insanity. Tyler made up his mind to veto the bill even before it left Congress, but he waited the full ten days provided by the Constitution before he issued his veto. As his secretary delivered the message to the Senate chamber, the senators stopped their work to listen. The message was pure strict constructionist bliss.

Tyler began his veto message by stating, "The power of Congress to create a national bank to operate *per se* over the Union has been a question of dispute from the origin of the Government.... [and] my own opinion has been uniformly proclaimed to be against the exercise of any such power by this Government." Tyler then pointed out that his oath to "preserve, protect, and defend the Constitution" prohibited him from signing a bill containing provisions he had long deemed to be unconstitutional. Should he change course at this time, Tyler insisted, he would surrender "all claim to the respect of honorable men, all confidence on the part of the people, all self-respect, all regard for moral and religious obligations, without an observance of which no government can be prosperous and no people can be happy. It would be to commit a crime which I would not willfully commit to gain any earthly reward, and which would justly subject me to the ridicule and scorn of all virtuous men."[6]

After listing his objections to several components of the bill, notably those that forced the states to accept bank branches without their consent, Tyler concluded, "I regard the bill as asserting for Congress the right to incorporate a United States bank with power and right to establish offices of discount and deposit in the several States of this Union with or without their consent—a principle to which I have always heretofore been opposed and which can never obtain my sanction...."[7] After the message was read, a few cheers mixed with hisses from the chamber. One pro-administration senator imprudently moved to arrest those whose verbal outbursts had offended the president and his message. A drunken mob gathered at the executive mansion that night to protest the veto, and Tyler was burned in effigy a day later.[8] Today, such a scene would result in an immediate arrest and perhaps a Justice Department "hate crime" investigation.

Tyler coolly responded with a speech that downplayed the incident. Several participants were rounded up and thrown in jail, but when they were brought to trial, Tyler issued a letter to the court which excused their behavior within their right of free speech and suggested that none of the men should face prosecution. The charges were immediately dropped and the defendants issued an apology.[9]

Clay did not behave as gracefully. His failed attempt to have the veto overridden was probably little more than an opportunity to publicly lambaste Tyler for his supposed inconsistencies. The public and other members of Congress regarded Clay's behavior as a lengthy temper tantrum disguised as a firm stand against Tyler's principles and his character. Tyler, Clay said, should just resign. And other Whigs accused Tyler of selfishly attempting to splinter the Whig Party to gain ascendency for himself— suggesting that the veto was a calculated move for purely personal gain. How anyone could come to this conclusion is beyond comprehension. Tyler gained only scorn from most men in his own Whig Party with his move against the Bank, and Democrats, while applauding the veto, still did not trust Tyler because he had abandoned them and joined their arch-nemesis Clay in the Whig Party. Tyler had insisted both publicly and privately since before the 1840 election that he would oppose a national bank. His veto was consistent with his principles and his determination to uphold the oath of office. We should take a man with such deep convictions at his word.

The Whigs moved quickly to pass another bank bill. Unfortunately, Tyler had given mixed messages in cabinet meetings, leading to another round of contentious political wrangling. The public pressure against him may have caused Tyler to waffle a bit at this juncture. He was being excoriated in the press, scolded in the Congress, and lambasted in the cabinet. He told Secretary of State Daniel Webster that if the Congress could meet a series of demands in regard to another bank bill, he might sign it, but he thought it would be better to wait until the next session to let the smoke clear. Webster immediately approached House leaders with Tyler's recommendations, and on September 3, 1841, they rammed through a bill that they believed would theoretically meet the president's approval. They were wrong.

Tyler set the bill aside for six days while preparing a second veto message. This bill created a stronger national bank than the first, and Tyler, though interested in "compromise," pointed out that his "constitutional duty" required him to veto the bill. Tyler then provided a lengthy explanation of the veto power, perhaps the best summary written since the ratifying debates of 1787 and 1788. He wrote:

> I readily admit that whilst the qualified veto with which the Chief Magistrate is invested should be regarded and was intended by the wise men who made it a part of the Constitution as a great conservative principle of our system, *without the exercise of which on important occasions a mere representative majority might urge the Government in its legislation beyond the limits fixed by its framers or might exert its just powers too hastily or oppressively*, yet it is a power which ought to be most cautiously exerted, and perhaps never except in a case eminently involving the public interest or one in which the oath of the President, acting under his convictions, both mental and moral, imperiously requires its exercise. In such a case he has no alternative. *He must either exert the negative power intrusted to him by the Constitution chiefly for its own preservation, protection, and defense or commit an act of gross moral turpitude. Mere regard to the will of a majority must not in a constitutional republic like ours control this sacred and solemn duty of a sworn officer....* [The veto] must be exerted against the will of a mere representative majority or not at all. It is alone in pursuance of that will that any measure can reach the President, and to say that because a majority in Congress have passed a bill he should therefore sanction it is to abrogate the power altogether and to render its insertion in the Constitution a work of absolute supererogation. The duty is to guard the fundamental will of the people themselves from (in this case, I admit, unintentional) change or infraction by a majority in Congress; and in that light alone do I regard the constitutional duty which I now most reluctantly discharge.[10] [emphasis added]

In a few sentences, Tyler affirmed the veto power as an executive check against the tyranny of the majority, a tool that should be used to *defend* the Constitution and the American people from oppressive or hasty unconstitutional legislation. Like Jefferson, Tyler believed that the president had a constitutional obligation to veto any and all unconstitutional legislation that crossed his desk. He had taken an oath to "preserve, protect and defend the Constitution of the United States," and fulfilling that oath required giving the negative to unconstitutional legislation. This is precisely the way the veto power was sold to the states during ratification. Tyler had concluded that the bank bill violated the delegated powers of Congress by attempting to incorporate a national bank, the constitutionality of which had long been in dispute. Congress, he said, had no power to create corporations of a national character.

Tyler knew that this second veto of a national bank could be a fatal blow to his political career. The closing paragraph of his veto message hinted at the probable outcome. "I will take this occasion to declare that the conclusions to which I have brought myself are those of a settled conviction, founded, in my opinion, on a just view of the Constitution; that in arriving at it I have been actuated by no other motive or desire than to uphold the institutions of the country as they have come down to us from the hands of our godlike ancestors, and that I shall esteem my efforts to sustain them, even though I perish, more honorable than to win the applause of men by a sacrifice of my duty and my conscience."[11] "Duty," "conscience," and the "desire...to uphold the institutions of the country as they have come down to us" were more important than the "applause" of the moment. Tyler was a statesman, and the politicians of the Whig Party, led by Clay, punished him for it.

The Whig response is perhaps the most bizarre and certainly the most partisan display of spite for a sitting president in American history. In contrast to congressional action against Nixon and Clinton, it had nothing to do with illegal abuse of power or a violation of the law. The nationalist Whigs hated Tyler because he would not toe the party line, and they wanted him out of office, period. Two days after Tyler's second veto message, the Whigs convened a committee charged with drafting resolutions expelling the president from the Whig Party. More than fifty members of the Party met on September 13 at the steps of the Capitol building and issued a statement to the American people denouncing Tyler's policies and actions as president and formally expelling him from the Party. The group hoped that "vast numbers of our fellow citizens, who have been hitherto separated from us, will unite with us under such a glorious standard; and that majorities in both houses of congress sufficiently large may be secured to carry any measure demanded by the welfare of the nation, in spite of the interposition of the power with which any one man may have been accidentally invested."[12]

Henry Clay wasn't finished with Tyler. On the day Tyler issued his veto, Secretary of the Navy George Badger had organized a supper party at his home for the members of the cabinet and Henry Clay. Everyone but the postmaster general attended. The group decided, reportedly at Clay's insistence, that they would all resign in dramatic fashion. Daniel Webster, who had no intention of leaving his post as secretary of state at this time, withdrew from the event before this decision was made. Webster and Clay had been at odds over their treatment of the president, and more importantly over who was the real leader of the Whig Party. Webster was not happy with Tyler's veto of the second bank bill, but he had an independent streak and accordingly determined to resist Clay's political stunt, the point of which was to embarrass Tyler and force *him* to resign.

For five hours on September 11, 1841, the members of the cabinet filed one by one into Tyler's office and offered their resignations, which he gladly accepted. When Webster stepped into the room he asked Tyler, "Where am I to go, Mr. President?" to which Tyler responded, "You must decide that for yourself, Mr. Webster." Webster had already determined to stay, and Tyler, who had no ill feelings toward him or any other member of the cabinet (though he privately wanted all of them to resign), stood, and in a gesture of true statesmanship stuck out his hand and said, "Give me your hand on that, and I will say to you that Henry Clay is a doomed man."[13] Webster eventually would resign, but not before completing an important treaty with Great Britain that established a permanent border between Canada and the United States in 1842.

Clay's plan to get rid of Tyler failed. Tyler did not believe he had to step down just because the overwhelming majority of the cabinet had resigned. On the contrary, the resignations emboldened the president and allowed him to appoint sympathetic voices to a new cabinet, chief among them fellow Virginian Abel P. Upshur, a man of little renown today but one of the more important states' rights advocates of his generation. By the time of the resignations, Tyler already had a slate of candidates ready to go to the Senate for approval. They were quickly confirmed, leaving Clay embarrassed and Tyler firmly in control of his own destiny as president. That had been his agenda from the beginning.

Tyler wielded a potent veto pen for the remainder of his administration. In August 1842 he vetoed a bill which would have increased the tariff to levels that were unacceptable to virtually everyone but leading American industrialists. Attached to the bill were provisions to close the federal deficit and balance the budget. The deficit was projected to reach stratospheric levels the following year (about $16 billion in 2015 dollars), and something had to be done to close the gap. Tyler had long been opposed to protective tariffs and held the 1833 compromise tariff to be sacrosanct. As a senator from Virginia, Tyler had opposed the Tariff of 1832 and supported South Carolina's nullification effort. He was not going to betray his deeply held convictions on the matter, but the Whigs in Congress wanted to force the issue to lay the blame at his feet should the legislation fail and the budget remain out of balance. As in previous political battles, Tyler would win, but not before a comedy of errors enacted by the Whig-controlled Congress.

Tyler's veto message again relied on sound constitutional principles. He had already vetoed a stop-gap tariff bill in June because it violated the Constitution, and the August bill not only increased the tariff but added a provision for "unconditional distribution of the land proceeds"—recklessly distributing federal resources at a time when "the Treasury is in a state of extreme embarrassment, requiring every dollar which it can make available, and when the government not only has to lay additional taxes, but to borrow money to meet pressing demands." Tyler called the provision "highly impolitic, if not unconstitutional."[14] The language of the veto message, however, was not as firm as that of his previous veto messages and the Congress seized the opportunity to rake him over the coals again. The historian Oliver Chitwood aptly described the situation:

> The Whig leaders in Congress proceeded to act on the assumption that Tyler had again betrayed his party and to punish him for this alleged treason. To talk of a President's disloyalty to a party from which he had been expelled would under ordinary circumstances have appealed irresistibly to the sense of humor of politicians. But by this time the hatred which the Whigs had for Tyler seems to have paralyzed their risibles, and in all seriousness they undertook to flay him for his political irregularity.[15]

Tyler's old friend turned political foe John Minor Botts drafted impeachment articles. The charge? Tyler had had the audacity to use the constitutional power of the veto in the manner the founding generation suggested it would be used. Botts's resolution to convene a committee to explore formally impeaching Tyler failed in the House by a crushing majority. The Whigs' vengeful behavior was bordering on lunacy and virtually everyone, Whig and Democrat alike, could see it.

The House of Representatives did, however, appoint a committee of thirteen led by the irascible John Quincy Adams—a man who called Tyler a "slave-monger"—that condemned Tyler's use of executive power and suggested that Tyler *deserved* to be impeached. The Whigs also floated a constitutional amendment that would have negated the veto power by reducing from two-thirds to a mere majority the number of votes needed for an override. Tyler immediately penned a protest defending his actions as constitutional. Tyler requested that his protest be logged into the official journal of the House. His request was denied, and the Congress censured him for his actions, though the censure passed by only eight votes. As Tyler himself pointed out, if the Congress was so offended by his "illegal acts," they should have impeached him.

Tyler's final use of the veto occurred in 1844, this time on an "internal improvements" bill. Congress had passed legislation that would have allocated federal funds for the "improvement of certain harbors and rivers." Tyler considered the bill unconstitutional. He had opposed "internal improvement" legislation throughout his political career, and his veto provided the chance to explain his position. "At the adoption of the Constitution," he wrote, "each State was possessed of a separate and independent sovereignty and an exclusive jurisdiction over all streams and water courses within its territorial limits. The Articles of Confederation in no way affected this authority or jurisdiction, and the present Constitution, adopted for the purpose of correcting the defects which existed in the original Articles, expressly reserves to the States all powers not delegated. No such surrender of jurisdiction is made by the States to this Government by any express grant, and if it is possessed it is to be deduced from the clause in the Constitution which invests Congress with authority 'to make all laws which are necessary and proper for carrying into execution' the granted powers."[16]

Tyler's opinion paralleled that of James Madison and James Monroe, who had both vetoed "internal improvements" bills while president. They insisted that any federal legislation to this effect was illegal without an amendment to the Constitution. No "internal improvements" amendment has ever been ratified, but the current general government spends billions annually on roads and other "internal improvements" projects without any hesitation about their constitutionality. Americans have become so accustomed to this type of unconstitutional federal legislation that Tyler's veto is a quaint relic of the past. But his was still a viable constitutional position to take until 1861.

TEXAS

The annexation of Texas represented the signature achievement of the Tyler administration. Texas achieved its independence from Mexico in 1836 and immediately petitioned the United States for annexation. The United States officially recognized the government of Texas in 1837, but the Congress twice rejected her overtures for admission to the Union, and eventually Texas withdrew the petition. When Tyler assumed office in 1841, Texas had been an independent republic for five years. Her principles and government were on the American model, and she was led by a hearty group of settlers from the United States, including the famous war hero Sam Houston. It was Houston who had suggested that Texas stop courting the United States in 1837, though he never stopped advocating annexation.

Tyler firmly believed that Texas should be added to the Union and broached the subject with Secretary of State Webster almost immediately after taking office. Webster did not support annexation—nor did many Northern men, because they feared that the large territory would bolster Southern interests in the Congress and relegate New England to backwater status in the government. The South had controlled the executive branch either formally or informally for nearly the entire history of the United States, the lone exceptions being the brief Adams administrations. And beginning in 1801 it had also dominated the Congress. At this juncture party still trumped section—there were many Southern Whigs who favored Henry Clay's "American System" of high tariffs, a national bank, and "internal improvements"—but that alliance was fragile and the majority of the South was opposed to the nationalist Whig program. Adding at least two more Southern senators and a host of House members did not appeal to Northern nationalists.

Tyler remained undeterred. After Daniel Webster resigned in 1843, Tyler appointed his own political ally Abel Upshur as secretary of state. Upshur was as interested in Texas as Tyler, and though he found the office to be draining, he pursued annexation with vigor. The situation in Texas necessitated a determined effort if the United States was going to be successful in bringing the republic into the Union. In 1842, Texas submitted two more proposals for annexation. Both were rejected. Texas then began courting the British, possibly to make the United States jealous but more likely because Texas needed military support. Mexico had never recognized Texan independence and had been rattling her sabers about a possible invasion of the Lone Star republic for several years.

Upshur agreed with the Texas government on the outlines of a treaty, and Tyler pledged military support, going so far as to dispatch both the navy and army to the region to protect against Mexican incursions along the border. Diplomatic negotiations were complicated by Upshur's death in a naval accident in early 1844. Tyler then appointed John C. Calhoun as secretary of state, and Calhoun was able to complete Upshur's work in early April 1844. Tyler submitted a treaty of annexation to the Senate. It was rejected.

The issue of slavery had become a vexing problem in American politics in the early 1840s. Texas was explicitly tied to the issue. Texas was a slaveholding republic, and the possibility—if the state joined the Union—of at least one if not several new slave states sent Northern abolitionists into a frothing rage. Tyler and Calhoun further complicated the issue by defending the potential acquisition explicitly as a way to protect slave property in the United States. Yet the slavery issue did not decide the Senate vote to reject the treaty. The vote split on purely partisan lines, with Southern Whigs voting in line with their Northern comrades. National politics certainly played a role. The Whigs had already nominated Henry Clay for president, and he had come out decidedly against the annexation of Texas. To Southern Whigs, party loyalty superseded sectional devotion.

Whigs thought they had sealed the fate of Texas. But Tyler still had hope and quickly began pushing for a joint resolution of Congress to bring this sister republic into the Union. In June he sent all materials relating to the failed treaty to the House of Representatives and urged them to come to a prompt conclusion, adding that "while I regarded the annexation to be accomplished by treaty as the most suitable form in which it could be effected…" he would support "any other expedient compatible with the Constitution and likely to accomplish the object.…"[17] The Senate protested, with Senator Thomas Hart Benton of Missouri suggesting that Tyler's appeal to the House of Representatives was unconstitutional and worthy of impeachment.

The 1844 presidential election sealed the deal. Democrat James K. Polk was elected on an expansionist platform, making the annexation of Texas certain in the next administration. In December 1844, Tyler recommended that Congress pass a joint resolution annexing Texas. "A controlling majority of the people and a large majority of the States have declared in favor of immediate annexation," he wrote, and Texas "Free and independent herself…asks to be received into our Union."[18] Congress acted quickly. The House passed a joint resolution bill in January 1845, and though the Senate debated the measure more strenuously, it eventually capitulated and sent a finalized joint resolution bill to Tyler in March 1845, a bill he gladly signed. Texas agreed to enter the Union in October.

Texas had been annexed to the United States, but the constitutional question remained. Did Congress have the constitutional authority to skip the treaty process and acquire Texas by a simple majority vote? Did Tyler sign an unconstitutional bill into law? Critics believed the entire process after the Senate rejected the treaty was a blatant abuse of executive power. But they were on shaky ground. As Tyler insisted, the treaty method was the preferable course in admitting Texas into the Union, but Article IV, Section 3, of the Constitution explicitly states that "New States may be admitted by the Congress into this Union." A joint resolution was perfectly consistent with the Constitution as ratified by the founding generation so long as Texas, an independent republic, agreed to enter the Union with other states. It did. All states, whether carved out of existing United States territory or already existing as free and independent republics, had to accede to the compact. The thirteen original states did so in 1787 and 1788. Texas was following protocol and entered the Union "on an equal footing with the existing states." Tyler did nothing illegal or unconstitutional during the entire process.

If Mt. Rushmore could be re-carved according to the simple yet lofty standard of "defending their oath," John Tyler would have to be given a place next to Washington and Jefferson. No such accolades awaited the tenth president. He retired in 1845 and disappeared from public life until the events that led to the War Between the States stirred him to action. Tyler worked to avoid war, but when Virginia seceded in April 1861, Tyler supported the actions of his native state and was elected to the Confederate Congress. He died shortly thereafter. The Confederate government recognized his death, but the Lincoln administration remained silent. The Union army responded by plundering his property, his only reward from the government he once led. Tyler remained faithful until his last breath to the Constitution as ratified by the founding generation. His presidency should be emulated for its consistency, not only in Tyler's steadfast determination to adhere to his oath of office, but in his unwavering belief that the powers of the general government, including those of the executive office, should be strictly limited. That would be a wonderful change of pace.

CHAPTER 12

GROVER CLEVELAND

Twenty-Second and Twenty-Fourth
President, 1885–1889 and 1893–1897

L ike John Tyler, Cleveland is better known for trivial reasons than for
what is really important in his presidential record. He was the man who
served two non-consecutive terms; he was the first man married in the
White House; and his daughter, Ruth, inspired the Baby Ruth candy bar.
Recent historical presidential rankings have Cleveland in the middle of the
pack. Allan Nevins, whose 1933 biography of Cleveland, titled *A Study in
Courage*, is still considered the standard treatment, wrote that Cleveland
"was too conservative to be a great constructive statesman."[1] Historian
Mark W. Summers said in a 2005 History Channel documentary on Cleve-
land that "I just wish he had only been elected to one term. I think the
second term was a great misfortune to him and the country." Those on the
Left cannot stand him, which is precisely why conservative Americans

should pay attention to the last Jeffersonian to occupy the executive office. Woodrow Wilson once wrote, "You may think Cleveland's administration was Democratic. It was not. Cleveland was a conservative Republican."[2] Translation: Cleveland was not a progressive and did not illegally usurp power from the other branches of governments and the states at large. Coming from Wilson, this is a ringing endorsement.

Cleveland was the first Democrat elected president since James Buchanan in 1856. He assumed office with the bitter taste of Reconstruction still in the air and at the precipice of the "Gilded Age." Americans had become weary of corruption and scandal in government. They had a right to be. Two previous presidents had been assassinated, several leading members of Congress and one vice president had been indicted for corruption, the fusion of finance and government was creating an economic climate destructive to middle class Americans, and Congress was spending money like drunken sailors on shore leave. The Constitution had been ignored for years, and confidence in government at all levels was at historical lows. Cleveland promised to turn things around in Washington, D.C. He thought American politics attracted two classes of men: a class of "spoilsmen, little and big, all the disappointed office seekers after personal interest, all those hoping to gain personal ends, and all those who desire a return to the old, corrupt, and repudiated order of things in party management"; and a class of, "the true and earnest men."[3] He was nicknamed "Grover the Good," and Joseph Pulitzer's four reasons for endorsing Cleveland in the 1884 election cycle were "1. He is an honest man. 2. He is an honest man. 3. He is an honest man. 4. He is an honest man."[4]

Cleveland issued more vetoes than all the men who had previously held the office *combined*. Why? Because Congress kept passing unconstitutional legislation, and Cleveland had taken an oath to "preserve, protect and defend the Constitution," not some pet congressional project. To Cleveland, the veto was a wrecking ball to be wielded in obligation to his oath. Most of the vetoes were issued against pension bills, a form of government welfare Cleveland despised. He also waged war with Congress over the unconstitutional Tenure of Office Act and ultimately forced its repeal. Cleveland suggested legislation to Congress but never had a legislative agenda codified by some slogan to make it popular with the American people. That would come in later administrations. He also worked to block the annexation of Hawaii. The pro-American government there had come to power through illegitimate means, and Cleveland thought that the United States should not support clandestine operations in foreign policy. Cleveland argued that sound government should be the aim both at home and abroad.

While Cleveland never wrote a treatise on his political philosophy, he believed in what he called "true Democracy." Its principles included "the limitation of Federal power under the Constitution, the absolute necessity of public economy, the safety of a sound currency, honesty in public place, the responsibility of public servants to the people, care for the people who toil with their hands, a proper limitation of corporate privileges, and a reform in the civil service."[5] Cleveland added to this list an independent executive branch charged with defending the interests of the states and the people against politically motivated attacks on the Constitution. No man to this point in American history had worked harder as president— he sometimes worked twenty-hour days—and no man in the Gilded Age better exemplified the Founders' executive than Cleveland. He twice righted a distressed ship lost in the fog of corruption.

DEFENDING HIS OATH

Cleveland set the tone for his eight years in office in his first inaugural address. "In the discharge of my official duty," he said, "I shall endeavor to be guided by a just and unrestrained construction of the Constitution, a careful observance of the distinction between the powers granted to the Federal government and those reserved to the State or to the people, and by a cautious appreciation of those functions which, by the Constitution and laws, have been especially assigned to the executive branch of the government."[6] His belief in a strong executive branch within its defined sphere of influence guided the Cleveland administrations through turbulent political waters. The Congress had successfully usurped power from the executive branch in the preceding decades, and though the founding generation considered the legislative branch to be the most important and powerful of the three, they never intended it to have unchecked authority over the general government. Cleveland immediately ensured that the president would be an independent voice in Washington.

His first line of attack was on the Tenure of Office Act, passed in 1867 in an effort to restrain President Andrew Johnson and softened in 1869 after Republican U. S. Grant took office. Cleveland considered the law to be a grave affront to both good government and the separation of powers. The Constitution states that the president may "nominate, and by and with the Advice and Consent of the Senate, shall appoint Ambassadors, other public Ministers and Consuls, Judges of the supreme Court, and all other Officers of the United States, whose Appointments are not herein otherwise provided for, and which shall be established by Law...." Nothing, however, is said about *removing* said "Officers of the United States" once the Senate has confirmed the nominations.

To the Congress, the Constitution's silence implied the power to restrict presidential authority in regard to executive appointments. The Tenure of Office Act did just that. It was little more than a partisan tool designed to keep Republicans in office should Democrats take control of the White House. At its core, Reconstruction was a struggle for political supremacy in Washington, D.C., and in the states. Elections came with spoils, and corruption quickly followed. The Tenure of Office Act was used as the centerpiece of the Andrew Johnson impeachment case, and while the 1869 revision had removed several horrendous and blatantly unconstitutional provisions of the law, it still infringed on the president's control of his cabinet and the executive branch. The president could terminate federal appointees while the Senate was in recess, but he had to submit a suitable list of potential replacements to the Senate within thirty days for the removal to stick. Essentially, once "hired," executive branch employees could not be "fired" without the consent of the Senate.

In January 1885, the Senate issued a resolution demanding all documents pertaining to the removal of the United States District Attorney of southern Alabama. Cleveland, senators charged, had acted in a partisan manner and had broken the law. Four more resolutions followed, each an attempt by Senate Republicans to kneecap Cleveland and the executive branch. Cleveland expertly repulsed their attack. He issued a special message to the Senate on March 1, 1886, challenging the constitutionality of the Tenure of Office Act. "I believe," he wrote, "the power to remove or suspend such officials is vested in the President alone by the Constitution, which in express terms provides that 'the executive power shall be vested in a President of the United States of America,' and that 'he shall take care that the laws be faithfully executed.'" Cleveland conceded that the Senate had the authority to check the power of the executive branch, but that authority was limited by the language of the Constitution and applied only to the powers to "advise and consent" and hold impeachment trials. The Tenure of Office Act created "express and special grant of... extraordinary powers, not in any way related to or growing out of general Senatorial duty, and in itself a departure from the general plan of our Government..." and therefore "should be held, under a familiar maxim of construction, to exclude every other right of interference with Executive functions."

Cleveland insisted that the law be repealed, arguing that he was "not responsible to the Senate" and thus was "unwilling to submit my actions and official conduct to them for judgment." This was an important statement. Cleveland was asserting his independency and reaffirming the separation of powers between the legislative and executive branches. He never denied that he had a responsibility to execute the laws passed by Congress, but Cleveland correctly understood that only *constitutional* laws had to be enforced. The Tenure of Office Act did not pass that test. He wrapped up his message to the lawmakers by pointing out that if the Congress disagreed with his stance they could impeach him. Otherwise,

Cleveland was going to follow the Constitution and adhere to his oath to protect and defend the document.[7] Within a year, Cleveland gladly signed a bill repealing the law. His argument had won the day.

This was the opening salvo in what would be a contentious two terms in office, particularly in regard to the president's relationship with the Senate. One famous anecdote was of Cleveland's wife waking him in the middle of the night to warn him of "burglars in the house!" Cleveland gently responded, "No, my dear. In the Senate maybe, but not in the House."[8] Cleveland, however, tended to let Congress legislate without trying to influence them directly. His detachment from the legislative process was by design. The president, he reasoned, could recommend measures to Congress, but it was not the responsibility of the executive office to see them through. He could—and would—deploy the veto against legislative overreach, but like Jefferson, Cleveland was not going to get into the political trenches with Congress. Cleveland made his position clear in his first annual message to Congress: "While the Executive may recommend such measures as he shall deem expedient, the responsibility for legislative action must and should rest upon those selected by the people to make their laws."[9] When Congress failed to act on his recommendations, Cleveland did nothing. But when they exceeded their charge constitutionally, he had a deep well of ink and a sharp pen at hand.

THE TARIFF AND WELFARE

Cleveland believed he had a sacred charge to block government patronage and handouts in all forms. He thought that using the power of the government to enrich some at the expense of others was not only immoral but potentially unconstitutional. Tariffs were an example of this type of government redistribution. The Democratic Party had traditionally held protective tariffs to be unconstitutional—little more than government handouts to rich industrialists who stood to gain from a reduction in foreign competition for their goods. In his first annual message to Congress, Cleveland wrote that excessive taxation in the form of tariffs violated the principles of republican government:

> It is the duty of those serving the people in public place to closely limit public expenditures to the actual needs of the Government economically administered, because this bounds the right of the Government to exact tribute from the earnings of labor or the property of the citizen, and because public extravagance begets extravagance among the people.... and that our system of revenue shall be so adjusted as to relieve the people of unnecessary taxation, having a due regard to the interests of capital invested and workingmen employed in American industries, and preventing the accumulation of a surplus in the Treasury to tempt extravagance and waste.[10]

Some members of Congress were receptive to tariff reduction during Cleveland's first term, but there were enough Republicans and protectionist Democrats in the Congress to block a tariff reform bill. Cleveland blocked all of the protectionist Democrats from government patronage and then decided to make tariff reduction the centerpiece of his reelection campaign in 1888. This was not a particularly "sexy" issue. Tariff reform did not have the political voltage of identity politics, but Cleveland thought unconstitutional government waste should be a primary issue for the American voter. Taxes destroyed American enterprise and initiative and reduced wages. That alone should have made the electorate take notice.

Cleveland sent his third annual address to the Congress in December 1887. It was devoted exclusively to tariff reduction, and it read like an anti-tax manifesto. "The public Treasury," he wrote, "which should only exist as a conduit conveying the people's tribute to its legitimate objects of expenditure, becomes a hoarding place for money needlessly withdrawn from trade and the people's use, thus crippling our national energies, suspending our country's development, preventing investment in productive enterprise, threatening financial disturbance, and inviting schemes of public plunder." The tariff represented a "vicious, inequitable and illogical source of unnecessary taxation." Congress, he asserted, should act immediately to reduce taxes and return those dollars to the pockets of the American working class.[11]

Congress listened but failed to act. Another tariff reform bill died in the Republican-controlled Senate, but Cleveland believed he had fulfilled his constitutional responsibility as president. This is where historians tend to rattle off invective about his "do-nothing" stance. If Cleveland had only used the bully pulpit to harangue congressional leaders and rammed his "agenda" through the halls of Congress, he might have accomplished something, but Cleveland let Congress legislate and his recommendations ended up in the Senate waste receptacle. In reality, Cleveland should be admired for this stance. According to the Constitution, the president has no power to initiate legislation. Cleveland accepted the limitations the Constitution places on the executive because not doing so would have resulted in an unconstitutional usurpation of power from the Congress. He did not always like the outcome, but Congress could choose how to receive his recommendations.

His plan to use the tariff issue to win reelection backfired. Cleveland was defeated in the 1888 election—probably with the help of extensive voter fraud—but by the time he was re-nominated by the Democrats in 1892 the tariff had once again become a contentious issue. The Republicans had passed the McKinley Tariff, a highly protective measure that created a system of government handouts for already wealthy industrialists, in 1892. The Democrats protested the measure and made their opposition to it a core component of their Party platform. "We declare...that the Federal Government has no constitutional power to impose and collect tariff duties, except for the purpose of revenue only, and we demand that the collection of such taxes shall be limited to the necessities of the Government when honestly and economically administered."[12]

For his part, Cleveland rejected the tariff statement in the platform, but did not make his own position on the tariff explicit. In fact he did not think protective measures were necessarily unconstitutional, but he did consider the McKinley Tariff, with its 49 percent levies on almost all imported industrial goods, to be a bad and immoral policy. After he secured reelection in 1892, Cleveland uncharacteristically went to work crafting tariff legislation. He would not partake in the legislative debates, but he had William L. Wilson of West Virginia present "his" tariff bill to the House in 1893. The bill would be chopped, sliced, and diced in both the House and the Senate. Cleveland remained relatively silent, though he wrote a letter late in the game expressing disappointment that so many Democrats had ultimately abandoned "the cause of the principles upon which" the success of the Democratic Party relied.[13]

When this Frankenstein bill finally made it to the White House as the "Wilson-Gorman Tariff Bill," Cleveland refused to sign it. Signing it would have signaled that Cleveland agreed with the content. He did not veto it either. His veto would not have been overridden, meaning that the abhorrent McKinley Tariff would have remained in effect. So the bill became law without any explicit support from the president. This was probably the best course of action, constitutionally. Modern presidents would have issued a long signing statement with the bill outlining how they disagreed with certain provisions and would thus choose not to enforce them. That tactic is an abuse of executive power. Cleveland did not think the bill was unconstitutional. He deemed it bad policy and a betrayal of the Democratic Party platform, but bad policy did not warrant a veto, and a signing statement was out of the question. Cleveland can be faulted for breaking his pledge to leave legislation to the legislature, but he acted properly in letting the controversial legislation become law without interference. The Democratic platform articulated the proper constitutional position. Cleveland disagreed. Given his belief that the tariff bill was constitutional, though bad policy, his action in allowing the bill to become law maintained his principled stand on the proper role of the executive in the legislative process, as established by the Washington administration—let all constitutional legislation pass and veto the rest. He would do just that 584 times.

Cleveland has received the harshest criticism from historians for vetoing a Texas seed bill in 1887. The bill would have provided federal funds to help drought-stricken Texas farmers procure seed for the upcoming planting season. The amount was minimal—$10,000—but Cleveland viewed it as an unconstitutional appropriation of funds. He famously wrote, "I can find no warrant for such an appropriation in the Constitution, and I do not believe that the power and duty of the General Government ought to be extended to the relief of individual suffering which is in no manner properly related to the public service or benefit. A prevalent tendency to disregard the limited mission of this power and duty should, I think, be steadfastly resisted, to the end that the lesson should be constantly enforced that though the people support the Government the Government should not support the people."[14]

Progressives went mad over Cleveland's supposed indifference to the common man. Government, after all, should be used to alleviate the suffering of the people and soften the rigors of "natural selection." As the famous progressive thinking Lester Frank Ward postulated, government could be used to mitigate the evils of evolution. Cleveland could find no constitutional justification for such a position. He also vetoed bills providing for new post offices in Pennsylvania and Massachusetts (Cleveland wrote that the power to erect "post roads" did not equal the power to build "post offices"), the unrestricted use of public land by timber and cattle interests in the west, and the setting aside of public land in Arizona for education. Like the tariff, such legislation would have amounted to a government handout to special interests at the expense of the American public at large. This was government welfare in the form of patronage—what is known as "corporate welfare" or "crony capitalism" today. Tariffs enriched the industrial class at the expense of the farmer and the consumer; the Texas seed bill and other related legislation enriched the farmer at the expense of the industrialist. Neither was moral or legal. Cleveland displayed a cogent constitutional philosophy—something unmatched in the modern era. One constitutional wrong could not be remedied by another. Later presidents could have learned from his example.

PENSIONS

Cleveland did not have a happy relationship with the Grand Army of the Republic (GAR), a Union army veterans group that had transformed into a Republican lobbyist association. As a Democrat with Southern support, Cleveland had promised to heal the wounds of Reconstruction and appointed several Southern or pro-Southern men to high-level executive positions. He had also removed many Republicans who were incidentally Union veterans and replaced them with Democrats who were incidentally Confederate veterans. The GAR saw that as nothing less than a betrayal from a man they considered to be a draft dodging Southern sympathizer.

During the Civil War, Cleveland had paid a substitute $150 to take his place in the Union Army. This was legal but frowned upon in some circles. Both Democrats and Republicans who had the means used this method to avoid dying on the bloody battlefields. They could still say they were supporting the War, without having to be maimed by it. It could shield Democrats from a claim of disloyalty and perhaps a stint in a federal prison. Cleveland supported the war effort, though like many other Democrats he believed the Lincoln administration had gone too far in its zeal to quell dissent on the home front.

Following the war, a Union Army veteran could apply to the Federal Bureau of Pensions for financial relief. If the Bureau rejected the claim, the veteran could appeal to his congressman to present a bill overriding the bureau's decision. This happened with such regularity that when Cleveland assumed office in 1885, the Congress was setting aside one day a week during the legislative session for pension bills. It had become a form of open corruption, a way for congressmen to buy votes and curry favor with their constituents. The American people viewed it as an expensive and corrupt waste of time. Cleveland considered fraudulent pension bills to be a form of government welfare and an abuse of taxpayer dollars that had to be stamped out. As president he vetoed over two hundred pension bills for Union Army veterans. That accounted for nearly half of his total number of vetoes while in office. Yet, he also allowed over two thousand pension bills to pass unmolested, and he never objected to credible claims.

Cleveland's veto messages were brief but hard hitting. For example, he explained that he could not understand why a man who took the fee to serve as a substitute in March 1865, only three weeks before the war ended, contracted measles, spent the next month in a hospital, and then was mustered out of service in May 1865 needed a government pension because his "brilliant service and this terrific encounter with the measles" did not warrant government aid. [15] He vetoed another bill when the claimant had insisted that "sore eyes among the results of his diarrhea" merited an increase in his pension.[16] Another veto was inspired by the fact that the widow of a deceased veteran applied for a pension because her husband had fallen off a ladder in 1881, fully sixteen years after the conclusion of the War. Cleveland could not ascertain how this accident was related to his war injury. He wrote that "we are dealing with pensions and not gratuities."[17] Cleveland vetoed pensions for deserters, one of which was filed for by a family after their son drowned in a canal while trying to make it back home. Another widow claimed her husband died of a cerebral apoplexy that was related to a hernia injury he had incurred in 1863 while in the army.[18] Cleveland's war against government waste was best summarized by one pension veto: "I believe this claim for pension to be a fraud from beginning to end...."[19]

When Congress sought to transform individual pensions for wounded soldiers into a general federal welfare system for veterans, Cleveland vetoed the bill. The "Dependent Pension Bill," otherwise known as the Blair Bill after sponsor Henry W. Blair of New Hampshire, who himself was a veteran, would have granted a $12 monthly pension to all Union veterans who had served at least three months and were honorably discharged and to their dependent parents. No longer were combat wounds a prerequisite for government money. The drunk, the vagabond, and the shiftless rent-seeker would have been on equal terms with the men who had lost a limb in the wheat field at Gettysburg or in the trenches at Petersburg. The GAR lobbied hard for the bill's passage. They sold the bill on emotion, claiming that thousands of Union veterans were languishing in poor houses across America. When critics countered with fears of fraud, Blair and other supporters insisted that the GAR would ensure that the millions of dollars set aside for the project would be administered in good faith.

Cleveland's veto message emphasized the already voluminous number of fraudulent pension bills that crossed his desk on a weekly basis. He believed that no wounded veteran who had suffered from his valiant efforts in defense of the Union would approve of a bill that placed his efforts on the same plane with the behavior of shirkers and deserters. Cleveland insisted that "there can be no doubt that the race after the pensions offered by this bill would not only stimulate weakness and pretended incapacity for labor, but put a further premium on dishonesty and mendacity." The Blair Bill would strain the treasury and keep the American people saddled with "Federal taxation... still maintained at the rate made necessary by the exigencies of war. If this bill should become a law, with its tremendous addition to our pension obligation, I am thoroughly convinced that further efforts to reduce the Federal revenue and restore some part of it to our people will, and perhaps should, be seriously questioned."[20]

Cleveland offered no criticism of the bill on constitutional grounds, but this veto, and every other bill for individual relief, could have been defended with that argument. The Constitution does not empower Congress to provide stipends for individual citizens for any reason, including military service once discharged. Certainly, veterans who had been wounded or maimed by American wars, including those of the American War for Independence, had been granted pensions, but not until many years after the conclusion of hostilities and only in dire circumstances. This did not make them constitutional. Americans regarded pensions as morally responsible, and yet only around one hundred twenty thousand pensions had been granted between 1789 to 1861. Then from 1861 until 1886, the general government granted over half a million pensions to Union war veterans. The constitutional question, however, had never been answered. Pensions were the first round in a dramatic expansion of federal benefits for individuals—something never approved by the framers and ratifiers of the Constitution. As we have seen, Cleveland vetoed pension bills because they were fraudulent and a waste of taxpayer money, but he could have vetoed them because they were unconstitutional. For this and other vetoes, he has been viewed as a callous ideologue, but his oath of office meant something. More than anything, Cleveland wanted a republic of laws, not of men. Even the progressive historian Allan Nevins called his veto "an act of principle, without a trace of partisanship...."[21]

For his stand against pension abuse, the GAR made Cleveland public enemy number one. Several members of Congress were beholden to the veterans' organization for their seats in Congress, and every Republican appealed to the GAR on election day. This was a milder form of "waving the bloody shirt," a Republican electoral tactic made famous during the days of Reconstruction. Republicans, with the backing of the GAR, were still insisting that a vote for a Democrat equated to a vote for treason. No self-respecting American, they said, would vote for anyone but a Republican, the party that had won the War and saved the Union. Many, if not most, Americans could see through this lie, but the GAR had deep pockets and tremendous influence in the North and thus could swing elections. This had happened to be the case in 1888 when Cleveland won the popular vote but lost in the Electoral College because the GAR influenced the outcome in New York and Indiana through widespread voter fraud. Government welfare was fostering political corruption. It would only get worse in successive administrations.

SILVER AND THE GREAT PANIC OF 1893

Eighteen-ninety-three saw the worst depression in American history to that point. Banks failed, businesses failed, unemployment hit record highs, and many financial speculators were ruined. The historian Henry Adams wrote, "Men died like flies under the strain, and Boston grew suddenly old, haggard, and thin."[22] People were broke, starving, and desperate, and many began looking to the general government for solutions. At the very least they urged Cleveland to call a special session of Congress immediately after he re-assumed office in 1893.

There were many similarities between the Panic of 1893 and the Great Depression of 1929. Unemployment was near the same level, hundreds of banks failed, and thousands of businesses closed. During the interregnum between Cleveland's two terms, the Congress had passed several pieces of legislation that created both a credit and inflationary crisis in the United States, namely the Sherman Silver Purchase Act of 1890 and the McKinley Tariff of 1890. The Sherman Silver Purchase Act mandated that the government purchase every scrap of silver in the United States and inflate the money supply by printing paper currency to the tune of $50 million annually. This flood of cheap cash sent speculators into a wild frenzy. Men flung dollars into risky ventures, mal-invested their money, and paid the price when the economy tanked and the bubble burst. The stock market would eventually collapse.

The government further contributed to the problem by pumping millions into railroads and other "public works" projects that were laden with fraud and corruption. The McKinley Tariff of 1890 placed rates at their highest level in history. American industry, protected by the tariff and awash in easy money, produced expensive goods that would not sell. Inflation spiked, and the American consumer felt the pinch. This was state capitalism run amok. The American people were the losers in a rigged game created by plutocratic government. It was not free market economics that sank the economy—that would save it—but the fusion of big business, big banks, and big government, the first billion-dollar Congress.

246 9 PRESIDENTS WHO SCREWED UP AMERICA

Cleveland understood the situation better than most. He blamed the financial crisis on poor government policy and refused to intervene on behalf of big business when he took office in 1893. If a bank or a business failed, it was up to the private sector to correct the situation. Cleveland worried that the mass exodus of gold from the American treasury was making the problem worse by driving up inflation (he was right), so he tried to stimulate investment by agreeing to allow the Treasury Department to issue a series of bonds. The goal was to restock the treasury with gold and thus correct the rampant inflation that had paralyzed the economy. It was also the proper move to make legally. According to law, the general government had to maintain a certain level of gold reserves in relation to its stock in silver. The ratio was way out of proportion in 1893, with gold having almost disappeared from the United States Treasury. When the bond program did not work, Cleveland had to cajole Congress to act.

He called a special session of Congress in August 1893 with the express purpose of repealing the Sherman Silver Purchase Act. He wrote, "The existence of an alarming and extraordinary business situation, involving the welfare and prosperity of all our people, has constrained me to call together in extra session the people's representatives in Congress, to the end that through a wise and patriotic exercise of the legislative duty, with which they solely are charged, present evils may be mitigated and dangers threatening the future may be averted." Notice that Cleveland did not suggest that he alone could counter the situation. It was Congress's "wise and patriotic" duty to act in such a crisis.[23] Cleveland recommended the "prompt repeal" of the Sherman law, but then he could do nothing more than wait on Congress's response to his recommendation.

In the meantime, Cleveland was barraged with requests for government assistance in one form or another. He did nothing except keep pressing for the repeal of the Sherman Act and modification of the tariff. Farmers blamed the administration for ignoring their plight. Business leaders were frustrated by what seemed to be government inactivity in a major financial crisis. Cleveland stayed the course, and when in late 1893 a bill for the repeal of the Sherman Silver Purchase Act crossed his desk, he gladly signed it. The issue was not finally settled; "silverite" Democrats would gain control of the party in the next election cycle. But Cleveland had temporarily won the day and the argument.

Later presidents would use this type of crisis to unconstitutionally expand government power. Cleveland had that option available to him. He could have thrown off his oath to defend the Constitution and supported programs that would have pumped millions of dollars into federal relief initiatives. He certainly would have been more popular for doing so, but that is not the mark of a good president—let alone the type of statesman the founding generation envisioned should occupy the executive office. Cleveland had already made it clear in 1887 that it was not the government's job to "support the people." A severe economic downturn had not shaken that belief, or the president's commitment to uphold the Constitution. Neither business nor individuals received one handout from the Cleveland administration, and when the Panic of 1893 evaporated by 1895, Cleveland could with great pride point to his anti-inflationary policies and refusal to bow to political pressure and pump more government dollars into the economy as the strategies that turned things around. Instead of the Square Deal, New Deal, Fair Deal, Great Society, or "compassionate conservatism," Cleveland relied on the Constitution and defended his oath. That, more than anything else, saved the American economy.

FOREIGN POLICY

Cleveland's foreign policy echoed that of the founding generation. He made that clear in his first inaugural address:

> The genius of our institutions, the needs of our people in
> their home life, and the attention which is demanded for the

settlement and development of the resources of our vast territory dictate the scrupulous avoidance of any departure from that foreign policy commended by the history, the traditions, and the prosperity of our Republic. It is the policy of independence, favored by our position and defended by our known love of justice and by our power. It is the policy of peace suitable to our interests. It is the policy of neutrality, rejecting any share in foreign broils and ambitions upon other continents and repelling their intrusion here. It is the policy of Monroe and of Washington and Jefferson—"Peace, commerce, and honest friendship with all nations; entangling alliance with none."[24]

In contrast to most of his successors, Cleveland was not interested in making the United States into an imperial power. Hawaii is the best example of Cleveland's preference to abide by the founding tradition and his oath of office.

The United States had long been interested in Hawaii. In 1875 the Ulysses S. Grant administration had negotiated a treaty with Hawaii that allowed its massive sugar crops to be imported to the United States duty free. There was an almost simultaneous call for the annexation of the islands. During Cleveland's first term in office, he negotiated a renewal of the trade agreement and also worked a deal for a permanent United States military installation—later known as Pearl Harbor—on the island. But Cleveland resisted annexation. If Hawaii wanted to become part of the United States, he would agree, but only if she expressed that wish through the vote of her people. It did not seem that the Hawaiian public was ready for such a step, so Cleveland recommended maintaining Hawaiian independence.

His successor in 1889, Benjamin Harrison, was more interested in American occupation of the island. He dispatched the U.S. Navy to protect the Hawaiian monarch and maintained continual naval patrols of the area.

Near the end of his administration, a group of American and British businessmen staged a coup and ousted the nativist Hawaiian queen. It was bloodless, but only because the American navy backed the queen's overthrow. The commanding officer of the one American warship in the region, the USS *Boston*, did not have permission from the United States government to act, but in the crisis he and the American minister to Hawaii threw in their lot with the pro-American resistance. Once the coup was successful, Hawaii immediately petitioned for annexation.

President Harrison and his secretary of state, James G. Blaine (who had been Cleveland's opponent in the 1884 election) supported the overthrow of the Hawaiian monarch and crafted a treaty of annexation. Harrison submitted it to the Senate, but it still had not been ratified when Cleveland came back into office in 1893. After a lengthy investigation into the Hawaiian situation, Cleveland withdrew the treaty from the Senate and decided against annexation. The Hawaiian people did not want it, he concluded, and American involvement had been illegal and unjust. Cleveland, however, was forced to recognize the new Hawaiian government after the ousted queen promised to publicly execute anyone involved in the coup, including several Americans, should she come back into power. Cleveland would maintain the *status quo* in Hawaii for the remainder of his administration.

Cleveland was an advocate of the American navy and urged Congress to modernize and expand its fleet of battleships. Teddy Roosevelt would eventually get credit for what became known as the "Great White Fleet," but construction on these modern warships began during Cleveland's tenure in office. Cleveland would also use the navy to enforce the Monroe Doctrine in Latin America, often to the detriment of European interests in the region. Cleveland wanted to ensure that independent Latin American governments remained that way. At the same time, he avoided conflict in Cuba because he could see no tangible benefit to the United States.

Cuba was controlled by the Spanish government. It was one of the last Spanish colonial possessions in the world, and though Cuban rebels had been agitating for independence for several years, the United States under Cleveland refused to get involved. Cleveland once said he predicted disaster if the United States became embroiled in an independence movement on the island; he urged his successor William McKinley to stay out. McKinley did not listen, and Cuba, along with the Philippines, was annexed to the United States in 1898. The United States won the war, but traditional American foreign policy had been defeated by American imperialists. Cleveland was the last president to resist this type of American adventurism, and his foreign policy was a model of constitutional restraint.

Cleveland is often regarded as a "do nothing" president, the stooge of big business during the unrestrained excesses of the "Gilded Age." His record does not fit that characterization. Cleveland used the powers of the executive branch to trim excessive spending, halt unconstitutional legislation, and rein in big government. If Cleveland could be faulted for anything in office it was his signing of the Interstate Commerce Act of 1887 (legislation he deemed unconstitutional but necessary) and his advocacy of an income tax. But in neither case did Cleveland act as "chief legislator." Cleveland brought an energy to the executive branch that had been lacking for much of the late nineteenth century, but in contrast to the "energy" of Jackson, Lincoln, or any of Cleveland's successors, he used that energy to defend the Constitution. That is what his oath required. Executive energy is not inimical to constitutional government. As the Cleveland and John Tyler administrations both illustrated, it is often necessary to arrest a legislative branch that has attempted to abuse its powers. Executive "energy" is problematic only when it is used in violation of the Constitution and the presidential oath of office.

CHAPTER 13

CALVIN COOLIDGE

Thirtieth President, 1923–1929

Finding a twentieth-century president who "tried to save" America is a daunting task. It's a poor field. Most of the presidents in the last one hundred years have unconstitutionally expanded executive power. Twentieth- and twenty-first-century chief executives were generally the worst presidents in American history, at least in regard to upholding their oath to defend the Constitution. Many were popular, and they had some of the highest approval ratings in American history, but popularity is not how Americans should judge a president's record. To his credit, Calvin Coolidge was more principled than popular.

He took office amid a cloud of scandals from his predecessor's administration and following over twenty years of progressive meddling in government. Coolidge's model of executive restraint would not last, but he has been cited as the quintessential modern conservative president, the faithful steward of limited government. To a man like "Silent Cal," defending his oath did not mean bending to the fashionable opinion of the day. He was the last man to occupy the White House before the dramatic transformation of the office under Herbert Hoover and Franklin Roosevelt. That may be why there is some level of innocence to the Coolidge administration. It was a peaceful, simpler time. But had Coolidge been in office during the Great Depression and beyond, his principles would have dictated a different course from that of the men who tackled those monumental problems.

The thirtieth president's reputation has received a boost in recent years, due in large part to Ronald Reagan's admiration for the man and his administration. Coolidge has become a polarizing figure, lauded by conservatives for his tax cutting frugality and despised by the Left for his intractability and unwillingness to expand government power to "help" the people. He was, in many ways, a Jeffersonian, a throwback to the Cleveland and Tyler administrations. Coolidge used the office the way the founding generation intended, and he understood his oath. He protected the balance between the federal and state governments and used the veto power as a check on unconstitutional legislation. Coolidge was not a "weak" president who allowed Congress to run roughshod over the Constitution. He had a backbone and did what needed to be done to safeguard the proper separation of powers. He was also innovative, a pioneer in new technologies and strategies that allowed him to directly address the American public, if for no other reason than to articulate his positions. He was not the first president to address the public, but in contrast to men like Andrew Jackson or Teddy Roosevelt, Coolidge was not a demagogue, and he did not believe "popular will" should justify executive action.

To be sure, Coolidge was not infallible. He signed legislation that drastically expanded the so-called Commerce Clause of the Constitution beyond what was contemplated or advanced by the founding generation. These bills were politically popular, especially legislation that provided federal aid for flood victims—but popular does not mean constitutional. Coolidge, in fact, believed disaster relief *was* unconstitutional, but he bowed to political pressure and signed two relief bills into law. Coolidge also advanced a national program for education and character improvement. Such an agenda was out of step with the Constitution as ratified. Coolidge, however, believed that some of the legislation he recommended, namely to provide better wages for working women and to restrict child labor—would require a constitutional amendment. He was correct. Congress eventually passed legislation to this effect after Coolidge left office without the benefit of a constitutional amendment. That should not taint his legacy.

Coolidge may represent just a pause in the progressive onslaught that eventually overwhelmed the Constitution, but it would probably be better to remember him as the last of an era. Even Reagan, so often lauded by conservatives for his principled stand against Leftist innovation, could not match Coolidge's record in relation to defending his oath of office. If that is our yardstick, then Coolidge should rank as one of the best presidents in American history, and certainly one of the last men who "tried to save" the country.

COOLIDGE AND THE CONSTITUTION

Coolidge assumed office in 1923 after Warren Harding died during a summer trip across the United States. Coolidge, on vacation himself, was awoken in the middle of the night with the news. His father administered the oath of office and Coolidge calmly went back to bed. Upon returning to Washington, Coolidge woke to an attempted robbery in his hotel room. He stopped the would-be thief and asked him not to take one of his personal possessions, a charm that had been given to him by the state of Massachusetts. When the man realized he was speaking with the president, he immediately apologized and explained that he and his college buddy were short on cash and needed to get back to school. Coolidge reached into his wallet (which the burglar had since returned), pulled out $32, and gave it to the man as a "loan." The police were not alerted to the situation and Coolidge did not let anyone speak of the incident during his lifetime.[1]

His reactions in these stressful situations were indicative of how he would behave as president. Coolidge saw himself as a man of the people, a conscientious defender of the Constitution, and the roadblock to bad legislation. He wrote in his *Autobiography* of the office of president that "a power so vast in its implications has never been conferred upon any ruling sovereign. Yet the President exercises his authority in accordance with the Constitution and the law. He is truly the agent of the people, performing such functions as they have entrusted to him." His approach to issues was at times pragmatic, and he cited Jefferson's waffling over the Louisiana Purchase as a fine example of the requirement that the president "wait to decide each question on its merits as it arises." To Coolidge, the office, though taxing, came down to one fundamental rule: "All situations that arise are likely to be simplified, and many of them completely solved, by an application of the Constitution and the law."[2]

Not everyone agreed. And certainly not everyone believed that Coolidge would be an effective executive. Henry Cabot Lodge expressed shock and disdain when he heard that Harding had died. "My God! That means Coolidge is president." Harold Ickes, who would become infamous for his role in the unconstitutional New Deal fiasco just a decade later, said, "If this country has reached the state where Coolidge is the right sort of a person for president, then any office boy is qualified to be chief executive."[3] The social critic H. L. Mencken took great pleasure in ridiculing the new president. His biting columns lambasted Coolidge for his common man approach and poor speech-writing skills. "Nero fiddled while Coolidge snored," he once quipped.[4]

Coolidge did bring a workmanlike approach to the White House. He was neither flamboyant nor reckless. He did not crave the limelight, and he thought the president should be only one part of the American general government. After nearly two decades of progressive presidents bent on remaking America, and one half-term of a showman more comfortable chasing skirts than defending his oath, Coolidge seemed like a breath of fresh air to many Americans. They responded with overwhelming support.

Like most presidents, Coolidge did not leave a political manifesto behind, but his annual addresses to Congress outlined some of his political beliefs. They read like well-organized business memos, clear and concise, but often lacking substance. His first message, in December 1923, included short statements such as "The foreign service of our Government needs to be reorganized and improved." This tendency to make recommendations without any further discussion matched the president's public persona as "Silent Cal," the man who said and spoke little and expected Congress to work things out. The recommendation was made, and Congress, as the legislative branch, needed to hammer out the details if they chose to act.

Coolidge did insist that Congress rein in spending and cut taxes. In that regard, a direct line could be run from the first Jefferson administration in 1801 to Coolidge's first months in office in 1923. Coolidge was a Republican in the mold of the Party of Lincoln but with a tinge of Jeffersonian "republicanism" that colored his political philosophy. He admired business and industry but believed that the small towns and rural communities of America were the backbone of society. He presided over a massive federal bureaucracy but sought to trim it wherever possible. Like Jefferson he was a farmer at heart. He was descended from early American stock, contemporaries of the Sage of Monticello, men and women with a fierce independent streak that ultimately defined Coolidge and his views on government and society.

The "war taxes" that had been implemented during American involvement in World War I remained in effect when Coolidge took office. He pressed for their reduction or repeal. "To reduce war taxes is to give every home a better chance," he said in 1923, and then explained why:

For seven years the people have borne with uncomplaining courage the tremendous burden of national and local taxation. These must both be reduced. The taxes of the Nation must be reduced now as much as prudence will permit, and expenditures must be reduced accordingly. High taxes reach everywhere and burden everybody. They gear most heavily upon the poor. They diminish industry and commerce. They make agriculture unprofitable. They increase the rates on transportation. They are a charge on every necessary of life. Of all services which the Congress can render to the country, I have no hesitation in declaring to neglect it, to postpone it, to obstruct it by unsound proposals, is to become unworthy of public confidence and untrue to public trust. The country wants this measure to have the right of way over any others.[5]

The Jeffersonian pamphleteer John Taylor of Caroline once said excessive taxation reduced the American people to the condition of "asses" to be used and abused by government. Coolidge was more tactful but no less insightful.

Coolidge was not going to use the executive branch to unravel decades of unconstitutional legislation. The president cannot do so constitutionally. Coolidge had to work within the governmental structure he was handed in 1923. To expect a president to roll back mountains of illegal acts of Congress would be to expect the executive branch to become an elected monarchy. Coolidge, like Cleveland, had to work subtly at times—and at others more forcefully, through the veto. By the 1920s, the executive had virtually dropped providing constitutional justification for negating acts of Congress; the veto had become a partisan weapon for political gain. Coolidge accepted unconstitutional legislation in regard to "internal improvements" and even promoted it, but in other areas he sought constitutional means to achieve reform.

His first annual message included a call for a constitutional amendment that would outlaw child labor. At the same time, he argued, "There is no method by which we can either be relieved of the results of our own folly or be guaranteed a successful life. There is an inescapable personal responsibility for the development of character, of industry, of thrift, and of self-control. These do not come from the Government, but from the people themselves." And though he favored more investment in education, Coolidge rejected direct federal aid, stating "I do not favor the making of appropriations from the National Treasury to be expended directly on local education...."[6] No "Common Core," NSEA, Title IV funds, or "No Child Left Behind" in the Coolidge administration. Coolidge could be faulted for opening the door to such ideas, but the concepts had already been advanced by previous administrations. His recommendations were more of a brake than a spur to the federal takeover of education. Coolidge's attitude was: Look to better education, but don't use unconstitutional means to do it.

Coolidge's resistance to spending federal dollars on local issues was a clear indication of his belief in federalism. This was a recurring theme in his annual messages. In his third annual message, Coolidge spoke these powerful words:

> The functions which the Congress are to discharge are not those of local government but of National Government. The greatest solicitude should be exercised to prevent any encroachment upon the rights of the States or their various political subdivisions. Local self-government is one of our most precious possessions. It is the greatest contributing factor to the stability, strength, liberty, and progress of the Nation. It ought not to be in ringed by assault or undermined by purchase. It ought not to abdicate its power through weakness or resign its authority through favor. It does not at all follow that because abuses exist it is the concern of the Federal Government to attempt their reform.[7]

This statement was in perfect accord with the Constitution as ratified by the founding generation. True federalism relies on the power of local communities and the "sovereign people" to handle their own affairs. This may seem quaint in the twenty-first century, but Coolidge was articulating a principle that had been part of American traditions since before the American War for Independence. He later wrote,

> Society is in much more danger from encumbering the National Government beyond its wisdom to comprehend, or its ability to administer, than from leaving the local communities to bear their own burdens and remedy their own evils. Our local habit and custom is so strong, our variety of race and creed is so great, the Federal authority is so tenuous, that the area within which it can function successfully is very limited. The wiser policy is to leave the localities, so far as we can, possessed of their own sources of revenue and charged with their own obligations.[8]

Coolidge believed that the executive branch had a responsibility to check Congress, not only in relation to excessive spending or high taxes, but in its powers vis-à-vis the states. Coolidge was not a "do nothing" president the Left likes to insist he was. On the contrary, restraining Congress from exercising unconstitutional authority is one of the most important tasks a president can undertake.

Coolidge best articulated his position on the powers of the states in a 1925 speech on "The Reign of Law." "If there is to be a continuation of individual and local self-government, and of state sovereignty," he said, "the individual and locality must govern themselves and the state must assert its sovereignty. Otherwise these rights and privileges will be confiscated under the all-compelling pressure of public necessity for a better maintenance of order and morality." Coolidge argued that the founding generation had established a "dual system of state government and Federal Government, each supreme in its own sphere," but the States were to be the guardians of the "form and course of society." Coolidge insisted on the permanence of the states, no less than the permanence of the Union: "We have demonstrated in the time of war that under the Constitution we possess an indestructible Union. We must not fail to demonstrate in the time of peace that we are likewise determined to possess and maintain indestructible States."[9]

Coolidge returned to the theme of federalism in his fourth annual message in 1926. "It is too much assumed," he wrote, "that because an abuse exists it is the business of the National Government to provide a remedy. The presumption should be that it is the business of local and State governments. Such national action results in encroaching upon the salutary independence of the States and by undertaking to supersede their natural authority fills the land with bureaus and departments which are undertaking to do what it is impossible for them to accomplish and brings our whole system of government into disrespect and disfavor."[10] In an era when the States have been reduced to virtual provinces of the general government and the Tenth Amendment is readily ignored, Coolidge's statement seems both prophetic and outdated. A better respect for state authority by federal judges, legislators, and bureaucrats would alleviate the "disrespect and disfavor" for the general government among the American public.

The historian Michael Gerhardt believes that Coolidge came closest to expressing his "constitutional views" in a 1926 message to Congress. Coolidge emphasized separation of powers as the "guarantees of liberty." The founding generation, Coolidge said, had sought "to establish a free government, which must not be permitted to degenerate into the unrestrained authority of a mere majority or the unbridled weight of a mere influential few." If Coolidge could maintain the independence of the executive branch and the federalism of the founding generation, the United States and the American public would remain "free from oppression."[11] Americans today have come to believe that executive action in the form of a legislative agenda or a personal involvement in the legislative process is the mark of a "great" president. But Coolidge proved that greatness should be measured by restraint rather than unconstitutional action, by independence rather than demagoguery or kowtowing. Coolidge was his own man. He let Congress legislate, but he would often have the final word.

THE VETO

Coolidge did not have the veto record of Grover Cleveland, and his veto messages lacked the constitutional punch of John Tyler or even Andrew Jackson, but he used the power as an effective check on unconstitutional legislation. Nearly half of his vetoes were in the form of the "pocket veto," a practice begun by James Madison but used by every president since. The premise is simple. According to the Constitution, the president has ten days (excluding Sundays) to sign a bill into law. If Congress adjourns before the expiration of the ten-day window, the bill "shall not be a law" unless the president had already signed it.

The Whig Party challenged Andrew Jackson's use of the pocket veto and attempted to outlaw the practice. When that failed, Congress devised a way to theoretically stay in session even when they adjourned by appointing an "agent" to receive a veto message from the president while the Congress was in recess. This did not always stop the president from exercising a pocket veto. Abraham Lincoln used a pocket veto to override the controversial Wade-Davis Bill of 1864 even with a congressional agent on hand to carry his veto message back to the House of Representatives. The bill would have killed his lenient "Ten Percent" reconstruction plan and implemented a much more harsh (and unrealistic) set of requirements for the Southern States to form pro-Union governments. Lincoln ignored the agent and refused to act on the bill.

Critics claimed the pocket veto smacked of the absolute veto that the king of Great Britain had possessed before the American War for Independence. Not really, though a pocket veto left Congress no recourse until the next session, when the bill would have to be passed again and sent to the president for approval. There was certainly nothing unconstitutional about a pocket veto. The text of the Constitution clearly states that if "Adjourn-ment prevents" a bill from returning to Congress, it is void.

Coolidge knew this, and thus used a pocket veto to void a 1926 bill that would have allowed several Northwestern American Indian tribes to sue the general government for damages incurred in the loss of their tribal lands. The bill passed the Senate on June 24, and the Congress adjourned on July 3, three days before the expiration of the ten-day window. Coolidge did not act on the bill. The tribes then sued Coolidge, and the case made it to the Supreme Court, which in 1929 ruled 9–0 in the "Pocket Veto Case" that "Adjournment" was any cessation of congressional business—because if the phrase were interpreted more narrowly, Congress could force the president to act on a bill more quickly than the Constitution plainly required. This would be an unconstitutional usurpation of power by the legislative branch. Coolidge had already been succeeded by Herbert Hoover when the Court decided the case, but his veto stood.

The Court subsequently, in 1938, defined "Adjournment" more strictly. "Recess" and adjournment *sine die* were two different things. In Coolidge's case, the Congress (both houses) had adjourned for five months before starting a new session. Subsequent presidents had claimed that a "recess" of only the originating branch of Congress constituted a congres-sional "Adjournment" for the purpose of a pocket veto. The Court cor-rectly viewed that as an unconstitutional abuse of power by the executive branch. As a result, both houses of Congress have to formally adjourn *sine die* before a pocket veto can be issued. A recess is not an adjournment. But the appointment of a legislative "agent" for the time during an adjourn-ment *sine die* does not preclude the president from using the pocket veto. This ruling maintains the appropriate balance between the two branches of government.

Coolidge outraged congressional leaders in 1927 and 1928 by twice vetoing the popular McNary-Haugen Bill, which would have created a new government agency called the Federal Farm Board with the ability to buy excess agricultural products and sell them overseas, ostensibly to boost prices or set a price floor for certain commodities. It amounted to little more than a resumption of the price-fixing methods the general government had used at the behest of Woodrow Wilson to control agricultural output during World War I. Coolidge had already made clear his desire to return the United States to a pre-war footing in regard to taxes and government expenditures. The same held true for unconstitutional federal regulations.

The bill had the support of Coolidge's secretary of agriculture, Henry C. Wallace (father of the closet communist and future Secretary of Agriculture Henry A. Wallace), and Vice President Charles Dawes, but Coolidge and his powerful Secretary of the Treasury Andrew Mellon opposed the bill. It was an obviously unconstitutional expansion of the federal government, a program with antecedents in the illegal congressional acts during World War I and descendants in New Deal legislation. The "farm block" in Congress placed tremendous pressure on the president to sign the bill, but Coolidge stood firm and vetoed it. His three-thousand-word veto message listed several objections to the legislation, not the least of which were the cost of the bill and the poor economic theory that underpinned it: "To expect to increase prices and then maintain them on a higher level by means of a plan which must of necessity increase production while decreasing consumption is to fly in the face of economic law as well established as any law of nature."[12] It was bad policy.

The Congress was undeterred and passed a similar bill the following session. This time, Coolidge took a different approach in his veto message, which included a devastating twenty-three-page report by Attorney General John G. Sargent pointing to the bill's unconstitutional application of the Commerce Clause. In a tone that stands in stark contrast to the position later administrations would take in regard to government regulatory "boards," Coolidge stressed that the government did not have the authority to create bureaucratic agencies infused with legislative authority and lacking oversight. Additionally, the bill would addict American farmers to a constant drip of taxpayer dollars through subsidies, thus eliminating the independence that had made American agriculture one of the strongest aspects of the economy. Farmers would subsequently require more subsidies to stay afloat, these subsidies would raise prices for the American consumer and lead to over-production of certain goods (in a phenomenon similar to mal-investment in industry), and thus the law would create a never-ending cycle of government dependency that would assuredly lead to more government spending and regulation. Congress failed to override either veto.

Coolidge had assessed the situation accurately. He was not callous about the growing problems of American agriculture, but he thought the solution was lower taxes and less, not more, government regulation. If there is one constant theme in the Coolidge presidency, it is the belief that lowering taxes would lead to greater American prosperity. Coolidge's recommended solutions for stagnant agricultural prices centered on individual initiative and "individual responsibility":

> We should avoid the error of seeking in laws the cause of the ills of agriculture. This mistake leads away from a permanent solution, and serves only to make political issues out of fundamental economic problems that cannot be solved by political action.... I have believed at all times that the only sound basis for further Federal Government action in behalf of agriculture would be to encourage its adequate organization to assist in building up marketing agencies and facilities in the control of the farmers themselves. I want to see them undertake, under their own management, the marketing of their products under such conditions as will enable them to bring about greater stability in prices and less waste in marketing, but entirely within unalterable economic laws. Such a program, supported by a strong protective tariff on farm products, is the best method of affecting a permanent cure of existing agricultural ills. Such a program is in accordance with

264 9 PRESIDENTS WHO SCREWED UP AMERICA

the American tradition and the American ideal of reliance on and maintenance of private initiative and individual responsibility, and the duty of the Government is discharged when it has provided conditions under which the individual can achieve success.[13]

While these were the highest-profile vetoes of the Coolidge administration, others reflected the president's consistent advocacy for fiscal restraint and constitutional government. He vetoed the Bursum Pension Bill of 1924, a law designed to increase pensions for veterans of the Mexican and Civil Wars. Coolidge thought the bill violated the principles of sound government. It would have cost American taxpayers $400 million to increase the pensions of these veterans and their dependents, a group that included many "widows" who had married old men to acquire the pension. Warren G. Harding had vetoed an earlier version of the bill, but even with the tighter restrictions on dependent widows in the new version, Coolidge still considered the bill to be too expensive and a waste of taxpayer dollars. This was a form of government welfare that he could not support.

In his annual messages Coolidge consistently criticized an ongoing federal project in Alabama to develop the region known as Muscle Shoals along the Tennessee River. The idea was to bring electric power to rural Alabama and Tennessee, both of which had suffered from widespread poverty since the conclusion of the War Between the States, but, more importantly, to produce nitrates for both agricultural and military use. Coolidge thought that the cost to develop the plant was prohibitive and that the project was better left in private hands. When in 1928 Congress sent him a bill that would have authorized the Treasury to spend $150 million for the power plant, Coolidge issued a pocket veto. Like other "internal improvements" projects throughout American history, the Muscle Shoals development was an appropriation of national funds for a local project that benefitted only a small segment of the American population. The bill was pushed with the argument that the nitrates produced in the region would benefit the American military, but any thoughtful person could see that Muscle Shoals was the type of legislation whose real point was to buy votes and maintain power for connected politicians in Washington. Nearly every unconstitutional federal spending project from the time of Washington forward could be characterized this way. Coolidge was one of the last presidents—if not the last—who frowned upon such legislative trickery.

Coolidge vetoed eight bills on May 18, 1928, many of them designed to increase the wages, benefits, and expenditures for the United States Post Office and its employees. One of the bills would have increased the pay of nighttime postal workers by over $6,000 per year. These were well-intentioned measures, but Coolidge declared them a waste of government money. This political stance would be nearly impossible for any viable politician in modern America to take, and it showed Coolidge's willingness to single out even popular measures for their gross abuse of the public treasury. Grover Cleveland had taken a veto pen to similar legislation, and Coolidge was the same type of nineteenth-century fiscal warrior—in the twentieth century. Government had to be frugal, honest, constitutional, and above all moral.

The one blemish on Coolidge's record, from a constitutional standpoint, occurred in 1927. The Mississippi River flooded that year to levels not seen in American history. Every state the river touched suffered some type of flooding. In some places, the water reached over thirty feet above its normal level. Entire communities were under water. Hardest hit were black communities along the floodplain. Nearly 75 percent of the affected people were black, and it seemed that the poorest populations in the region had been targeted by nature's fury.

The Southern states most affected by the flood began begging for federal assistance. The cost in property damage and infrastructure alone equaled nearly half a billion in 1927 dollars. Coolidge hesitated to directly involve his office in the cleanup, arguing that the federal government had no constitutional authority to funnel taxpayer dollars to the flood-stricken region. "Coolidge did not deem it appropriate for a president to march south like a general into governors' territory to manage a flood rescue.... It was wrong, on principle, for a president to intrude upon a governor; that was basic federalism."[14] Like Cleveland's Texas seed bill veto in 1887, Coolidge's refusal to involve the general government in flood relief was met with great consternation across the United States, but particularly in the South. The Southern black population had been loyal Republicans since they were given the vote in 1870, and it seemed that the Party of Lincoln was abandoning them in their greatest need since Reconstruction. Coolidge stood firm, and many Southern governors supported his federalist approach to the problem, but he decided to send Herbert Hoover to the region as a sign of good faith. He also began pitching private relief for flood victims and eventually sent federal resources to the region to aid in rescue operations.

In his Fourth Annual Message, Coolidge addressed the Mississippi flood, suggesting that "The Government is not an insurer of its citizens against the hazard of the elements. We shall always have flood and drought, heat and cold, earthquake and wind, lightning and tidal wave, which are all too constant in their afflictions. The Government does not undertake to reimburse its citizens for loss and damage incurred under such circumstances." Coolidge, however, left the door open to some type of federal aid, saying that "the National Government should not fail to provide generous relief" and that the general government was "chargeable ... with the rebuilding of public works and the humanitarian duty of relieving its citizens from distress."[15]

Hoover's Southern tour paid great political dividends for the Coolidge administration (and more importantly for Hoover in 1928), and private money began pouring into the region, mostly through the hard work of the American Red Cross. Coolidge pragmatically dropped his resistance to federal aid for reconstruction and began pushing for a flood relief bill. It did not come easy. He called the first draft to cross his desk "the most radical and dangerous bill that has had the countenance of Congress since

I have been president."[16] For the first time in his administration, Coolidge became directly involved in the legislative process. He brokered a deal with congressional leaders on a compromise bill that provided $500 million in federal aid to the region and involved the Army Corps of Engineers in future flood prevention and abatement assistance. Coolidge signed two flood relief bills into law in 1927. These two bills signaled a temporary shift in his principles, one that he alluded to in his post-presidency *Autobiography*. This was Coolidge's Louisiana Purchase. He had to weigh the situation on its merits and decide on a proper course of action. The bills were the first in a long line of federal assistance for disaster relief and the most expensive until the twenty-first century. They were also unconstitutional, but Coolidge chose to ignore constitutional arguments in favor of political expediency.

FOREIGN POLICY

The 1920s are often viewed as a decade of excesses and a coming of age, the last period of innocence before the Great Depression and World War II. In the traditional narrative, men like Coolidge could not see how destructive their policies would be for future Americans, how the light taxes, low spending, and conspicuous prosperity of the "Roaring 20s" would lead to the poverty and dislocation of the 1930s, or how a naïve "isolationist" America was allowing the rise of totalitarian regimes in Europe that would plunge the world into the most destructive war in human history. In both cases, Coolidge gets the blame.

At heart he was an optimist whose firm religious convictions guided both his foreign and domestic policies. In contrast to modern politicians who view government as a civic religion—thanks in large part to men like Lincoln who elevated politics to that level—Coolidge argued that all good government relied on Divine Providence. Echoing the eighteenth-century Congregationalist minister John Wise, Coolidge once called democracy "Christ's government.... The ultimate sanction of law rests on the righteous authority of the Almighty."[17] Coolidge's determination to maintain a Christian peace drove his foreign policy. It was neither naïve nor "isolationist," as critics contend. Rather, Coolidge sought to save the United States and the American public from the progressive foreign adventurism of his predecessor, Woodrow Wilson, in order to bring prosperity to the Union and ensure the health and safety of its people. War and social engineering could never accomplish those things.

Coolidge wrote in 1924, "To continue to be independent we must continue to be whole-hearted American.... We cannot become the partisans of one nation or the opponents of another.... To be independent to my mind does not mean to be isolated, to be the priest or the Levite, but rather to be the good Samaritan." Coolidge channeled the foreign policies of Washington and Jefferson better than anyone in the twentieth century. He understood that conflict could be abated by a firm but gentle hand. The United States should not engage in the "entangling alliances" that had brought Europe into World War I, but should instead strive for a "permanent peace," for "[t]he cause of freedom has been triumphant. We believe it to be, likewise, the cause of peace." He concluded that while the United States should be an example for the world, "We cannot make over the people of Europe. We must help them as they are, if we are to help them at all." Coolidge did not shrink from this responsibility, but in contrast to a Wilsonian imperialism, Coolidge urged American involvement on the world stage "not at the sacrifice of our independence, not for the support of imperialism, but to restore to those great peoples a peaceful civilization."[18]

In 1926, Coolidge refused to join European powers in the World Court. The Senate had placed conditions upon American involvement in the venture, one of which was rejected by the other parties to the agreement, namely that the United States would not have to abide by World Court decisions that violated the United States Constitution. This had been Coolidge's primary objection to the Court from the beginning, and he informed the signatories to the Court that he did not have the authority to make changes to the conditions without Senate approval, something he most assuredly would not acquire. As a result, the United States did not join the World Court during the Coolidge administration. And more importantly, Coolidge had deferred to Congress—the proper constitutional method for establishing American foreign policy.

The fullest expression of Coolidge's commitment to "ordered liberty and world peace" was the signing of the Kellogg-Briand Pact in 1928. Named after Coolidge's secretary of state, Frank B. Kellogg, and French foreign minister Aristide Briand, the treaty sought to remove the gun from international politics by replacing war with peaceful negotiation. Germany, France, and the United States were the initial signatories to the deal, and Kellogg was awarded the Nobel Peace Prize in 1933 for his work on the Pact. Constitutionally, Coolidge followed every executive requirement to the letter, including the incorporation of several Senate recommendations into the final deal—so that it was ultimately ratified by an 87–1 vote. This was truly "advice and consent." Coolidge made no unilateral commitments but instead led where he could and placed a formalized treaty on the Senate docket for approval. The Senate, therefore, had the final say in foreign policy—a principle Coolidge continually upheld during his six years in office.

Did Coolidge's foreign policy reflect a shortsightedness that eventually brought World War II to America's doorstep? No, Kellogg-Briand did not help bring Hitler to power in Germany, and it was American *meddling* in Europe during the 1930s—through financial assistance to the British, not peaceful neutrality—that led to American entry into World War II. If anything, Kellogg-Briand prolonged American neutrality and kept the United States out of the broiling European mess in the 1920s, a mess that had been created in the first place partly by American intervention during the Wilson administration. Americans wanted peace, and Coolidge delivered. At the same time, he reaffirmed, if only briefly, executive commitment to the foreign policy of the founding generation and the Constitution as ratified in 1788.

"It costs a great deal to be President," Coolidge wrote in 1929.[19] While in the White House, he took considerable blame for his reluctance to "help" the American people, and the wave of popularity on which he rode out of office quickly receded after the stock market crash of 1929. Coolidge could have done more to steer clear of disaster, the narrative went. He took these charges personally. Coolidge largely retired from public life after leaving office, but for one year he penned a syndicated newspaper column that served as a soapbox for his views on society and government, in particular his belief that the Great Depression was the result of forces that had been generally out of his control. Certainly, Coolidge could have checked the power of the Federal Reserve Bank during his time in office, at least by recommending tighter controls on interest rates, cheap money, and fractional reserve policies, but the FED was designed to be independent of the control of the government. The American economy has paid the price time and time again, but that was not Coolidge's fault. More blame for widening the Depression could be placed upon the reckless policies of the Herbert Hoover administration (tax and spend) than on those of Coolidge. A more Coolidge-like approach—cut taxes and cut spending—could have turned the economic disaster around without having it drag on for nearly another twenty years.

Coolidge died of a heart attack in 1933, only days before Franklin Roosevelt took office. He had written to a friend just a few weeks before, "We are in a new era to which I do not belong and it would not be possible for me to adjust to it."[20] Coolidge knew he was a dinosaur, a relic of the nineteenth century—a Jeffersonian whose vision had given way to the socialism of Franklin Roosevelt. Yet, his innovative use of audio recordings, the radio, and early film reels ensured that his message would endure long into the twentieth century. Ronald Reagan cited him as the intellectual godfather of modern American conservatism, at least in regard to executive power. Perhaps the best epitaph on Coolidge's public career was written by his longtime critic, H. L. Mencken:

We suffer most when the White House busts with ideas. With a World Saver [Wilson] preceding him (I count out Harding as a mere hallucination) and a Wonder Boy [Hoover] following him, [Coolidge] begins to seem, in retrospect, an extremely comfortable and even praiseworthy citizen.... If the day ever comes when Jefferson's warnings are heeded at last, and we reduce government to its simplest terms, it may very well happen that Cal's bones now resting inconspicuously in the Vermont granite will come to be revered as those of a man who really did the nation some service.[21]

Coolidge was more of a common man than Truman, more of a conservative than Reagan, and certainly the last man to occupy the executive office who truly believed in the Constitution as ratified. His vision was short-lived, and it returned only briefly as a shadow of its former self in the 1980s. If Americans were to somehow regain their reverence for the executive restraint so lauded by the founding generation, Coolidge would be the only twentieth-century example to emulate.

WHAT CAN BE DONE?

If the past is indicative of the future for the American executive, there is little hope in reform. Americans, it seems, have become accustomed to the "imperial presidency," the loss of power to their representatives in the Congress, and the destruction of federalism. We can "vote better," but with the mechanisms giving the executive branch and the general government unconstitutional power over the legislature and the states there is no reason to believe that much would change even if John Tyler or Calvin Coolidge were resurrected and put back in office. Congress has abandoned virtually every vestige of their legal authority to challenge the president, and the American people have decided that it is easier to vote every four years for a virtual dictator than to place their hope and confidence in Congress or in state or local government.

The slew of executive legislative initiatives since the 1930s has forced Americans to believe that American government *is* executive government, regardless of political party. We feel confident in *our* guy in office and think little of the potential ramifications should *our* guy be out of office and the *other* guy take his place. Republicans who insist on impeaching Obama for his unconstitutional acts are the same who defended George W. Bush and his unconstitutional acts, and vice versa. Inconsistency and excessive partisanship—something George Washington warned against in his Farewell Address—has inflicted terrible damage on the American experiment in republican self-government. Eliminating political parties would be both impossible and inexpedient, and simply voting in better candidates—if by that we mean candidates willing to take their oath to defend the Constitution seriously—doesn't seem to be a practical alternative. There are, however, potential reforms that could trim the powers of the executive branch, limit its unconstitutional overreach, and anchor the general government to sound republican principles, the bedrock of the Constitution as ratified in 1788.

Some of these reforms could be accomplished without the general government being involved in the process. An Article V convention called by the states to add salutary amendments to the Constitution could circumvent federal roadblocks. A constitutional convention has become a popular idea in recent years. Syndicated talk show host Mark Levin pushed it in his *Liberty Amendments* (2014), and he was not the first to champion this method for constitutional amendment. Talk show host Mike Church hosted a public forum in 2010 featuring historian Kevin Gutzman, law professor Randy Barnett, former White House aide Tony Blankley, and former Assistant Deputy U.S. Attorney General Bruce Fein that called for an Article V convention.[1]

There are, of course, critics of this method, notably Phyllis Schlafly at Eagle Forum. She fears that such a convention of the states would be infiltrated by Leftist organizations that would try to insert Roosevelt's Second Bill of Rights into our founding document, or perhaps scrap the Constitution itself and start over with a more radical document. But these dangers could be checked by calling a convention to address *only* certain amendments up for debate. The states can set the rules. If three-quarters of the States agreed to any of the following proposed amendments, they would become law:

1. An Amendment to the Constitution repealing the Twenty-Second Amendment and amending Article II, Section I, Clause 1. The new Amendment would read (changes in bold): "The executive Power shall be vested in a President of the United States of America. No person shall be elected to the office of the President more than **once**, and no person who has held the office of President, or acted as President, for more than two years of a term to which some other person was elected President shall be elected to the office of the President more than once. He shall hold his Office during the Term of **six** Years, and, together with the Vice President, chosen for the same Term, be elected, as follows...."

2. An Amendment to the Constitution altering the language of Article I, Section 7, to read (changes in bold): "Every Bill which shall have passed the House of Representatives and the Senate, shall, before it become a Law, be presented to the President of the United States; If he approve he shall sign it, but if not he shall return it, with his Objections to that House in which it shall have originated, who shall enter the Objections at large on their Journal, and proceed to reconsider it. **Any Objections must cite express constitutional justification for disapproval, and the President may disapprove any item of appropriation in any bill. If any bill is approved by the President, any item of appropriation contained therein which is not disapproved shall become law.** If after such Reconsideration **three**

fifths of that House shall agree to pass the Bill **or any item disapproved under this article**, it shall be sent, together with the Objections, to the other House, by which it shall likewise be reconsidered, and if approved by **three fifths** of that House, it shall become a Law. But in all such Cases the Votes of both Houses shall be determined by yeas and Nays, and the Names of the Persons voting for and against the Bill shall be entered on the Journal of each House respectively. If any Bill shall not be returned by the President within ten Days (Sundays excepted) after it shall have been presented to him, the Same shall be a Law, in like Manner as if he had signed it, unless the Congress by their Adjournment *sine die* prevent its Return, in which Case it shall not be a Law."

3. An Amendment to the Constitution altering the language of Article II, Section 2, to read (changes in bold): "The President shall be Commander in Chief of the Army and Navy of the United States, and of the Militia of the several States, when called into the actual Service of the United States, **but the President may not deploy the militia outside of American borders without the consent of the State legislatures or call the militia into the service of the United States without the consent of the State legislature nor can the President deploy the armed forces of the United States into actual combat unless the United States is suddenly attacked or invaded. In the case of a sudden attack or invasion, the President may not deploy the armed forces of the United States for a longer duration of one month without authorization by the Congress of the United States.**"

4. An Amendment to the Constitution altering the language of Article II, Section 2, to read (changes in bold): "He shall have Power, by and with the Advice and Consent of the

Senate, to make Treaties, provided **three fifths** of the Senators present concur, **and all agreements with foreign powers must have Senate approval before becoming law. No treaty can supersede the authority of the United States Constitution, the laws of the United States, or the laws of the several States.**"

5. An Amendment to the Constitution altering the language of Article II, Section 4, to read (changes in bold): "The President, Vice President and all civil Officers of the United States, shall be removed from Office on Impeachment for, and Conviction of, Treason, Bribery, **Incapacity, Negligence, Perfidy, Peculation, Oppression, Violation of the Oath of Office, Abuse of Power,** or other high Crimes and Misdemeanors **including violation of the laws of the United States, or the laws of the several States.**"

6. An Amendment to the Constitution altering the language about impeachment cases in Article I, Section 3, to read (changes in bold): "And no Person shall be convicted without the Concurrence of **three fifths** of the Members present."

7. An Amendment to the Constitution limiting unilateral executive authority, to read: "**The President of the United States shall not issue proclamations, orders, statements, or decrees of a legislative nature or in regard to foreign policy; create commissions, committees, boards, regulatory agencies, or appoint 'dictators,' 'czars' or any other non-elected government official, organization, or agency unless prescribed by the Constitution for the United States; submit a budget for the executive branch or the government of the United States; withhold non-classified information from the Congress of the United States; or undertake any acts of a legislative or judicial nature.**"

History has shown that presidents tend to abuse their power in their second term, and that the best presidents tend to serve less than eight years in office. The first proposed amendment would eliminate that problem by limiting the president to one six-year term without the possibility of reelection. Should the president violate his oath or abuse power, he could be impeached—for a greater range of misbehavior, as described in the fifth amendment above, and removed from office by a more easily attainable three-fifths majority, as in proposed amendment six, rather than the nearly impossible two-thirds majority. Opponents of the Constitution in 1788 complained that the impeachment process was too difficult to execute. This would correct that problem.

The second proposed amendment would solve four problems. First, it would require the president to provide a constitutional rationale for vetoing legislation. No longer would the president be able to wield a political hammer for purely partisan gain. Second, it would allow for the line-item veto. This would eliminate the need for "signing statements" and serve as a check on unconstitutional congressional spending. Third, it would reduce the legislative threshold for a veto override to three-fifths, making it easier to attain and thus more closely aligning with the Founders' wish for a less than absolute veto. Fourth, it would specify the rules for the "pocket veto" and eradicate the battle over the vague word "Adjournment."

The third proposed amendment would curtail executive abuse in regard to foreign policy, specifically the propensity to engage in undeclared wars, participate in extended military conflicts without congressional approval, or use the militias of the several states without their consent for federal purposes, including foreign deployments. The founding generation feared a standing army. Modern technologies and threats have made a professional military a necessity, but the militia (or the unconstitutional modern National Guard) has been used by the president in overseas wars and in domestic disputes in ways that are inconsistent with the language of the Constitution. This amendment would specify how and where the president could exercise his authority as "Commander in Chief."

The fourth proposed amendment would render "executive agreements" invalid and illegal and give the Senate back its proper role of providing "Advice and Consent." Reducing the "Consent" threshold to three-fifths would make it more likely for treaties or foreign agreements to pass, but the president would be unable to unilaterally pledge money or domestic or military aid to a foreign power. Congress would have the final say.

The seventh amendment would render much of the expansion of executive power over the last one hundred years illegal. Actually, it already is, but vague language and the inability of Congress to check presidential usurpation of power makes an amendment specifically prohibiting such activity necessary.

Moving an agenda like this through the states would be difficult but not impossible. Several states have already signed on to potential amendments requiring a balanced budget, for example, but Americans have to understand that the most destructive element of government is not the Congress or even the laws that are passed but the illegal expansion of executive power in the last one hundred and fifty years. The very brief interruptions in the growth of executive power from the founding period forward prove that sustained resistance to encroachment on constitutional government is nearly impossible without amendments to the Constitution. No one person can "save" America, nor should we expect to be saved by a president, even the best possible man to hold the office. The president has become the elected king the founding generation feared. Only through true structural reform can Americans hope to reclaim any semblance of self-government or real liberty. Otherwise, we are bound to endure ever more powerful executive government—and the continual shredding of the Constitution.

NOTES

INTRODUCTION

1. Jonathan Elliot, ed., *The Debates in the Several State Conventions on the Adoption of the Federal Constitution as Recommended by the General Convention in Philadelphia in 1787* (New York: Burt Franklin Reprints, 1974), V: 140–41.

2. Ibid.

3. Ibid., IV: 17–18.

4. Ibid., V: 140–41.

5. Ibid., IV: 107–8; III: 497–98.

6. Ibid., IV: 125; III: 509–10.

7. Max Farrand, ed., *The Records of the Federal Convention of 1787* (New Haven, CT: Yale University Press, 1937, 1966), I: 100–3.

8. Ibid., II: 585–87.

9. Merrill Jensen et al., ed., *The Documentary History of the Ratification of the Constitution* (Madison, WI: State Historical Society of Wisconsin, 1976–2010), XVI: 387–90.

CHAPTER ONE: ANDREW JACKSON AND THE ANTECEDENTS OF THE IMPERIAL PRESIDENCY

1. Max Farrand, ed., *The Records of the Federal Convention of 1787* (New Haven, CT: Yale University Press, 1937, 1966), I: 101–3.

2. All quotes from the debate are taken from Morton J. Frisch, ed., *The Pacificus-Helvidius Debates of 1793–1794: Toward the Completion of the American Founding* (Indianapolis, IN: Liberty Fund, 2007).

3. Kevin R. C. Gutzman, *James Madison and the Making of America* (New York: St. Martin's Press, 2012), 266.

4. Forrest McDonald, *The Presidency of George Washington* (Lawrence, KS: University Press of Kansas, 1974), 147.

5. James D. Richardson, ed., *A Compilation of the Messages and Papers of the Presidents 1789–1897* (Washington, DC: Bureau of National Literature and Art, 1900), II: 581–82.

6. Ibid.

7. Elliot, *Debates*, II: 362.

8. Merrill Jensen et al., ed., *The Documentary History of the Ratification of the Constitution* (Madison, WI: State Historical Society of Wisconsin, 1976–2010), XIV: 387.

9. Clyde N. Wilson, ed., *The Essential Calhoun: Selections from Writings, Speeches, and Letters* (New Brunswick, NJ: Transaction Publishers, 1992), 300.

10. Ibid., 274.

11. President Jackson's Proclamation Regarding Nullification, December 10, 1832, retrieved from: http://avalon.law.yale.edu/19th_century/jack01.asp#1.

12. Wilson, ed., *The Essential Calhoun*, 63.

13. Ibid., 64.

14. Ibid.

CHAPTER TWO: ABRAHAM LINCOLN

1.   Joseph Story, *Commentaries on the Constitution of the United States; With a Preliminary Review of the Constitutional History of the Colonies and States, Before the Adoption of the Constitution* (Clark, NJ: The Law Book Exchange, 2008), I: 244.

2.   Jon White, ed., *Northern Opposition to Mr. Lincoln's War* (Abbeville, SC: Abbeville Institute Press, 2014), 116–50.

3.   Benjamin R. Curtis, ed., *A Memoir of Benjamin Robbins Curtis, L.L.D. with Some of His Personal and Miscellaneous Writings* (Boston: Little, Brown and Co., 1879), II: 307.

4.   Ibid., 318–19.

5.   Ibid., 332.

6.   Merrill Jensen et al., ed., *The Documentary History of the Ratification of the Constitution* (Madison, WI: State Historical Society of Wisconsin, 1976–2010), IV: 154.

CHAPTER THREE: THEODORE ROOSEVELT

1.   James D. Richardson, ed., *A Compilation of the Messages and Papers of the Presidents 1789–1897* (Washington, DC: Bureau of National Literature and Art, 1900), Supplement: 323.

2.   Official report of the proceedings of the Democratic national convention held in St. Louis, Mo., July 6, 7, 8, and 9, 1904: resulting in the nomination of Hon. Alton B. Parker (of New York) for president and Hon. Henry G. Davis (of West Virginia) for vice-president, 125.

3.   Merrill Jensen et al., ed., *The Documentary History of the Ratification of the Constitution* (Madison, WI: State Historical Society of Wisconsin, 1976–2010), X: 1773; XIV: 213–14.

4.   Richardson, ed., *Messages and Papers of the Presidents*, Supplement: 329.

5.   *Northern Securities Co. v. United States*, http://www.law.cornell.edu/supremecourt/text/193/197#writing-USSC_CR_0193_0197_ZD1.

6.   Jack London, "What Jack London Says of *The Jungle*," *Chicago Socialist*, November 25, 1905: 2.

7.   John Morton Blum, *The Republican Roosevelt* (Cambridge: Harvard University Press, 1967), 70.

8.   Quoted in David McCullough, *The Path Between the Seas: The Creation of the Panama Canal 1870–1914* (New York: Simon and Schuster, 1977), 383–84.

9.   Theodore Roosevelt, *Theodore Roosevelt: An Autobiography* (New York: Charles Scribner's Sons, 1922), 357.

CHAPTER FOUR: WOODROW WILSON

1.   Stephen Samuel Wise, *Challenging Years* (New York: G. P. Putnam's Sons, 1949), 161.

2.   Woodrow Wilson, *Congressional Government: A Study in American Politics* (New York: Houghton Mifflin Company, 1885, 1913), 253–54.

3.   Woodrow Wilson, *Constitutional Government in the United States* (New York: Columbia University Press, 1908), 59–60.

4.   Ibid., 68.

5.   Woodrow Wilson, *The New Freedom: A Call for the Emancipation of the Generous Energies of a People*, http://www.gutenberg.org/files/14811/14811-h/14811-h.htm.

6.   Arthur S. Link, *Woodrow Wilson and the Progressive Era 1910–1917* (New York: Harper and Row, 1954), 41.

7.   Ibid., 53.

8.   Ibid., 59.

9.   John Morton Blum, *Woodrow Wilson and the Politics of Morality* (Boston: Little, Brown and Co., 1956), 137.

10.   Paul D. Moreno, *The American State from the Civil War to the New Deal: The Twilight of Constitutionalism and the Triumph of Progressivism* (Cambridge, NY: Cambridge University Press, 2013), 168.

11.   Blum, *Woodrow Wilson and the Politics of Morality*, 144.

CHAPTER FIVE: FRANKLIN D. ROOSEVELT

1.   All quotes from Franklin D. Roosevelt, first inaugural address, March 4, 1933, retrieved from: http://avalon.law.yale.edu/20th_century/froos1.asp.

2.   John Robert Moore, "Senator Josiah W. Bailey and the 'Conservative Manifesto' of 1937," *Journal of Southern History* 31 (Feb. 1965): 24.

3.   Franklin Roosevelt, State of the Union Address, 1944, http://www.presidency. ucsb.edu/ws/?pid=16518, accessed April 28, 2015.

4.   See, for example, Wofgang Schivelbusch, *Three New Deals: Reflections on Roosevelt's America, Mussolini's Italy, and Hitler's Germany, 1933–39* (New York: Picador, 2006).

CHAPTER SIX: HARRY S. TRUMAN

1.   Robert Dallek, *Harry S. Truman* (New York: Times Books, 2008), 3–4, 51.

2.   David McCullough, *Truman* (New York: Simon and Schuster, 1992), 547.

3.   Ibid., 548.

4.   Harry Truman, State of the Union address, 1949, http://www.presidency.ucsb. edu/ws/index.php?pid=13293.

5.   Harry Truman, Radio and Television Report to the American People on the National Emergency, December 15, 1950, http://trumanlibrary.org/public papers/viewpapers.php?pid=993.

CHAPTER SEVEN: LYNDON B. JOHNSON

1.   Lyndon B. Johnson, State of the Union address, 1964, http://www.lbjlib.utexas. edu/johnson/archives.hom/speeches.hom/640108.asp.

2.   Karl E. Campbell, *Senator Sam Ervin, Last of the Founding Fathers* (Chapel Hill: University of North Carolina Press, 2007), 346 (n. 44).

CHAPTER EIGHT: RICHARD M. NIXON

1.   Jonathan Aitken, *Richard Nixon: A Life* (Washington DC: Regnery, 1993), 397.

2.   Ibid., 398.

3.   Richard Nixon, State of the Union address, 1970, http://www.presidency.ucsb. edu/ws/?pid=2921.

4.   Aitken, *Richard Nixon: A Life*, 400.

5.   See Thomas E. Woods Jr. and Kevin R. C. Gutzman, *Who Killed the Constitution?: The Federal Government vs. American Liberty from World War I to Barack Obama* (New York: Three Rivers Press, 2008), 55–70.

6.   Richard Nixon, Executive Order 11478, Equal Employment Opportunity in the Federal Government, http://www.presidency.ucsb.edu/ws/index. php?pid=59072, accessed 28 April 2015.

7.   Stephen A. Ambrose, *Nixon: The Triumph of a Politician 1962–1972* (New York: Simon and Schuster, 1989), 473–74.

8.   Terry H. Anderson, *The Pursuit of Fairness: A History of Affirmative Action* (New York: Oxford University Press, 2004), 127.

9.   Ibid., 122–23.

10.   Karl E. Campbell, *Senator Sam Ervin, Last of the Founding Fathers* (Chapel Hill: University of North Carolina Press, 2007), 232–33.

11.   "At Age 40, A Hearty Toast to Title IX," http://articles.orlandosentinel. com/2012-06-24/news/sns-mct-editorial-at-age-40-a-hearty-toast-to-title-ix-20120624_1_title-ix-sports-opportunities-minor-sports, accessed February 17, 2015.

12.   Ambrose, *Nixon*, 458–59.

13.   Richard Nixon, Veto of the War Powers Resolution, 1973, http://www. presidency.ucsb.edu/ws/?pid=4021, accessed April 28, 2015.

14.   Jonathan Elliot, ed., *The Debates in the Several State Conventions on the Adoption of the Federal Constitution as Recommended by the General Convention at Philadelphia in 1787* (New York: Burt Franklin Reprints, 1974), IV: 107–8.

15.   Raoul Berger, *Executive Privilege: A Constitutional Myth* (Cambridge: Harvard University Press, 1974), 1.

16.   Sam Ervin Jr., *The Whole Truth: The Watergate Conspiracy* (New York: Random House, 1980). This is still the best treatment of the Watergate scandal.

17.   Berger, *Executive Privilege*, 49.

18.   Ibid., 59.

CHAPTER NINE: BARACK OBAMA

1. Jennifer K. Elsea and Richard F. Grimmett, "Declarations of War and Authorizations for the Use of Military Force: Historical Background and Legal Implications," Congressional Research Service, CRS Report for Congress, March 17, 2011, 11–12.

2. Merrill Jensen et al., ed., *The Documentary History of the Ratification of the Constitution* (Madison, WI: State Historical Society of Wisconsin, 1976–2010), XV: 458, 510.

3. Korean War, Lebanon, Vietnam War, Grenada, Panama, the Dominican Republic, the Congo, and the Persian Gulf War.

4. There are various interpretations on signing statements. Presidents issue them for a variety of reasons, and if all are included, then there would have been around a thousand before Bush took office in 2001. James Monroe issued the first in 1822.

5. Thomas E. Woods Jr. and Kevin R. C. Gutzman, *Who Killed the Constitution?: The Federal Government vs. American Liberty from World War I to Barack Obama* (New York: Three Rivers Press, 2008), 188–89.

6. The best single study on Bush's use of signing statements is Phillip J. Cooper, "George W. Bush, Edgar Allan Poe, and the Use and Abuse of Presidential Signing Statements," *Presidential Studies Quarterly* 35 (September 2006): 515–32.

7. Caroline Houck, "Barack Obama on Surveillance, Then and Now," PolitiFact, June 13, 2013.

8. Guy Benson, "Pure Gold: Obama Slams Bush for Expanding Executive Power, Ignoring Congress," Townhall, February 13, 2014.

9. Stephen Dinan, "Obamacare has been amended or delayed 19 times: study," *Washington Times*, Sept 11, 2013; David Nather and Susan Levine, "A Brief History of Obamacare Delays," *Politico*, March 25, 2014.

10. Reid J. Epstein, "Yoo: GOP Abandoning Principles on War Powers," *Politico*, June 17, 2011.

CHAPTER TEN: THOMAS JEFFERSON

1.   Thomas Jefferson, first inaugural address, 1801, http://www.presidency.ucsb. edu/ws/?pid=25803.

2.   Thomas Jefferson Randolph, ed., *Memoir, Correspondence and Miscellanies from the Papers of Thomas Jefferson* (Charlottesville, VA: F. Carr and Co., 1829), IV: 372–73.

3.   Charles Warren, *The Supreme Court in United States History* (Boston: Little, Brown and Co., 1923), I: 294–95.

4.   Ibid.

5.   Ibid., 193.

6.   Henry Adams, *History of the United States During the First Administration of Thomas Jefferson* (New York: Charles Scribner's Sons, 1921), II: 90.

7.   Ibid.

8.   Thomas Jefferson, first inaugural address, 1801, http://www.presidency.ucsb. edu/ws/?pid=25803.

9.   Andrew Adgate Lipscomb and Albert Ellery Bergh, eds., *The Writings of Thomas Jefferson* (Washington, DC: The Thomas Jefferson Memorial Association, 1903–1904), X:123.

CHAPTER ELEVEN: JOHN TYLER

1.   Oliver Perry Chitwood, *John Tyler: Champion of the Old South* (New York: Russell and Russell, 1964), 206.

2.   Ibid., 270.

3.   Ibid., 207.

4.   Lyon G. Tyler, *The Letters and Times of the Tylers* (Richmond, VA: Whittet and Shepperson, 1885), II: 33–34.

5.   John Tyler, first inaugural address, 1841, http://www.presidency.ucsb.edu/ ws/?pid=533.

6.   James D. Richardson, ed., *A Compilation of the Messages and Papers of the Presidents 1789–1897* (Washington, DC: Bureau of National Literature and Art, 1900), IV: 63–64.

7. Ibid., 68.

8. Chitwood, *John Tyler,* 228–29.

9. Ibid.

10. Richardson, ed., *Messages and Papers of the Presidents,* IV: 68–69.

11. Ibid., 72.

12. *Niles National Register* LXI (September 18, 1841): 35–36.

13. Tyler, *Letters and Times,* II: 122.

14. Richardson, ed., *Messages and Papers of the Presidents,* IV: 186–87.

15. Chitwood, *John Tyler,* 300.

16. Richardson, ed., *Messages and Papers of the Presidents,* IV: 330.

17. Ibid., 327.

18. Ibid., 344–45.

CHAPTER TWELVE: GROVER CLEVELAND

1. Quoted in Vincent P. De Santis, "Grover Cleveland," in Morten Borden, *America's Eleven Greatest Presidents* (Chicago: Rand McNally, 1971), 159.

2. Ibid., 164.

3. Brion McClanahan and Clyde N. Wilson, *Forgotten Conservatives in American History* (Greta, LA: Pelican Publishing, 2012), 96.

4. Ryan S. Walters, *The Last Jeffersonian: Grover Cleveland and the Path to Restoring the Republic* (Bloomington, IN: WestBow Press, 2012), 41.

5. *Public Papers of Grover Cleveland, Twenty-Second President of the United States, 1885–1889* (Washington DC: U.S. Government Printing Office, 1889), 287.

6. George F. Parker, ed., *The Writings and Speeches of Grover Cleveland* (New York: Cassell Publishing Company, 1892), 34.

7. James D. Richardson, ed., *A Compilation of the Messages and Papers of the Presidents 1789–1897* (Washington, DC: Bureau of National Literature and Art, 1900), VIII: 375–83.

8. Paul F. Boller Jr., *Presidential Anecdotes* (New York: Penguin Books, 1981), 182.

9. Richardson, *Messages and Papers of the Presidents,* VIII: 325.

10. Ibid., 301.

11. Ibid., 581.

12. *The Campaign Textbook of the Democratic Party for the Presidential Election of 1892 Prepared by the Authority of the Democratic National Committee* (New York: M. B. Brown), 6.

13. Richard E. Welch Jr., *The Presidencies of Grover Cleveland* (Lawrence, KS: University Press of Kansas, 1988), 136.

14. Richardson, *Messages and Papers*, VIII: 557.

15. Ibid., 443.

16. Ibid., 436.

17. Ibid., 425.

18. Allan Nevins, *Grover Cleveland: A Study in Courage* (New York: Dodd, Mead and Co., 1944), 328–29.

19. Richardson, *Messages and Papers*, VIII: 667.

20. Ibid., 555–56.

21. Nevins, *Grover Cleveland*, 331.

22. Henry Adams, *The Education of Henry Adams: An Autobiography* (Boston: Houghton Mifflin Company, 1918), 338.

23. Richardson, *Messages and Papers of the Presidents*, IX: 401–6.

24. Richardson, *Messages and Papers of the Presidents*, VIII: 301.

CHAPTER THIRTEEN: CALVIN COOLIDGE

1. Amity Shlaes, *Coolidge* (New York: Harper, 2014), 259.

2. Calvin Coolidge, *Autobiography* (New York: Cosmopolitan Book Corporation, 1929), 198–99.

3. David Greenberg, *Calvin Coolidge* (New York: Times Books), 45.

4. Vincent Fitzpatrick, *H. L. Mencken* (Macon, GA: Mercer University Press, 2004), 66.

5. Calvin Coolidge, First Annual Message, http://www.presidency.ucsb.edu/ws/index.php?pid=29564.

6. Ibid.

7. Calvin Coolidge, Third Annual Message, http://www.presidency.ucsb.edu/ws/index.php?pid=29566.

8. Ibid.

9.   Calvin Coolidge, *Foundations of the Republic: Speeches and Addresses* (New York: Charles Scribner's Sons, 1926), 230–33.

10.   Calvin Coolidge, Fourth Annual Message, http://www.presidency.ucsb.edu/ws/index.php?pid=29567.

11.   Michael J. Gerhardt, *The Forgotten Presidents: Their Untold Constitutional Legacy* (New York: Oxford University Press, 2013), 195.

12.   Shlaes, *Coolidge*, 354.

13.   Calvin Coolidge Veto Message, *Congressional Record*, May 23, 1928, 9524–9526.

14.   Shlaes, *Coolidge*, 357–58.

15.   Calvin Coolidge, Fourth Annual Message, http://www.presidency.ucsb.edu/ws/index.php?pid=29568.

16.   Gerhardt, *The Forgotten Presidents*, 211.

17.   Coolidge, *Foundations of the Republic*, 230–33.

18.   Ibid., 97–100.

19.   Coolidge, *Autobiography*, 192.

20.   Greenberg, *Coolidge*, 155.

21.   H. L. Mencken, *On Politics: A Carnival of Buncombe* (Baltimore: Johns Hopkins University Press, 2006), 140.

WHAT CAN BE DONE?

1.   Kevin Gutzman et al., "The Federal Solution for a Federal Crisis," http://www.kevingutzman.com/articles/assets/ArticleVConvention_04212010.pdf.

BIBLIOGRAPHY

I n addition to the public papers of the presidents, the following books
were used in my research. They represent the best (though not always
entirely accurate) material on a particular president. Some presidents
have a more substantial bibliography than others.

The books listed on the Constitution are either primary material or
the finest examples of constitutional scholarship from an originalist position.

ON THE CONSTITUTION

Berger, Raoul. *Executive Privilege: A Constitutional Myth*. Cambridge:
Harvard University Press, 1974.

————. *Federalism: The Founders' Design*. Norman, OK: University of Oklahoma Press, 1987.

————. *Impeachment: The Constitutional Problems*. Cambridge: Harvard University Press, 1972.

Bradford, M. E. *Original Intentions: On the Making and Ratification of the United States Constitution*. Athens, GA: University of Georgia Press, 1994.

Elliot, Jonathan, ed. *The Debates in the Several State Conventions on the Adoption of the Federal Constitution as Recommended by the General Convention at Philadelphia in 1787.* 5 vols. New York: Burt Franklin Reprints, 1974.

Farrand, Max, ed. *The Records of the Federal Convention of 1787.* 4 vols. New Haven: Yale University Press, 1937, 1966.

Jensen, Merrill, et al., ed. *The Documentary History of the Ratification of the Constitution*. 27 vols. Madison, WI: State Historical Society of Wisconsin, 1976–2014.

Gutzman, Kevin R. C. *The Politically Incorrect Guide to the Constitution*. Washington, DC: Regnery, 2007.

McClanahan, Brion. *The Founding Fathers Guide to the Constitution*. Washington, DC: Regnery History, 2012.

Taylor, John. *New Views on the Constitution of the United States*. Washington, DC: Way and Gideon, 1823.

Tucker, St. George. *View of the Constitution of the United States with Selected Writings*, edited by Clyde N. Wilson. Indianapolis: Liberty Fund, 1999.

Upshur, Abel P. *A Brief Inquiry into the True Nature of Our Federal Government: Being a Review of Judge Story's Commentaries on the Constitution of the United States*. New York: Van Evrie, Horton, and Co., 1868.

Woods, Thomas E., and Kevin Gutzman. *Who Killed the Constitution? The Federal Government vs. American Liberty from World War I to Barack Obama.* New York: Three Rivers Press, 2008.

ON THE FOUNDERS AND ANDREW JACKSON

Cole, Donald B. *The Presidency of Andrew Jackson.* Lawrence, KS: University Press of Kansas, 1993.

Ellis, Richard E. *The Union at Risk: Jacksonian Democracy, States' Rights, and the Nullification Crisis.* New York: Oxford University Press, 1987.

Freeman, Douglas Southall. *George Washington: A Biography.* 7 vols. New York: Charles Scribner's Sons, 1951. Vol. 7 by John A. Carroll and Mary W. Ashworth.

Frisch, Morton J. *The Pacificus-Helvidius Debates of 1793–1794: Toward the Completion of the American Founding.* Indianapolis, IN: Liberty Fund, 2007.

McDonald, Forrest. *Alexander Hamilton: A Biography.* New York: W. W. Norton and Company, 1979.

———. *The Presidency of George Washington.* Lawrence, KS: University Press of Kansas, 1974.

Remini, Robert V. *Andrew Jackson and the Course of American Democracy, 1833–1845.* New York: Harper and Row, 1984.

Parton, James. *Life of Andrew Jackson.* New York: Mason Brothers, 1860.

Schlesinger, Arthur M., Jr. *The Age of Jackson.* Boston: Little, Brown and Co., 1945.

Wilson, Clyde N., ed. *The Essential Calhoun.* New Brunswick: Transaction Publishers, 1992.

Woods, Thomas E., Jr. *Nullification: How to Resist Federal Tyranny in the 21st Century.* Washington, DC: Regnery, 2010.

ON ABRAHAM LINCOLN

DiLorenzo, Thomas. *The Real Lincoln.* New York: Crown Forum, 2002.

Fletcher, George P. *Our Secret Constitution: How Lincoln Remade America.* New York: Oxford University Press, 2001.

Gray, Wood. *The Hidden Civil War: The Story of the Copperheads.* New York: The Viking Press, 1964.

Hyman, Harold M. *Era of the Oath: Northern Loyalty Tests During the Civil War and Reconstruction.* New York: Octagon Books, 1978.

———. *A More Perfect Union: The Impact of the Civil War and Reconstruction on the Constitution.* New York: Knopf, 1973.

Klement, Frank. *Lincoln's Critics: The Copperheads of the North.* Shippensburg, PA: White Mane Books, 1999.

Magness, Philip W. *Colonization After Emancipation: Lincoln and the Movement for Black Resettlement.* Columbia, MO: University of Missouri Press, 2011.

Randall, James G. *The Civil War and Reconstruction.* New York: D. C. Heath and Co., 1937.

———. *Constitutional Problems under Lincoln.* Gloucester, MA: Peter Smith, 1951.

———. *Lincoln the President.* 2 vols. New York: Dodd, Mead and Co., 1945.

Rehnquist, William H. *All The Laws But One: Civil Liberties in Wartime.* New York: Knopf, 1998.

White, Jonathan, ed. *Northern Opposition to Mr. Lincoln's War.* McClellanville, SC: Abbeville Institute Press, 2014.

ON THEODORE ROOSEVELT

Beale, Howard K. *Theodore Roosevelt and the Rise of America to World Power.* Baltimore: Johns Hopkins Press, 1953.

Blum, John M. *The Republican Roosevelt.* Cambridge, MA: Harvard University Press, 1954.

Gould, Louis L. *The Presidency of Theodore Roosevelt.* Lawrence, KS: The University Press of Kansas, 1991.

Marks, Frederick W., III. *Velvet on Iron: The Diplomacy of Theodore Roosevelt.* Lincoln, NB: University of Nebraska Press, 1979.

McCullough, David. *The Path Between the Seas: The Creation of the Panama Canal 1870–1914.* New York: Simon and Schuster, 1971.

Moore, Edmund. *Theodore Rex.* New York: Random House, 2001.

Roosevelt, Theodore. *An Autobiography.* New York: Charles Scribner's Sons, 1920.

ON WOODROW WILSON

Berg, A. Scott. *Wilson.* New York: Simon and Schuster, 2013.

Blum, John M. *Woodrow Wilson and the Politics of Morality.* Boston: Little, Brown and Co., 1956.

Bragdon, Henry W. *Woodrow Wilson: The Academic Years.* Cambridge, MA: Harvard University Press, 1967.

Brand, H. W. *Woodrow Wilson*. New York: Times Books, 2003.

Cooper, John Milton, Jr. *Woodrow Wilson: A Biography*. New York: Vintage Books, 2009.

Corwin, Edwin S. *Presidential Power and the Constitution: Essays*. Ithaca: Cornell University Press, 1976.

George, Alexander L. *Woodrow Wilson and Colonel House: A Personality Study*. New York: Dover Publications, 1964.

Latham, Earl. *The Philosophy and Policies of Woodrow Wilson*. Chicago: University of Chicago Press, 1958.

Link, Arthur S. *Wilson*. Princeton, NJ: Princeton University Press, 1947.

———. *Woodrow Wilson and the Progressive Era, 1910–1917*. New York: Harper, 1954.

Wilson, Woodrow. *Congressional Government: A Study in American Politics*. New York: Houghton Mifflin Co., 1913.

———. *A History of the American People*. 10 vols. New York: Harper Brothers, 1918.

ON FRANKLIN D. ROOSEVELT

Brinkley, Alan. *The End of Reform: New Deal Liberalism in Recession and War*. New York: Knopf, 1995.

Dallek, Robert. *Franklin D. Roosevelt and American Foreign Policy, 1932–1945*. New York: Oxford University Press, 1979.

Davis, Kenneth. *FDR*. 5 vols. New York: Random House, 1971–2000.

Flynn, John T. *The Roosevelt Myth*. New York: Delvin-Adair, 1956.

Freidel, Frank. *Franklin D. Roosevelt.* 4 vols. New York: Little, Brown and Co., 1952–1973.

Jenkins, Roy. *Franklin Delano Roosevelt.* New York: Henry Holt and Company, 2003.

Schlesinger, Arthur M., Jr. *The Age of Roosevelt.* 3 vols. Boston: Houghton Mifflin, 1957–1960.

Tansill, Charles Callan. *Back Door to War: The Roosevelt Foreign Policy, 1933–1941.* Chicago: Henry Regnery Company, 1952.

ON HARRY TRUMAN

Dallek, Robert. *Harry S. Truman.* New York: Henry Holt and Company, 2008.

Hamby, Alonzo L. *Beyond the New Deal: Harry S. Truman and American Liberalism.* New York: Columbia University Press, 1973.

———. *Man of the People: A Life of Harry S. Truman.* New York: Oxford University Press, 1998.

McCullough, David. *Truman.* New York: Simon and Schuster, 1992.

Truman, Harry S. *The Autobiography of Harry S. Truman.* Columbia: University of Missouri Press, 2002.

ON LYNDON B. JOHNSON

Caro, Robert A. *Means of Ascent: The Years of Lyndon B. Johnson.* New York: Alfred A. Knopf, 1990.

———. *The Path to Power: The Years of Lyndon B. Johnson.* New York: Alfred A. Knopf, 1982.

Dallek, Robert. *Flawed Giant: Lyndon Johnson and His Times, 1961–1973.* New York: Oxford University Press, 1998.

———. *Lyndon B. Johnson: Portrait of a President.* New York: Penguin Books, 2004.

Jones, Howard. *Death of a Generation: How the Assassination of Diem and JFK Prolonged the Vietnam War.* New York: Oxford University Press, 2003.

Peters, Charles. *Lyndon B. Johnson.* New York: Henry Holt and Company, 2010.

ON RICHARD NIXON

Aitken, Jonathan. *Nixon: A Life.* Washington, DC: Regnery, 1993.

Ambrose, Stephen E. *Nixon: The Triumph of a Politician 1962–1972.* New York: Simon and Schuster, 1989.

Binkiewicz, Donna M. *Federalizing the Muse: United States Arts Policy and the National Endowment for the Arts, 1965–1980.* Chapel Hill: University of North Carolina Press, 2004.

Black, Conrad. *Richard M. Nixon: A Life in Full.* New York: Perseus Books, 2008.

Burke, Vincent J. *Nixon's Good Deed: Welfare Reform.* New York: Columbia University Press, 1974.

Ervin, Sam J., Jr. *The Whole Truth: The Watergate Conspiracy.* New York: Random House, 1980.

Friedman, Leon. *The United States v. Nixon: The President Before the Supreme Court.* New York: Chelsea House Publishers, 1974.

ON GEORGE H. W. BUSH, BILL CLINTON, GEORGE W. BUSH, AND BARACK OBAMA

Bose, Meena, and Rosanna Perotti, eds. *From Cold War to New World Order: The Foreign Policy of George Bush*. Westport, CT: Greenwood Press, 2002.

Bovard, James. *The Bush Betrayal*. New York: Macmillan, 2004.

————. *"Feeling Your Pain": The Explosion and Abuse of Government Power in the Clinton-Gore Years*. New York: St. Martin's Press, 2000.

————. *Lost Rights: The Destruction of American Liberty*. New York: St. Martin's Press, 1995.

————. *Terrorism and Tyranny: Trampling Freedom, Justice, and Peace to Rid the World of Evil*. New York: Macmillan, 2004.

Cooper, Danny. *Neoconservatism and American Foreign Policy: A Critical Analysis*. New York: Routledge, 2011.

Freddoso, David. *Gangster Government: Barack Obama and the New Washington Thugocracy*. Washington, DC: Regnery, 2011.

Graham, John D. *Bush on the Home Front: Domestic Policy Triumphs and Failures*. Bloomington, IN: Indiana University Press, 2010.

Klein, Aaron. *Impeachable Offenses: The Case for Removing Barack Obama from Office*. Washington, DC: WND Books, 2013.

McCarthy, Andrew. *Faithless Execution: Building the Political Case for Obama's Impeachment*. New York: Encounter Books, 2014.

Nelson, Michael, and Barbara A. Perry, eds. *41: Inside the Presidency of George H. W. Bush*. Ithaca: Cornell University Press, 2014.

Peleg, Ilan. *The Legacy of George W. Bush's Foreign Policy: Moving Beyond Neoconservatism*. Boulder, CO: Westview Press, 2009.

Shapiro, Ben. *The People vs. Barack Obama: The Criminal Case Against the Obama Administration*. New York: Threshold Editions, 2014.

Tiefer, Charles. *Veering Right: How the Bush Administration Subverts the Law for Conservative Causes*. Berkeley, CA: University of California Press, 2004.

ON THOMAS JEFFERSON

Adams, Henry. *History of the United States of America During the Administration of Thomas Jefferson*. New York: Library of America, 1986.

Malone, Dumas. *Jefferson and His Time*. 6 volumes. Boston: Little, Brown and Co., 1948–1981.

McDonald, Forrest. *The Presidency of Thomas Jefferson*. Lawrence, KS: University Press of Kansas, 1976.

Peterson, Merrill D., ed. *Thomas Jefferson: Writings*. New York: Library of America, 1984.

Risjord, Norman K. *The Old Republicans: Southern Conservatism in the Age of Jefferson*. New York: Columbia University Press, 1965.

ON JOHN TYLER

Abell, Alexander Gordon. *Life of John Tyler*. New York: Harper and Brothers, 1843.

Chitwood, Oliver Perry. *John Tyler: Campion of the Old South*. Newtown, CT: American Political Biography Press, 1990.

Holt, Michael F. *The Rise and Fall of the American Whig Party: Jacksonian Politics and the Onset of the Civil War.* New York: Oxford University Press, 1999.

Monroe, Dan. *The Republican Vision of John Tyler.* College Station, TX: Texas A&M University Press, 2003.

Peterson, Norma Lois. *The Presidencies of William Henry Harrison and John Tyler.* Lawrence, KS: University Press of Kansas, 1989.

Tyler, Lyon G. *The Letters and Times of the Tylers.* 3 vols. Richmond, VA: Whittet and Shepperson, 1884–86.

ON GROVER CLEVELAND

Cleveland, Grover. *Good Citizenship.* Philadelphia: Henry Altemus Company, 1908.

———. *Presidential Problems.* New York: The Century Company, 1904.

Jeffers, H. Paul. *An Honest President: The Life and Presidencies of Grover Cleveland.* New York: William Morrow, 2000.

McClanahan, Brion, and Clyde Wilson. *Forgotten Conservatives in American History.* Gretna, LA: Pelican Publishing, 2012.

McElroy, Robert. *Grover Cleveland: The Man and the Statesman. An Authorized Biography.* 2 vols. New York: Harper Brothers Publishers, 1923.

Nevins, Allan. *Grover Cleveland: A Study in Courage.* New York: Dodd, Mead and Co., 1944.

Pafford, John M. *The Forgotten Conservative: Rediscovering Grover Cleveland.* Washington, DC: Regnery History, 2013.

Walters, Ryan S. *The Last Jeffersonian: Grover Cleveland and the Path to Restoring the Republic.* Bloomington, IN: WestBow Press, 2012.

ON CALVIN COOLIDGE

Coolidge, Calvin. *The Autobiography of Calvin Coolidge.* New York: Cosmopolitan Book Corporation, 1929.

Ferrell, Robert. *The Presidency of Calvin Coolidge.* Lawrence, KS: University Press of Kansas, 1998.

Fuess, Claude Moore. *Calvin Coolidge: The Man from Vermont.* Boston: Little, Brown and Co., 1940.

Green, Horace. *The Life of Calvin Coolidge.* New York: Duffield and Company, 1924.

Greenberg, David. *Calvin Coolidge.* New York: Times Books, 2006.

Shlaes, Amity. *Coolidge.* New York: Harper, 2013.

Sobel, Robert. *Coolidge: An American Enigma.* Washington, DC: Regnery, 1998.

White, William Allen. *A Puritan in Babylon: The Story of Calvin Coolidge.* New York: Macmillan, 1938.

INDEX

8/16